GODLINESS AND GOOD LEARNING

Godliness
& Good Learning

FOUR STUDIES

ON A VICTORIAN IDEAL BY

DAVID NEWSOME

John Murray

ALBEMARLE STREET LONDON

Made and printed in Great Britain by
William Clowes and Sons, Limited
London and Beccles

Contents

v

Illustrations

ILLUSTRATIONS

Line Drawings in Text

Preface

The Benson papers in the library at Trinity College, Cambridge, provided me with the idea from which this book has grown. From the pages of the remarkable correspondence which passed between Edward White Benson, later Archbishop of Canterbury, and J. B. Lightfoot, later Bishop of Durham, when they were boys together at King Edward's School, Birmingham, in the 1840's, there stands out one central figure—James Prince Lee, the headmaster who commanded from both these boys a veneration comparable to that which Stanley and Clough felt for the most famous schoolmaster of the nineteenth century, Thomas Arnold. Curiosity to know more led me to Birmingham and to Manchester, there to discover that the man who had the power to cast a spell over his pupils which lasted a lifetime could as easily provoke contempt and hatred from those who met him in other capacities, especially from the diocesan clergy of the see of Manchester, whose first bishop Prince Lee became in 1847. There seemed to be sufficient material to warrant a biographical sketch of this enigmatic and important figure.

By this time I had made the acquaintance of another interesting historical figure, indirectly connected with Prince Lee. In the Trinity Library I found the original of a document which I had seen only once before in typescript in the crypt of Truro Cathedral: a long and moving account written by Archbishop Benson of the life and death of his eldest son Martin, a Winchester Scholar who died in 1878 from meningitis at the age of seventeen. Benson always remained what Prince Lee had made him—a passionate idealist. To his eldest son he passed on that enthusiasm for godliness and good learning which he himself had derived from Lee. Martin therefore emerges from the grief-stricken narrative, which Benson intended posterity to read, as the exemplar of the ideal of his father's generation. A father, however, is not always the best guide to the personality and character of his son. The son must speak for himself. A large collection of Benson family papers in the Bodleian Library yielded what I wanted: Martin's own letters and papers, an astonishing series of letters that passed between the boy and his parents from the date when he first learnt to write to the very eve of the illness which ended his life.

At this point the pattern of the book became clear: Prince Lee, the idealist; Martin Benson, the exemplar. What was needed to round off the volume was a general study of the ideal which they represented, a discussion of the origins, development and significance of this ideal in the history of nineteenth-century England. I soon found myself on ground which I had already traversed. While working on the *History of Wellington College*, I had been forcibly struck by what many other students of nineteenth-century English history had previously observed, namely the revolutionary change in ideals which accompanied the transition from the mid-Victorian to the late-Victorian age, a change reflected in the difference commonly discerned between what Thomas Arnold taught and what Thomas Hughes, the creator of *Tom Brown*, practised. It seemed necessary, therefore, to conclude this series of studies with an investigation into the origins of 'muscular Christianity', to see how it was that the earlier ideal of 'godliness and good learning' came to be transformed into the popular cult of 'godliness and manliness'.

The number of those to whom acknowledgement and thanks are due is legion. I owe a great debt to those who helped me to locate the very scattered materials from which this book has been compiled: The Rev. R. G. Lunt, Chief Master of King Edward's, Birmingham, and Mr. T. H. Hutton, the author of the school's official history; Mr. V. H. Woods and Miss Norris of the Birmingham Reference Library; Mr. J. M. Lee who kindly scouted round the Manchester libraries in search of materials on Prince Lee; Mr. W. H. Shercliff, formerly the Local History Librarian of Manchester Central Library, and Miss Hilda Lofthouse of Chetham's Library, who took infinite pains to find everything of relevance. I am also greatly indebted to Mrs. Dorothy Owen, formerly of the Lambeth Palace Library, for all her valuable suggestions; to Mr. A. Halcrow of the Trinity Library and to Mr. R. W. Hunt and Mr. W. O. Hassall of the Bodleian Library for the speed with which they supplied me with photostat copies of Benson papers; to Mr. Kittermaster of the Temple Reading

Room at Rugby School and to Mr. J. M. Blakiston, Librarian of Winchester College, who were both kind enough to make transcriptions for me of important documents; to Mr. A. A. M. Batchelor, late Headmaster of Temple Grove School, who lent me records of the school to assist in my study of Martin Benson; to Mr. F. R. Salter, Fellow of Magdalene College, Cambridge, who endured with great patience my many questions on the Benson family; and to my former pupil Giles Ecclestone who supplied me with a mass of information about William Cory.

The Master of Emmanuel (Mr. Edward Welbourne) and the Master of Selwyn (Professor Owen Chadwick) were kind enough to read this book in typescript and to make helpful suggestions. I am also very grateful to my wife who, in the midst of coping with four young children, found time to help me in the compilation of the index; to Mr. E. O. Tancock who generously offered his expert assistance with the proofs; and to my two colleagues Alan Gauld and John Derry who have watched the book grow from small beginnings and who were always ready to goad me when I was tired and to cheer me up when I was despondent.

I have quoted very liberally in the course of this book both from source materials and from printed letters which appear in the standard Victorian biographies. For this I make no apology. This book attempts to bring to life an influential group of eminent Victorians and to convey to readers who live in very different times something of the ethos of that earlier period, something of its ideals, its enthusiasms, its values and its loves. No one can describe these better than the men who lived through this age. This book could never have been written, therefore, without the kind co-operation of copyright owners, trustees of libraries and publishers who have generously allowed me to make substantial quotations in my text.

Among those whom I should like to thank for such permission are: The Provost of King's College, Cambridge, Dr. V. H. H. Green, The Rev. K. S. P. McDowall, Sir Compton Mackenzie, The Master and Fellows of Trinity College, Cambridge, the Master and Fellows of Magdalene College, Cambridge, The Governors of Rugby School, the Governors of King Edward's School, Birmingham, the Governors of Wellington College, the

Manchester Public Libraries Committee and the Committee of Chetham's Library, Manchester. The publishers who have been good enough to allow me to use extracts from published works are: Edward Arnold Ltd., Jonathan Cape Ltd., Cassell and Co. Ltd., Constable and Co. Ltd., Macgibbon and Kee, Macmillan and Co. Ltd., Methuen and Co. Ltd., John Murray Ltd., and James Nisbet and Co. Ltd.

I must conclude with a special word of thanks to my publisher who turned not a hair when I presented him with a manuscript nearly double the length of the book which I had contracted to produce! The author admits that he is an admirer of the Victorians. He must, however, concede that the one quality which he seems to have learnt from those whom he has been studying is one of their faults. Like them, he has become prolix.

Emmanuel College,   DAVID NEWSOME
Cambridge.

Introduction

"What is a college without a chapel?" Bishop Christopher Wordsworth once asked a friend, a canon of Winchester Cathedral. "An angel without wings," was the prompt reply.[1] The Bishop went on his way rejoicing. We need not wonder at his pleasure. His friend had expressed in a single phrase the ideal of 'godliness and good learning' and had confirmed the Bishop's own conviction that to separate education from religion was as grievous as to set a man to climb a mountain and then deprive him of a guide. The phrase has for us, besides, the authentic ring of mid-Victorian England, evoking a picture of that influential world of eminent ecclesiastics, intellectual giants and earnest idealists—rulers in school, university and diocese—who demonstrated to their generation the grandeur and power which comes from the steadfast pursuit of noble aims. Their world provides the setting for this book; their noblest aim—the ideal of godliness and good learning—provides the theme.

If the history of this ideal properly begins many years before Thomas Arnold of Rugby became a famous headmaster, at least it is to Arnold that we should turn for its most forceful exposition. In his Inaugural Lecture, delivered at Oxford as Regius Professor of Modern History in December 1841, he bore witness to the importance of his life's work, relating his educational ideals to the needs of the nation at that time and to the duties—as he saw them—of a truly Christian society.

> There are certain principles [he observed], which the State wishes to inculcate on all its members, certain habits which it wishes to form, a certain kind and degree of knowledge which it wishes to communicate; such, namely, as bear more or less immediately on its great end, its own intellectual and moral perfection, arising out of the perfection of its several members. Now . . . as far as this instruction is applied to the young, it goes under the name of education; as far as it regards persons of all ages, it generally takes the form of religion.[2]

Schools, he maintained, should never be mere teaching academies.

1

He who educates must take a higher view, and pursue an end accordingly far more complicated. He must adjust the respective claims of bodily and mental exercise, of different kinds of intellectual labour; he must consider every part of his pupil's nature, physical, intellectual, and moral; regarding the cultivation of the last, however, as paramount to that of either of the others.[3]

According to Arnold, education and religion were really two aspects of the same thing—a system of instruction towards moral perfection. It was therefore the function of the State to enable and to encourage its members to aspire to the highest standards of Christian living.

All societies of men, whether we call them states or churches, should make their bond to consist in a common object and a common practice, rather than in a common belief: in other words, their end should be good rather than truth.[4]

Many of Arnold's contemporaries may have shrunk from this conclusion. Nevertheless his claim that godliness and good learning should walk together was entirely in accordance with the sentiments and opinions of his age. To A. C. Tait, Arnold's successor as headmaster of Rugby, the schoolmaster's calling was quite 'a proper profession for a clergyman. My opinion', he wrote, '. . . is that there is no situation of so directly pastoral a nature as mine'.[5] Christopher Wordsworth's convictions have been noted already. Headmaster of Harrow while Arnold was at Rugby, he took up his post when not yet thirty years of age 'with very high and noble aims, with a longing to unite religion and scholarship in education, as he felt that he had the power beyond most men of his time to do'.[6]

There was nothing particularly novel about these aspirations. The Church had from time immemorial dominated education in England. Very few assistant masters in public school or grammar school failed to take orders; not until the last decades of the nineteenth century was the clerical monopoly in the universities effectively assailed; and a layman headmaster of a public school was unknown before the 1890's. The ancient academic foundations had been committed to the pursuit of godliness and good learning long before Arnold was born. The Collect of Thanksgiving for the founder of Winchester College, William of Wykeham, runs as follows:

2

We give thee humble and hearty thanks, O most merciful Father, for our Founder William of Wykeham and all other our benefactors by whose benefits we are in this college brought up to godliness and good learning; and we beseech Thee to give us grace so to use these Thy blessings to the glory of Thy Name, that we may become profitable members in the Church and Commonwealth and may be at last partakers of the immortal glory of the Resurrection.

This collect has passed from Winchester with certain appropriate emendations to many other schools.

Despite the antiquity of the ideal, there is no doubt that it experienced something of a 're-birth' in the first decades of the nineteenth century after a long period of torpor. Fresh emphasis was laid on the pastoral functions of the schoolmaster; greater importance came to be ascribed to the public schools as prominent national institutions. At the same time, the prestige of the teaching profession rose rapidly, reaching its peak by about the 1860's and 70's, a fact reflected in the high salaries, the respected status and the prospects of handsome preferment which the position of schoolmaster could command. The schoolmaster-bishop became the acknowledged type of ecclesiastical ruler. Brooke Foss Westcott, while he was an undergraduate at Trinity in 1847, confided to his diary that he had been pondering over his future career: "A schoolmaster or a clergyman?" he mused. "I am fearful, if once I embrace the former profession, I shall be again absorbed in all the schemes of ambition and selfish distinction which used continually to haunt me."[7] He eventually took orders and accepted the offer of an assistant-mastership at Harrow. Seventeen years later he became canon of Peterborough, Regius Professor of Divinity at Cambridge and finally Bishop of Durham.

The explanation of the re-birth is not difficult to find. The cry had gone up for educational reform. Those who were in a position to carry out reform responded by looking to the past for their ideal. They strove to return to first principles, to original intentions; to fulfil what the founders had hoped for either by devising new methods or by breathing new life into the old. That there was a pressing need for the reform of public-school education at this time need not here be stressed. The subject has been the source of numerous lurid descriptions of sadistic floggings, savage bullying and merciless fagging not only in contemporary literature and pamphlets but also in many histories of English education. Critics, after the opening salvo of Sydney Smith's effective battery in the *Edinburgh Review* in 1810, combined in denouncing almost every aspect of public-school life —bullying, immorality, fagging, negligent masters, the antiquated curriculum.[8] While taking into account a good deal of polemical exaggeration, one cannot escape the conclusion that these critics had an abundance of material to substantiate their charges. The fact is, as R. L. Archer has rightly observed, that the state of British universities and secondary schools between 1789 and 1815 reveals 'one outstanding factor. They do not reflect any ideals of their own age. No new driving power had come to them for a century and a half.'[9]

There was wanting an ideal; and, to save the public schools from the wholesale desertion of the middle class, this ideal had exactly to express the wishes and sentiments of the parents whose sons the schools needed to retain and attract. At a time when the effects of the evangelical revival were being felt throughout the length and breadth of England, the way of salvation for the public schools was plain. The headmasters and assistant masters who came to the schools in the 1820's and 30's were drawn from the class whose patronage they sought. Two of them—Thomas Arnold and Christopher Wordsworth—while having no personal experience of the respective schools to which they had been appointed, certainly knew exactly what they intended to achieve and the methods they were going to employ before they took up their headmasterships. Arnold, because he was a greater personality and more realistic and because he was blessed with more sympathetic Trustees and parents, succeeded to a limited extent. Christopher Wordsworth, lacking these qualities and advantages, failed completely. But neither of them—nor many others like them—was consciously bowing to the force of public opinion in striving for the moral purification of Rugby and Harrow. They were doing what they passionately believed to be right and would have fought for the principles of godliness and good learning had all the world been against them.

They were conscious, however, of critics of a different sort.

4

Dr. Nicholas Hans, in his study of educational trends in the eighteenth century, has shown that the enormous advance in technology from 1760 onwards had done much to encourage a pragmatic and utilitarian concept of education.

> At the end of the century [he writes], the utilitarian motive becomes all-important and the religious and intellectual reasons recede into the background. 'Useful arts', 'application of science', 'diffusion of useful knowledge', are the sentences most often used by promoters of educational reform.[10]

He quotes from an anonymous pamphlet entitled *Letters on the Utility and Policy of Employing Machines to shorten Labour*:

> Read the history of mankind, consider the gradual steps of civilisation from barbarism to refinement, and you will not fail to discover that the progress of society from its lowest and worst to its highest and most perfect state has been uniformly accompanied and chiefly promoted by the happy exertions of man in the character of a mechanic or engineer. Let all machines be destroyed, and we are reduced in a moment to the condition of savages; and in that state men may indeed exist a long time without the aid of curious and complex machines; though without them they can never rise above it.[11]

This is the very antithesis of the concept of education as defined by Arnold in his Inaugural Lecture. The advocates of godliness and good learning were united in their horror of a materialistic philosophy such as this. The teaching of science and technology, enlightened and novel ideas about the training of children, the theories expounded by Bentham in the *Chrestomathia* and the practical experiments of the Hills at Hazelwood—all these they regarded with profound suspicion. Reform was needed—but not revolution; sound classical learning and firm religious principles —nothing radical or profane.

*   *   *   *   *

Who were these advocates of godliness and good learning? They are not an easy group to define precisely because they belonged to no single party, adhered to no single tradition of churchmanship, acknowledged no common commanding influence whom they could label as the father of their school. We cannot even list their names, for it is probable that by far the majority of the clergy of the early and mid-Victorian age—and many laymen too —applauded Arnold's contention that education is worthless without the leaven of religion.

Yet we cannot call them 'Arnoldians', for such a description would fail to take into account a number of educational reformers and moralists who, while admiring Arnold for his work at Rugby, thoroughly disapproved of his political views and churchmanship. G. H. Moberly and Charles Wordsworth at Winchester and Christopher Wordsworth at Harrow were as eager as Arnold to effect a moral reformation at their schools; but all three were High Churchmen and none of them was personally influenced by Arnold, although Moberly in a famous letter to Stanley clearly recognised Arnold's claims to be the first great influence for good in the public schools.[12]

Mr. Noel Annan, in his biography of Leslie Stephen and in the essay which he contributed to the volume of social studies presented to G. M. Trevelyan, has drawn an interesting picture of what he describes as the intellectual *élite* of the Victorian age. Certain families, which had risen from a common middle-class origin and had fallen under the spell of the evangelical revival, developed an intellectual ascendancy in England through a combination of inherited security, natural merits and inter-marriage. By this process of inter-marriage, 'the separate roots grew into a trunk most massive in the sixties and seventies'.[13] United by a common upbringing, training and interest, and stimulated by the zeal and earnestness which had characterised their religious education, they formed an 'establishment' which set the tone and dominated the social and intellectual life of their age.

> The same blood can be found appearing among the headmasters of the public schools, and the Fellows of Oxford and Cambridge colleges; the same tone of voice can be heard criticising, teaching and leading middle-class opinion in the periodicals; and the same families fill the vacancies among the senior permanent officials in a Civil Service open to talent.[14]

Such are the class, the background and the influence of the group of men whose names recur in the pages that follow. What makes them a group whose ideals and experiences can be discussed collectively is not so much their kinship by blood, but the common spirit which binds them together as men with a determined mission. For, having come from a similar home background, having been trained in the same disciplines in the same schools and having formed intimate friendships at the age when it is proper to see visions, they developed a common standard of values and shared a common resolve to impress their ideals upon the particular society into which their work was into take them.

'Evangelical morality was the single most widespread influence in Victorian England',[15] writes Mr. Annan. It is true that beside the austere scholarship and militant dogmatism of the Tractarians* and the daring rationalism and breadth of mind of the Mauriceans and the Broad Church party, Evangelicalism may appear to have been a spent force by the middle years of the nineteenth century. As Dean Church put it:

> It shrank . . . from coming into contact with the manifold realities of the spirit of man; it never seemed to get beyond the 'first beginnings' of Christian teaching, the call to repent, the assurance of forgiveness: it had nothing to say to the long and varied process of building up the new life of truth and goodness: it was nervously afraid of departing from the consecrated phrases of its school, and in the perpetual iteration of them it lost hold of the meaning they may once have had.[16]

Nevertheless, from the Evangelicals, Victorian England had learnt its philanthropy, its missionary zeal, its enthusiasm. If the scholarship of Evangelicalism had become barren and its attitude of mind narrow and unbending, the tradition of piety, earnestness and good works was active throughout the Victorian age: most particularly, it set the pattern of Victorian family life and

* The label given to the pioneers of the Oxford Movement who contributed to the series of pamphlets, edited by John Henry Newman, entitled *Tracts for the Times*, published between 1833 and 1841. The leading writers of these tracts were Newman, John Keble, E. B. Pusey, R. H. Froude, Charles Marriott and Isaac Williams. Their purpose was to emphasise the apostolical character of the doctrine of the Church of England by compiling catenas from the writings of the early Fathers and of Caroline divines. They also sought to rouse their fellow clergymen to a higher conception of their sacerdotal office, in the first place, by encouraging them to resist all secular encroachments on ecclesiastical power and, secondly, by repudiating the 'Protestant' elements in Anglicanism, especially the teaching and methods of the Evangelicals.

ethical training, perhaps the most important formative power behind the eminence of the eminent Victorians. Almost all this influential group of moral reformers owed something to the evangelical spirit. Sometimes, as in the case of Edward White Benson or Benjamin Jowett or F. W. Farrar, it was an evangelical father who saw that his children were brought up in godly ways; sometimes, as with Newman or A. H. Clough or F. J. A. Hort, the mother's influence prevailed. Even families not avowedly evangelical—like the Kebles, the Puseys, the Mannings or the Kingsleys—were infected with the spirit. Side by side with the early instruction in the catechism, bible-reading, family prayers and paternal benedictions, went the encouragement of precociousness in intellectual pursuits. Thomas Arnold was presented with Smollett's *History of England* at the age of three;[17] F. W. Farrar read the Milton given to him when a little child so thoroughly that he soon knew many passages from *Paradise Lost* by heart;[18] Charles Kingsley was delivering sermons at the age of four from a makeshift pulpit in the nursery, dressed in a pinafore as a surplice, while his delighted mother copied them down to show to the Bishop of Peterborough.[19]

Careful home training gave way to the classical discipline of school. Some—like Samuel Wilberforce, Mark Pattison and John Keble—were taught at home. However, Winchester educated Arnold, Moberly, Christopher Wordsworth and W. G. Ward; Charles Wordsworth, Manning and Isaac Williams were at Harrow; Gladstone and Pusey at Eton; James Prince Lee and Benjamin Jowett at St. Paul's. Some went to lesser known schools: Newman to a private school at Ealing; Kingsley to Helston Grammar School; Farrar to King William's, Isle of Man. In time, they arrived at their respective universities, loaded with school prizes, having read the same classical texts and having experienced a very similar discipline and training, albeit at schools as yet 'unreformed'.

Many of the second generation of Victorian intellectuals and scholars, however, had sat at the feet of the giants. They had absorbed the gospel of 'godliness and good learning' as ardent disciples listening to a revered master. Two of these groups receive special attention later in this book—the Rugbeians, the pupils of Arnold; and the influential group of pupils of James

Prince Lee, headmaster of King Edward's, Birmingham, notably
E. W. Benson, J. B. Lightfoot and B. F. Westcott.

One interesting feature of these two particular groups is that
the most formative influences on the lives of their members were
the teaching and personality of their headmasters and the
intimate friendships made at school. The sense of mission and the
spirit of dedicated resolution had been engendered before they
came up to the university. A. P. Stanley, for instance, dreaded
the day when he would have to leave Rugby to go up to Oxford,
partly because many of the leading figures of the university were
hostile to Arnold, partly because the prospect of community life
without Arnold's presiding inspiration seemed almost unendurable. 'I shall have to go from a place which I love with
more than ordinary affection to a place which I hate with more
than ordinary hatred.'[20] And Arnold wrote to J. T. Coleridge in
October 1835 to tell him that W. C. Lake had been spending the
last week of his Rugby life with the Arnold household,

> dreading the approach of the day which should take him to Oxford,
> although he was going up to a most delightful society of old
> friends; and when he actually came to take leave, I really think
> that the parting was like that of a father and son.[21]

However, on the earlier generation—on the pioneers of
godliness and good learning—their schooldays had made less
impression than the influence of their homes and the stimulating
society of the university. J. T. Coleridge, in the letter he contributed to Stanley's *Life of Arnold* and again in his *Memoir of
John Keble*, has given a vivid picture of college life and Oxford
society at the beginning of the nineteenth century. He, Keble
and Arnold were at Corpus Christi together, although Keble was
slightly senior to the other two. It was a small college—twenty
fellows, twenty scholars and four exhibitioners forming the
foundation, with the addition of some six gentlemen commoners.
Since several of the scholars were Bachelors of Arts, the actual
number of students under college tuition was about twenty.

> We were then a small society, the members rather under the usual
> age, and with more than the ordinary proportion of ability and
> scholarship. . . . One result of all these circumstances was, that we
> lived on the most familiar terms with each other: we might be,
> indeed we were, somewhat boyish in manner, and in the liberties

9

we took with each other; but our interest in literature, ancient and modern, and in all the stirring matters of that stirring time, was not boyish; we debated the classic and romantic question; we discussed poetry and history, logic and philosophy; or we fought over the Peninsular battles and the Continental campaigns with the energy of disputants personally concerned in them. Our habits were inexpensive and temperate.[22]

Both Arnold and Keble moved later to Oriel as fellows, where they joined the most stimulating society in Oxford, the circle known as the Noetics, already famed for its 'unusual dialectical cut and thrust' and for its tendency to fearless speculation.[23] In the 1820's, the Attic Society and its more famous offspring, the Oxford Union, became the arena where Samuel Wilberforce, Henry Edward Manning and W. E. Gladstone gained their early reputation for brilliant oratory. Indeed, the late twenties at Oxford were exceptionally rich in talent, at a time when the university was numerically very much smaller than it is to-day and when its brilliant members were all known to one another, often taught by the same tutors, frequently competing together for the same prizes. E. S. Purcell, the biographer of Manning, indulges in a somewhat highly coloured rhapsody on Manning's contemporaries who might have been present at the Union on the memorable occasion when Manning scored his first oratorical triumph:

> How little did the small band of his since illustrious contemporaries, who criticised or applauded an unknown undergraduate's first oratorical success at the Union, or on the morrow heard of its fame, dream of his or their own future career in life! And yet men say that the future is in mercy hid from our eyes; mercifully, perhaps, from the eyes of dunces or sinners, but scarcely in mercy hid from saints and sages.

He recalls Dick Whittington, hearing the chimes of Bow Bells.

> But infinitely greater would the amazement, and anguish perhaps in part, have been, had the bells of the city of Spires been alike gifted with prophetic tongues, and had proclaimed to the eighteen or nineteen young men of mark, present in body or in spirit at the Oxford Union on that memorable day, that out of their scanty number—the pick of the University, I grant—one would be four

10

times Prime Minister of England, disestablish a Church and attempt to wreck the unity of the Empire; three become Cabinet Ministers; three Governors-General of India; one Archbishop of Canterbury; six forsake the Anglican for the Catholic Church; and, wonder of wonders, two, without forfeiting the respect and reverence of their countrymen, become Cardinals of the Holy Roman Church.[24]

The generation that followed was scarcely less brilliant. The scholars of Balliol while A. C. Tait and W. G. Ward were tutors included A. P. Stanley, E. M. Goulburn, Benjamin Jowett, A. H. Clough, Sir Stafford Northcote, Frederick Temple and Matthew Arnold. This was Oxford of the *Tracts*, with its special ethos—*Credo in Newmannum*, 'Newmania' as some unkindly called it; the Oxford which Dean Church in a famous passage compared to the Florence of Savonarola, a small enclosed society torn asunder as if by *stasis*, so that emotions became abnormally high-pitched, rivalries unnaturally fierce, love and devotion more intense. For a decade and more, hardly anyone who entered the stronghold of Anglican orthodoxy could avoid being swept up in the maelstrom of religious controversy.

Cambridge experienced nothing quite like this. In the 1820's, Cambridge—and Trinity in particular—was the centre of classical scholarship. One has to picture a society to whom the greatest event in the year was the awarding of the Chancellor's Medals, a group of earnest, industrious, religious undergraduates competing for the top places within the First Class of the Classical Tripos, all familiar with each other's talents and enthusiasms, meeting for meals, talking together on long daily walks round the countryside, worshipping together in the College Chapel, joining together to make pious resolutions. This was the age of the classical triumphs of three prominent intellectual families—the Selwyns, the Kennedys and the Wordsworths. Fifteen years later, the pupils of a previous Craven Scholar and Fellow of Trinity, James Prince Lee, were to carry off all the classical honours. By that time the religious spirit had heightened in Cambridge, and while Oxford was lamenting or deriding the 'going-over' of Newman, Cambridge—or at least Trinity—was becoming more and more imbued with the theology of F. D. Maurice.[25] Certainly Cambridge was freer than Oxford from the distractions of violent religious controversy, those 'discussions unprofitable in

11

themselves' as Mark Pattison described them in his Memoirs, '. . . which had entirely diverted our thoughts from the true business of the place'.[26]

The two universities differed considerably in their religious standpoints; perhaps, too, as C. R. Sandars has maintained, a difference in philosophic influence can be discerned among those who might be labelled 'Broad Churchmen', belonging to either university. The Oxford rationalists, the Noetics and their successors—men like Stanley, Matthew Arnold and Jowett—were primarily Aristotelian in their philosophy, putting their faith in formal logic. The Cambridge school—Coleridge, Julius Hare, John Sterling, F. D. Maurice and, to some extent, Carlyle, Tennyson and Browning—were Platonists and disciples of Kant.[27] Nevertheless, despite these distinctions and despite the fact that the prevailing religious spirit undoubtedly led so many of these men into partisanship, the points of similarity between them are more striking than their differences.

At school they studied the same texts; at the university they competed for the same honours and prizes. They read and admired the same books. Indeed, one may go so far as to say that besides his Bible and his classical authors, the early Victorian intellectual was most conspicuously influenced by five literary works which did more to form his ideas, quicken his emotions and inspire his motives than any other influence of a cultural or philosophic kind. The five works were Butler's *Analogy*, Wordsworth's poems, Sir Walter Scott's novels, Coleridge's *Aids to Reflection* and Keble's *The Christian Year*. It is, of course, dangerous to generalise about the influence of books upon society and hence upon historical events, implying thereby that it is ideas which shape history rather than political opportunism or economic forces. Evidence that a man has read a certain important book does not prove that he has been moved by it, and, even if we can be sure that the reader admired what he had read, we often cannot say for certain that his subsequent actions were governed by the thoughts and ideas which he had absorbed. On the other hand, when the evidence points clearly to the almost universal reading among the class of men who form the intellectual aristocracy of the country of a few particularly significant books, which become the subject of their discussions and debates, of their letters and their sermons; which are taken with them on their walks to read in some quiet and shaded place; and from which extracts are taken and copied into commonplace books and diaries; then, it is justifiable to suppose that these books had a formative influence on the lives and thoughts of the men who prized them so highly.

And in argument and sentiment the affinities are plain. Newman wrote of Butler's *Analogy* that the study of it

> has been to so many, as it was to me, an era in their religious opinions. The inculcation of a visible Church, the oracle of truth and a pattern of sanctity, of the duties of external religion, and of the historical character of Revelation, are characteristics of this great work which strike the reader at once.[28]

On Hurrell Froude's death in 1836, Newman was asked to select one of his books as a keepsake. He chose Butler's *Analogy*, only to find that it had already been taken.[29]

Gladstone, in a letter to Manning written in 1865, stated

> I have no intention whatever of breaking with the traditions in which I have grown up, which I have learned from Oxford, which I have learned from four writers far beyond any, perhaps all, others—Butler, Aristotle, Dante, St. Augustine, my four doctors.[30]

Indeed, Butler's view of habit, which Gladstone always regarded as the 'foundation of character',[31] and which Newman would often recall for the benefit of his pupils, might be taken as one of the most appropriate mottoes of the Victorian moralists:

> Whatever we do on the call of duty we do easier next time; whatever we fail to do we find more difficult, that is we are still less disposed to do it. We fall back on the sure law of habit.[32]

From Wordsworth came the spirit of romanticism, the love of the mountains, insight into 'the deeper relations between nature and the human soul'.[33] J. T. Coleridge took pride in recalling that he had been the first to introduce Arnold to the Lake Poets. 'We felt their truth and beauty, and became zealous disciples of Wordsworth's philosophy.' This gave to Arnold 'that feeling for the lofty and imaginative which appeared in all his intimate conversation'.[34] Frances Woodward, in her study of four of

13

Arnold's disciples, cites with reference to their master the lines of his 'favourite poet':

> I made no vows, but vows
> Were then made for me; bond unknown to me
> Was given, that I should be, else sinning greatly,
> A dedicated spirit.[35] (*Prelude*, IV.334–7.)

From Scott came the mingling of the romantic vein with the rediscovery of the middle ages. The connection between the revival of interest in medievalism and the Tractarian Movement is obvious. As Elliott-Binns noted, 'the romantic atmosphere in which Tractarianism was to find itself so much at home undoubtedly owed much to the novels of Sir Walter Scott'.[36] But the enthusiasm for Scott was by no means confined to the Tractarian party. Westcott devoted the fruits of his first literary earnings to purchasing a set of Scott's novels for his wife;[37] Hort listened evening after evening to his father reading Scott to the family circle,[38] and F. W. Farrar re-read *Ivanhoe* so many times that 'the characters in it grew to be as real to him as the people in the streets'.[39]

The influence of Coleridge was perhaps the deepest force of all. J. S. Mill, writing in 1838, put Coleridge on a par with Bentham as one of the two great philosophers who had taught his own generation how to think.[40] Those who were horrified by Benthamite materialism—and, as we have seen already, almost all the early nineteenth-century moralists who believed in the essential union of godliness and good learning regarded Bentham as their enemy—naturally turned to Coleridge as their guide. In Coleridge's works lay almost everything they sought: an effective challenge to John Locke and his eighteenth-century admirers; a more profound comprehension of the evidences of Christianity than anything that Paley had to offer; the union of religion and morality. In reading his writings, they experienced that thrill which comes from the discovery that amidst a welter of nonsense and misdirected enthusiasm, the voice of wisdom had spoken; a whole system of thought, a true philosophy of life, had been enunciated, in which their own unarticulated beliefs and hopes had at last found expression, and which might—through their ardent advocacy of the cause—yet save their generation.

So it seemed, for instance, to young Frederick Temple in 1841 when he was an undergraduate at Balliol. He wrote to his sister Katy:

I have been reading Coleridge a good deal lately, and I can hardly tell you how much I admire him; I have a sort of feeling, however, that this admiration cannot last long. Reading him excites me so much that I can hardly do anything else after it; I am obliged never to read it except just before I am going to walk. What a wonderful power of conversation he must have had; no subject seems to have baffled him. [41]

Newman, temperamentally so very different from Temple, also felt the attraction. Coleridge it was, he wrote,

who, while he indulged a liberty of speculation, which no Christian can tolerate, and advocated conclusions which were often heathen rather than Christian, yet after all instilled a higher philosophy into inquiring minds, than they had hitherto been accustomed to accept. In this way he made trial of his age, and succeeded in interesting its genius in the cause of Catholic truth. [42]

Many of the ideals and precepts of the Arnoldians and of the Broad Church school can be traced back to Coleridge, especially to *Aids to Reflection*. Their hatred of sectarianism found expression in the famous passage:

He, who begins by loving Christianity better than truth, will proceed by loving his own sect or Church better than Christianity, and end in loving himself better than all. [43]

Coleridge's exaltation of the rational spirit ('Reason . . . is the organ of wisdom, and, as far as man is concerned, the source of living and actual truth') [44] and his criterion for the validity of doctrinal pronouncements ('Will the belief tend to the improvement of any of my moral or intellectual faculties?') [45] were prophetic of the tenets of the later school which was to combine a fearless rational criticism with an intense preoccupation with moral conduct. Cambridge, through the teaching of Julius Hare and F. D. Maurice and, later, through the scholarship and theological writings of F. J. A. Hort, fell deeply under the spell of this philosophy. Julius Hare, in his notes to *The Mission of the Comforter*, expressed exactly the debt which his generation owed to Coleridge and Wordsworth.

We whose entrance into intellectual life took place in the second and third decades of this century, enjoyed a singular felicity in

15

this respect, in that the stimulators and trainers of our thoughts were Wordsworth and Coleridge; in whom practical judgment and moral dignity and a sacred love of truth are so nobly wedded to the highest intellectual power. By them the better part of us were preserved from the noxious taint of Byron.[46]

John Keble's *The Christian Year* appeared in 1827. It was rapidly acclaimed as one of the classics of the language, combining originality of approach and expression with a singular awareness of what was needed to satisfy the deep spiritual yearnings of the time. Its depth of teaching, its mystery and sanctity, its consciousness of the living power of faith and love 'woke up in the hearts of thousands', as Newman testified, 'a new music, the music of a school, long unknown in England'.[47] It marked in the history of the Church the waning of the influence of the Noetics and the stirring of a new spiritual force, the appeal of which can be best comprehended in the phrase 'the beauty of holiness'. To the members of that school later to be called the Tractarians, it was an inspiration; indeed, as Mozley observed, 'most of its happy members knew *The Christian Year* by heart'.[48] But the appeal was widespread. To read it was the duty, and usually the joy, of every professing Christian. The following episode recounted by the Rev. C. W. Penny, one of Benson's assistant masters at Wellington, paints a typical Victorian scene. In January 1868, Benson and Penny were taking a walk together. About half-way to Wokingham, Benson

> led the conversation to Keble's *Christian Year*, of which he was a devout admirer, and seemed almost pained to find that I did not care much for Keble's sacred poetry. I pleaded in defence his great obscurity. Benson would not allow that it was great; and drawing a copy from his pocket proceeded to read to me as we walked along the poem for the day, and appealed to me to confess that I was wrong and prejudiced in my view—and that at all events in regard to that poem in particular my verdict could not stand. Then he took a pencil and added my name and the date to the margin of the poem, saying that it would remind him in after years of our walk and talk that day.[49]

Taking into account all their differences—in personality, religious temperament and philosophic standpoint—we may yet discern a definite pattern in the lives of these early and mid-

Victorian intellectuals who were brought up to godliness and good learning and who by precept and example endeavoured to bring up their own children likewise. They read seriously, talked earnestly, and sought to make the world a morally better place. They may have been dogmatic in their principles, but they were desperately anxious to increase their knowledge. Thus frivolities and worthless amusements played no part in their lives. They walked and talked indefatigably, but always with a purpose. There were churches or historical monuments to be seen and sketched, plants by the wayside to be noted and admired, the beauties of nature to be appreciated for the greater glory of God. As young men at the university they were drawn together by this bond of purposefulness. The older dons, relics of the more secular and leisurely eighteenth-century world, stood apart bewildered and perturbed. 'They wanted', Mr. V. H. H. Green tells us,

> their club gossip, their round of whist, their betting book, their port wine. . . . Hugh Platt recorded a conversation at St. John's just after the future Dean Stanley had come back from the Holy Land, which he was describing at some length. 'Jerusalem be damned,' an elderly fellow was heard to observe, 'give us wine, women and horses.' [50]

'Stirring matters of that stirring time' was the phrase which J. T. Coleridge used to describe the topics which engaged his Oxford contemporaries at the beginning of the century. These men were truly children of that age of anxious optimism which succeeded the French Revolution and the Napoleonic Wars. The consciousness of change and movement, inevitable at a time of rapid technological and economic advance, manifested itself in different forms. From France was blowing the chilly wind of reform, a source of invigoration to the Benthamites who welcomed a total reappraisal of the English legal system in the light of the efficient and practical Napoleonic Code. From Germany came the compelling philosophy of Herder and Hegel, reactionary and nationalist, with its stress on the organic nature of society and on gradual institutional development. Everywhere there seemed to be movement, controversy; the static had given way to the dynamic. It is not to be wondered at that those who were

17

making themselves masters in their own smaller world of school and university should see themselves equipped for and destined to leadership in the wider world outside. That England seemed particularly blessed to lead the world in industry and commerce was evident to any man who lived through the early railway age. 'In a petulant mood, he would talk, with Grote, of the Age of Steam and Cant', writes Mr. G. M. Young, 'but all the while he knew that in the essential business of humanity, the mastery of brute nature by intelligence, he had outstripped the world, and the Machine was the emblem and the instrument of his triumph.'[51] To the large and growing class of godly intellectuals it appeared increasingly important to ensure that progress was made in the right direction and never divorced from Christian principles. At the end of things, an account must be made to God for all these blessings.

This explains two leading characteristics of the members of this class: their ambition and their impatience. "I believe that, naturally, I am one of the most ambitious men alive",[52] * said Arnold in later life, referring to his early days at Laleham. In 1826, surveying the troubles of his time, he wrote: 'I cannot tell you how the present state of the country occupies my mind, and what a restless desire I feel that it were in my power to do any good.'[53] Samuel Wilberforce, in his late twenties, discussed with his brother whether he should accept the offer of a rich London living:

> As to ambitious feelings [he wrote], I trust I should not act from them. . . . I should say it was a lottery in which I staked certain comfort against the chance of rising to an uncomfortable eminence. But I earnestly desire and pray *constantly* to be able to put these thoughts aside.[54]

Indeed, neither ambition nor impatience exactly describes the impulses which made these men of thought into men of action. Their ambition was rather the awareness of important work to do which they were pre-eminently qualified to perform. There is little evidence of an ignoble grasping after power or of a studied

---

* Compare his reflections in 1823: 'I have always thought with regard to ambition, that I should like to be *aut Caesar aut nullus*, and as it is pretty well settled for me that I shall not be Caesar, I am quite content to live in peace as nullus.'

cultivation of useful contacts to make the ascent to the top smoother and more certain. Occasionally our suspicions are aroused: the career of Cardinal Manning has certainly been so represented; and William Wilberforce's advice to his son Samuel on going up to Oxford suggests that the usefulness of social contacts was not entirely discounted:

> Never omit any opportunity, my dear Sam[1], of getting acquainted with any good man or any useful man—of course, I mean that this usefulness in any one line should not be countervailed by any qualities of an opposite nature from which defilement might be contracted, —more perhaps depends on the selection of acquaintances than on any other circumstances in life, except, of course, still more close and intimate unions. Acquaintances are indeed the raw materials from which are manufactured friends, wives, husbands, etc. I wish it may please God to give you an opportunity of having some good ones to chuse out of on your first settling at Oxford.[55]

Notwithstanding the consciousness of dynamic change, the degree of assurance that talents would receive their due is very remarkable. There was not a hint of complacency in this attitude. Indeed, the virtually certain prospect of responsible office called for unending efforts to make oneself worthy and for intense self-examination. The summons was often awaited with rising dread and apprehension; but some day it would come. One had only to wait.

And to wait was not always easy when the world seemed in danger of running off the rails. Hence the impatience; more properly, perhaps, the sense of urgency. Nowhere is the realisation of this more evident than in the Inaugural Lecture of Arnold. "Without any presumptuous confidence", he said,

> if there be any signs, however uncertain, that we are living in the latest period of the world's history, that no other races remain behind to perform what we have neglected, or to restore what we have ruined, then indeed the interest of modern history does become intense, and the importance of not wasting the time still left to us may well be called incalculable. . . . So if our existing nations are the last reserve of the world, its fate may be said to be in their hands—God's work on earth will be left undone if they do not do it.[56]

Arnold's audience understood perfectly well. They knew their Coleridge. He had taught his followers that the very essence of a

Christian man was his capacity to live up to his faith, to win battles for his Master.[57] Carlyle was preaching the gospel of Work, wherein lay the salvation of mankind. Westcott summed it up admirably when he ascribed to the Cambridge of his generation the motto of Whichcote: 'I act, therefore I am.'[58]

*   *   *   *   *

This is the world and these are the people who form the subject of the studies that follow. Something, however, should be said of the circle within this group of earnest Victorian intellectuals whose activities and writings receive in this book by far the most attention—the friends, colleagues and associates of Edward White Benson, Archbishop of Canterbury from 1883 to 1896, a circle made up mainly of Cambridge figures, prominent scholars and churchmen, whose lives and work have been generally less studied than those of their Oxford contemporaries.

A brief account of the career of E. W. Benson may serve as an illustration of how an important and influential circle comes into being. Benson started life with no advantages of good birth and inherited riches. Born in 1829, he was a Birmingham boy of evangelical, middle-class parents whose family roots lay in Yorkshire. When Benson was only thirteen years old, his father died, leaving his widow and family of four boys and four girls virtually destitute. The generosity of two of his father's friends enabled Benson to complete his education at King Edward's School, Birmingham, and to enter Trinity College, Cambridge, as a sub-sizar, in 1848. He lived at Cambridge in conditions of extreme poverty and he became an orphan when his mother died in 1850. Nevertheless he was acquiring certain advantages. He had established himself within the *cursus honorum:* he had been taught at a school famed for its classical scholarship by a head-master who was 'generally considered one of the most distinguished classical scholars ever known in the university'[59] (James Prince Lee); he became a scholar and subsequently Fellow of the most distinguished college in Cambridge; he obtained a First Class in the Classical Tripos (8th Classic) and the Senior Chancellor's Medal. He was already one of the central figures of a group of scholarly, spiritually-minded friends. His contemporaries at

John Wordsworth
Elizabeth Wordsworth, Susan Wordsworth, Miss Wickenden
Mrs. Benson, E. W. Benson, Mary Wordsworth (Mrs. Trebecke)
Martin,   Arthur,   Canon Wickenden

A family group at Whitby, 1869

'A Friend in Need', from the illustrated edition of
F. W. Farrar's *Eric; or Little by Little*

school had been Brooke Foss Westcott (slightly senior to the others), Joseph Barber Lightfoot (his most intimate friend)—both subsequently Professors of Divinity at Cambridge and Bishops of Durham; J. F. Wickenden, later Prebendary of Lincoln; Charles Evans, later headmaster of King Edward's, Birmingham; E. J. Purbrick, later Provincial of the English Jesuits and Rector of Stonyhurst; and a number of future First Class classicists, including C. B. Hutchinson, A. A. Ellis and J. T. Pearse. All these men, with the exception of Hutchinson and Purbrick, were at Trinity together. Lightfoot and Benson became private pupils of Westcott at Cambridge, and the long period of unbroken and devoted friendship between these three scholars really began from this date. Into the circle of Prince Lee's pupils came F. J. A. Hort (from Rugby) and their particular friend and helper among the Fellows—Francis Martin, subsequently Vice-Master of Trinity.

Thus with academic standing and stimulating friends, Benson was placed in a position of high promise. Even before his academic successes he appears to have been conscious that he and his friends were destined for high office in the Church. His school-fellows and his family thought of him as a future Archbishop of Canterbury—he had resolved to take orders from the age of fourteen—and he would ponder quite calmly over the responsibilities of the future, having decided at an early stage in his career never to apply for any position but to wait until God's will should be made plain through the approaches of others.

Offers were soon to come. The first was an invitation from Dr. E. M. Goulburn, headmaster of Rugby, to accept a post of assistant master with special duties with the Sixth Form. The circle now widened. Benson became one of a group to whom offers of headmasterships came almost as a matter of course. For Arnold, as surely as he had raised the prestige of Rugby, had made of the Rugby staff a nursery of future headmasters. Into the circle came Frederick Temple, Goulburn's successor, who instantly became a firm and beloved friend; also G. G. Bradley, subsequently headmaster of Marlborough and Dean of Westminster; J. C. Shairp, Professor of Poetry at Oxford and Principal of St. Andrew's; T. S. Evans, Professor of Greek at Durham; T. W. Jex-Blake, Principal of Cheltenham, headmaster of Rugby and Dean of Wells; A. G. Butler, headmaster of Haileybury. Two former friends of Benson's schooldays were also on the Rugby staff—Charles Evans and C. B. Hutchinson.

While at Rugby, Benson lodged with his cousins—the Sidgwicks. He became engaged to Mary Sidgwick, his second cousin, whom he married in 1859. Henry and Arthur Sidgwick, Mary's brothers, were both taught by Benson at Rugby. Again the circle widened, in this instance providing an illustration of what Mr. Annan describes as a common phenomenon of the period—a particular type of middle-class family inter-marrying and producing children who became scholars and teachers.[60] Of their six children, Martin, the eldest son, and Eleanor, the eldest daughter, died young; Arthur Benson became a housemaster at Eton and eventually Master of Magdalene College, Cambridge; E. F. Benson (Fred) earned a considerable reputation as a writer and novelist; Maggy, after a brilliant career at Lady Margaret Hall, became interested in Egyptology and philosophy until incapacitated by mental illness; and Robert Hugh, the youngest, after taking orders in the Anglican church, subsequently renounced them and became a Roman Catholic priest. There the line ends, since none of the Benson children married.

In 1858, on Temple's recommendation, Benson accepted the offer of the Prince Consort to become first headmaster of Wellington College, an institution founded in memory of the Duke of Wellington to educate the orphan sons of army officers on virtually gratuitous terms. In the space of fourteen years he succeeded in converting Wellington into a great and important public school, despite the initial disadvantages of an inadequate endowment, unpromising material and somewhat limited aims. There is little doubt that this astonishing achievement largely accounts for the distinction of Benson's subsequent career. Having displayed such creative power and forcefulness in his work at Wellington, he was called in 1873 to establish an effective diocesan theological college—the Cancellarii Scholae—as Chancellor of Lincoln, and in December 1876 he was offered the Bishopric of Truro, a see newly created by act of Parliament. From Truro he was called to Canterbury in December 1882.

It is significant, however, that when Benson became Master of Wellington, he was already a member of an influential circle of friends;[61] * and the rapid rise in prestige of the new foundation was in no small part due to the determination of Benson's friends and former associates to assist him in every way they could.[62] The new post itself caused the numbers of the circle to swell. Only a few miles away from Wellington lived Charles Kingsley, rector of the neighbouring parish of Eversley, James Mozley, rector of Finchampstead, and John Walter of Bearwood, proprietor of *The Times*, all of whom took an active interest in the new educational experiment.

The most interesting addition to the Benson circle came, however, in 1866, when John Wordsworth, the third son of Christopher Wordsworth (a nephew of the poet), joined the staff at Wellington as Sixth Form assistant to the Master. John Wordsworth, who had already become deeply attached to Westcott while an assistant master at Harrow,[63] stayed at Wellington only two terms, but during that time he developed a great affection for the Benson family; and his father, who was then Archdeacon of Westminster, discovered in the course of a visit to Wellington that he and Benson had kindred interests in their pursuit of patristic studies and shared the same views on the active rôle which the cathedral should play in the spiritual life of a diocese. C. W. Penny has left the following account of this new friendship:

> Accompanied by Mrs. Wordsworth and two or three of his daughters, he [Christopher Wordsworth] visited Benson at the Master's Lodge for a few days. . . . The attraction of Wordsworth to Benson was very great. And from this date Miss Elizabeth Wordsworth (subsequently Principal of Lady Margaret Hall) often stayed at Wellington. During subsequent midsummer holidays the Bensons spent their holiday at Whitby in Yorkshire. And either in the same lodgings or quite near them were Wordsworth and his sister Elizabeth and Benson's schoolfellow J. F. Wickenden and his sister.

* This is borne out by a remarkable letter written by A. P. Stanley to A. C. Tait, in October 1856, shortly after Tait had become Bishop of London. Stanley recommended the names of a few bright young men who might be suitable as chaplains to the new Bishop. He had three Cambridge names to suggest: 'By far the best Cambridge man of fit age and the like that occurs to me is *Benson*, Fellow of Trinity, now at Rugby. . . . A man of the same kind . . . is *Westcott* of Harrow. One other Cambridge name occurs to me—*Lightfoot*, Fellow and, I think, Tutor of Trinity—of the same stamp as Westcott and Benson.'

. . . I have always considered that Benson's introduction to Bp. Christopher Wordsworth was the first step in the ladder which eventually landed him at Canterbury. As soon as Wordsworth became Bishop of Lincoln in 1869 he asked Benson to be one of his Examining Chaplains and in that capacity Benson preached the sermon at Bp. Wordsworth's Primary Ordination on Trinity Sunday, 1869. In 1870 he became Prebendary of Lincoln. Towards the end of 1872 he was Chancellor and had determined to leave Wellington College. Benson's admiration of Wordsworth as a Bishop knew no bounds, and still more did he appreciate his profound learning, monumental scholarship, and most lovable personal character. But he by no means agreed with the Bishop's rather peculiar theological views. [64]

Here the account of the Benson circle may rest. Within a few years Benson was drawn away into active ecclesiastical life, but the future of a young man in his thirties, who had risen from wholly unpropitious circumstances, was assured. The Master's Lodge at Wellington College, a gaunt structure of unweathered red brick in the midst of a wild and desolate heath, became the scene of meetings and discussions attended by some of the most eminent intellects of the day. Penny, in his reminiscences, recalled them in amazement:

I am afraid one hardly realised how infinitely better than the average society of the neighbourhood was that within which we were thrown—Benson—Kingsley—Mozley—Lightfoot and others. Temple among them. It is strange to think that two future Archbishops were sitting at table in the Head Master's House at Wellington College. [65]

Another day it might have been the Wordsworths, the Sidgwicks, G. G. Bradley, Westcott and Francis Martin. It is obvious that no single tradition of churchmanship was represented here. Indeed, these gatherings might seem to have their parallel in Stanley's famous reconciliation of opposites at his parties at the Deanery—or the meetings of the Sterling Club—the main differences, however, being that the bonds which held these men together were a common friendship with a man who was devoting his life to the ideal of 'godliness and good learning' and the fact that almost all of them were on the road to eminence and distinction, not yet having reached the end of their journey. From groups such as these, 'establishments' are formed.

* * * * *

This introduction has attempted to show that the ideal of godliness and good learning assumed that education and religion were essentially allied; and, furthermore, that the belief was not confined to a small group of Victorian headmasters who held a high and exaggerated view of the importance of their calling. In examining some of the roots of this ideal we have seen that this manner of thinking was natural to a large body of early Victorians who had been brought up in the atmosphere of pious homes and who had shared common experiences and enthusiasms at school and at the university. Despite doctrinal differences and rival philosophic systems, they can still be regarded as a single class, stamped with an unmistakable mintmark: a combination of intellectual toughness, moral earnestness and deep spiritual conviction.

The first of the studies that follow deals with the practical application of this ideal of godliness and good learning—the methods employed in the schools to convert 'dens of thieves' into 'temples of God', and the ways in which these attempts to inculcate spiritual zeal and love of learning reacted upon the younger generation of these times.

The second and third studies are biographical. The first of these is a particular study of one of the idealists who sought to make godliness and good learning the main principles of his teaching—James Prince Lee, headmaster of King Edward's School, Birmingham, and first Bishop of Manchester. He was the second of Arnold's appointments to his staff at Rugby and the first of Arnold's assistant masters to leave Rugby for a headmastership. The extraordinary succession of brilliant pupils who proceeded from Birmingham to Trinity College, Cambridge, has already been noted. His career has the added interest, that while he was revered as a headmaster by such pupils as Benson, Lightfoot and Westcott, his episcopate has been almost universally regarded as a complete failure.

In the second of the biographical studies the subject is not an idealist but rather an exemplar of the ideal. An attempt has been made to reconstruct the life of a schoolboy in the Victorian age, in particular a schoolboy in whom the ideal of godliness and good learning found a willing and eager recipient. The boy is Martin Benson, the eldest of E. W. Benson's children, who died from meningitis at Winchester in 1878 at the age of seventeen. For many reasons Martin seemed an obvious choice. Of all the Benson children he was most plainly the child of his father, and since in the study of Prince Lee a good deal emerges of E. W. Benson's childhood and upbringing, it is interesting to observe the transmission of the same ideals and enthusiasms from the father who learnt them from Prince Lee to the son who belonged to a generation which was slowly drawing away from the standards and values of the early and mid-Victorian age. Again, Martin's career is exceptionally well documented. His letters home from his private school—Temple Grove, East Sheen—and from Winchester have survived, as have also the letters which the parents wrote to the boy. In addition to this collection, there is a long and poignant account of the boy's life and death, written by his father a week after Martin died, a document of exceptional interest not only for the light that it sheds on Victorian family life but also for the testimony it bears of the emotionalism and high idealism of the age.

The final study in this book seeks to account for the gradual abandonment of the ideals of godliness and good learning in the last half of the nineteenth century. What is particularly striking is a change of spirit: moral earnestness became 'theumos'—the hearty enjoyment of physical pursuits, the belief that manliness and high spirits are more becoming qualities in a boy than piety and spiritual zeal. The change of spirit began to affect both the education system in public school and university and the standard of values that lay behind them. Games-playing, on an organised basis, became an important part of the school curriculum; excessive displays of emotion came in time to be regarded as bad form; patriotism and doing one's duty to country and Empire became the main sentiments which the new system sought to inculcate.

Perhaps the most interesting feature of the transition is this: in the 1870's, and in some respects earlier than that, godliness and good learning ceased to be essential concomitants. Godliness came more and more to be associated with manliness, especially by the school known to contemporaries and posterity alike as 'muscular Christian'. At the same time, good learning was becoming increasingly agnostic. There is a passage in Viscount Esher's study of William Cory—*Ionicus*—in which he describes a visit made by Cory to Trinity in 1873:

> I remember well [he writes], the evening of William Cory's arrival in Nevill's Court. Albert Grey was curled up on the sofa reading International Law. Henry Jackson, who had been lecturing us on Aristotle that morning, was playing whist with Ebrington and F. W. Maitland. I was the fourth. . . . That evening, when alone together, Henry Jackson, discussing our little group of undergraduates, picked out Gerald Balfour and F. W. Maitland as the two most likely to take pre-eminent places in the life of the country. It was not a bad shot, for both Arthur Balfour and his brother Frank had taken their degrees, but he missed Albert Grey, and William Cory, with a Whig bias, and a keener historical nose, bracketed him with the other two. During that short visit, either in Jackson's rooms, or Jebb's or mine, he met the two Balfours, Frederic and Arthur Myers, his old pupil Arthur Lyttelton, S. H. and J. G. Butcher, Hallam Tennyson, Edmund Gurney, and Maitland. They were the pick of a fine lot of Cambridge men, as fine—so he said—as his own contemporaries thirty years before. [66]

Who were 'the pick of a fine lot of Cambridge men' thirty years before? The names that stand out from memoirs of Cambridge in the 1840's are: B. F. Westcott, C. B. Scott, J. Llewellyn Davies, J. E. B. Mayor, Lord Alwyne Compton, E. H. Bickersteth, C. F. Mackenzie, Charles Evans, J. B. Lightfoot, E. W. Benson and F. J. A. Hort. Every one of these men took orders; three became great clerical headmasters; six became bishops. Those who stood in their place thirty years later and who won the prizes that they had gained were fired by very different enthusiasms. Almost all of them were agnostics. These young men saw visions even as their fathers had done. Manifestly they were not the same visions. And since ideals are born, often enough, out of doubts and dilemmas, we must try to understand if we can the problems that they sought to solve. Only thus can we hope to see when and why it was that these men closed their Bibles, and how —for them and for their generation—the angels lost their wings.

I

The Ideal: Godliness and Good Learning

The one thing which no Rugbeian of Arnold's time ever forgot was the weekly sermon by his headmaster. Outside the chapel, a boy—even in the School House—very probably spent several years of his school career without coming to close quarters with the Doctor. He had at times to endure the ordeal of a form review; he listened in the company of many others to the regular evening readings from a portion of the Greek Testament; now and then he was aware of some power behind the scenes, creating and directing the systems and policies of the society in which he lived. He accordingly reserved for that stern and distant figure the appropriate sentiment of admiration mingled with awe, and viewed with apprehension any circumstance which seemed likely to place his relations with his headmaster on a more personal footing. Not every Rugbeian sat under Arnold in the Sixth Form; not every member of Arnold's Sixth developed as close an understanding of his ways and ideals as did Stanley, Vaughan and Lake.

But once a week, after Arnold had obtained the chaplaincy of the school in 1831,[1] * came the Sunday afternoon sermon of some twenty minutes in length, when the whole school was assembled and Arnold could open his heart. Two famous descriptions of these sermons have survived: Stanley's picture of Arnold's pupils sitting beneath the pulpit 'with their eyes fixed upon him, and their attention strained to the utmost to catch every word that he uttered',[2] and Thomas Hughes's moving account in *Tom Brown's Schooldays* of that 'great and solemn sight'—

> The oak pulpit standing out by itself above the school seats. The
> tall, gallant form, the kindling eye, the voice, now soft as the low

* Up to 1831 Arnold contented himself with short sermonets delivered in the school hall.

28

notes of a flute, now clear and stirring as the call of the light infantry bugle, of him who stood there Sunday after Sunday, witnessing and pleading for his Lord, the King of Righteousness and love and glory, with whose spirit he was filled, and in whose power he spoke. . . . There always were boys scattered up and down the School, who in heart and head were worthy to hear and able to carry away the deepest and wisest words there spoken. But these were a minority always. . . . What was it that moved and held us, the rest of the three hundred reckless, childish boys, who feared the Doctor with all our hearts, and very little else besides in heaven and earth; who thought more of our sets in the School than of the Church of Christ, and put the traditions of Rugby and the public opinion of boys in our daily life above the laws of God? We couldn't enter into half that we heard: we hadn't the knowledge of our own hearts and the knowledge of one another; and little enough of the faith, hope and love needed to that end. But we listened, as all boys in their better moods will listen (aye, and men too for the matter of that), to a man who we felt to be, with all his heart and soul and strength, striving against whatsoever was mean and unmanly and unrighteous in our little world. It was not the cold clear voice of one giving advice and warning from serene heights to those who were struggling and sinning below, but the warm living voice of one who was fighting for us and by our sides, and calling on us to help him and ourselves and one another. And so, wearily and little by little, but surely and steadily on the whole, was brought home to the young boy, for the first time, the meaning of his life: that it was no fool's or sluggard's paradise into which he had wandered by chance, but a battle-field ordained from of old, where there are no spectators, but the youngest must take his side, and the stakes are life and death.[3]

Some of Arnold's attempts to demonstrate the pastoral nature of his work may have missed the mark. The opening of his study to any boy in the school who needed advice and help never wholly circumvented the natural shyness of boys to talk over personal matters and the deep-rooted apprehension that to seek such an opportunity might come very near to the schoolboy's cardinal sin—sneaking.[4] * But the sermons rarely failed to hit their target. It is true that the sermon, at this time, was very frequently

* A flag flying from the school tower was the signal that Arnold was at home to boys who might want to seek his advice.

employed—some may say exploited—as a vehicle to induce sound morals. Also, the boys who listened to Arnold with such rapt attention had, as like as not, been brought up to regard the sermon as the greatest event in the week; and may well have been obliged to take careful note of what the preacher was saying in order to acquit themselves creditably in a subsequent oral examination on the sermon's content.

Nevertheless, the apparent eagerness with which many Victorian schoolboys devoured their school sermons cannot be explained solely in terms of compulsion and the threat of punishment. Preserved in E. W. Benson's scrapbook, covering his career at Wellington College, is a charmingly worded petition from several of the first pupils of the school who had heard, on the first Sunday of the school's life, sermons delivered by Benson and Frederick Temple.

> We, the undersigned [the petition runs], steadfastly believing that the principles set forth in the sermons preached by yourself and Dr. Temple on Sunday the 23rd inst. will ever be cherished in the memory of the pupils to whom they were addressed; and their being the first two sermons preached in this College, do humbly beg that you will grant us your permission to have the above-mentioned sermons printed.[5]

F. W. Farrar, when headmaster of Marlborough, received a similar testimony to the effectiveness of his preaching. The letter, signed 'A Marlborough Boy' and headed 'Private', read: 'A Marlborough boy desires to express his greatest gratitude and thanks to Mr. Farrar, for a sermon which, he trusts, has done him more good, and brought him nearer Heaven, than anything he ever heard in his life'.[6]

Arnold, however, was the first headmaster to grasp this opportunity. The combination of the offices of headmaster and chaplain was almost unknown before 1831. For many years after that date several schools held back from following Arnold's example—notably Eton, where the sermons appear, from the testimony of schoolboy reminiscences,[7] to have been agonisingly dull and unedifying. Dr. Balston, headmaster of Eton, called to give evidence before the Public School Commissioners in 1862, was upbraided by Lord Clarendon for his failure to appreciate the great practical results which could come from the headmaster regularly preaching to the boys. Balston's reply was as follows:

If I may be allowed to express an opinion, I should say that Dr. Arnold was not an everyday man, and that it does not follow that what he achieved is obtainable by all other Head Masters. I should also be disposed to question the results of his preaching, eminently successful though it is said to have been. I think that the religious character formed by it was not so genuine as it should have been. Boys are so easily influenced and so easily impressed with anything which is said from the pulpit, that it requires great consideration whether the man who is placed over them as Head Master should be the man who should influence them so extensively as I consider the Head Master would have the power of doing if he had the right of preaching to them. I think it would rather tend to destroy the purity and freedom, and therefore the thorough simplicity of their religion. What I have noticed at Eton is the absence of all mannerisms, if I may so call it, a freedom from ostentation in the conscientious discharge of what they consider their duty as Christian men.[8]

Arnold would not have seen the force of this. Even if he had played no major part in the influencing of the astonishing schoolboy career of Spencer Thornton, whose excessive piety at Rugby reached such a pitch that he handed a tract on swearing to an older boy who had cuffed him, at least he emphatically approved its course.[9] * If, by 'mannerisms', Balston had meant the unhealthy cultivation of High Church practices, either ritualistic or devotional in character, Arnold might well have agreed. But to imply that one should not teach boys the supreme lessons of life at the age at which they were most teachable would have seemed to him culpable negligence.[10]

Wherein lay the power of Arnold's sermons? Firstly, their simplicity: the vocabulary was straightforward and intelligible, the sentences short and pointed. Secondly, the content was always wholly appropriate and rarely beyond the power of his congregation to assimilate. Doctrinal questions were avoided. Although Arnold was fiercely engaged in theological controversy throughout his headmastership, he seldom allowed a hint of these

---

* Arnold apparently expressed the wish that " there were many more of the spirit in the school."

contentions to enter his sermons. Almost all the teaching concerned behaviour—how to live a righteous life, why it was necessary constantly to combat sin.

We may take as an example the sermon preached on the text 'The law was our schoolmaster to bring us unto Christ'. Arnold quoted the remark of John Bowdler in his *Remains*: 'Public Schools are the very seats and nurseries of vice. It may be unavoidable, or it may not; but the fact is indisputable.' Time and again the phrase was flung out. 'Public Schools are the very seats and nurseries of vice.' Why was it so? How could we honestly thank God for our founders when the stigma of vice was upon us? 'Brought up to godliness and good learning, in places that are the very seats and nurseries of vice!' What was to be done about it? Was it 'unavoidable' or not?

> Our hope that this viciousness is not unavoidable, depends upon you, whether or no you choose to make it so. Outward order, regularity, nay, even advancement in learning, may be, up to a certain point, enforced; but no man can force another to be good, or hinder him from being evil. It must be your own choice and act, whether, indeed, you wish this place to be 'unavoidably a seat or nursery of vice' or whether you wish to verify the words of our daily thanksgiving, that, by the benefit of our founders, 'you are here brought up to godliness and good learning'.[11]

In a series of three sermons preached in 1840 on the subject of 'Christian Schools', Arnold returned to the same theme, his text being the passage from St. Luke (xix.45–7): 'It is written, My house is the house of prayer, but ye have made it a den of thieves.' How does a school dedicated to the pursuits of godliness and good learning become a den of thieves? How low can a school sink before it ceases to be a school at all? The worst state would be

> when with a great deal of vice of all sorts existing in it, there is nothing of a decided spirit of good;—so that those who are not led away into vice, have yet no example or influence before them to lead them to good or to uphold them in it, and become if not vicious in the common sense of the term, yet altogether unprincipled and unchristian.

There were, however, six evils which, when existing together, could make 'the profanation of the temple . . . complete'. They were sensual wickedness, the systematic practice of falsehood, deliberate cruelty (bullying), a spirit of active disobedience, general idleness and, finally, 'a prevailing spirit of combination in evil and of companionship'.[12]

In the course of these sermons, Arnold made quite clear what was his aim; equally forcefully, he explored the territory of the enemy and described it sufficiently accurately to ensure that none should enter it without knowing where he was. Of Arnold it is true to say that if one knows the aim, one knows the man. All his actions and writings are consistent. At Laleham, the Middlesex retreat where he spent nine happy years of placid incubation, gathering together a little colony of devoted pupils, the prospect had gradually taken shape. Christianity was nothing if it was not everything. The bond of society was the common recognition of Christian principles and therefore the concept of the Church as a separate corporation above, below or within the State was abhorrent to him. Church and State were virtually synonymous terms.[13] * As Professor Willey has written:

> For him the worst apostasy, the source of all woes, was the separation of things secular from things spiritual: this meant, on the one hand, the handing over of all temporal concerns to the devil or to the operation of natural laws, and on the other, the retreat of religion into priestly inutilities.[14]

When Arnold saw the possibility of his gaining the headmastership of Rugby he realised that here lay the opportunity to prove his point. Rugby was to become a microcosm of what the State ought to be.

> If I do get it [he wrote to his friend George Cornish, referring to his candidature for Rugby], . . . I should like to try whether my notions of Christian education are really impracticable, whether our system of public schools has not in it some noble elements which, under the blessing of the Spirit of all holiness and wisdom, might produce fruit even to life eternal.[15]

And he had a clear picture in his mind of the type of boy he wished to send out into the world. Perhaps the most famous

* In the postscript to 'Principles of Church Reform', Arnold writes: 'Mr. Dickenson . . . complains that I have identified the church in this country with the nation. I plead guilty to the charge, for I do believe them to be properly identical.'

description of the qualities which he sought to encourage comes in the words which he was wont to use when instructing his praepostors in the duties of their office:

> And what I have often said before I repeat now: what we must look for here is, 1st, religious and moral principles; 2ndly, gentlemanly conduct; 3rdly, intellectual ability.[16]

Not surprisingly, he demanded the same qualities in the appointments to his staff.[17]

Arnold's own boyhood had not been exceptional. His upbringing had perhaps been freer and less oppressive than that of most boys of his class and background. At Winchester he had been precocious, reading Gibbon and Hume for relaxation and studying his classical authors with obvious delight, but he had found time for boyish recreations and occasionally fell foul of authority.[18] It was only as a young man that Arnold developed the intense earnestness which impressed his Oxford contemporaries so forcibly that, as Tuckwell observed, "It used to be said, laughingly, that he had invented the word 'earnest'."[19] It was this spirit of determined activity which Arnold most wished to communicate to his boys. They, too, must be fired with an enthusiasm to dedicate their lives to a cause; they must be made to realise the sense of urgency compelling man to go forward, to grasp at knowledge, to improve the shining hour. It is significant that Arnold described the worst state of a school as being one of negativeness, when there was no positive force for good to stimulate the mind and body into action.

Now every age tends to develop a particular pattern of behaviour which is approved and encouraged by the body which is powerful enough to set the tone and define the standards of its day. Harold Nicolson, in his book *Good Behaviour*, has made a study of certain of these changing codes of behaviour which in the passage of time have caused the appearance of accepted 'types' who represent the ideals of their particular age. In the nineteenth century it is especially noticeable that the middle classes, already economically powerful and—as the century progressed—increasing steadily in their political significance, were gradually displacing the aristocracy as the arbiters of taste, the guardians of morality and as the power that dictated and defined contemporary conventions and values. Many of the peculiar features of nineteenth-century life and thought can be explained in these terms—the re-awakening of the religious spirit, the appreciation of educational needs and the high regard for learning, the acceptance of the principle of competition as the doorway to honours and responsible public service. One of the most important manifestations of this rising influence of the middle class was the emergence of the public schools as important national institutions. In the first place, it is clear that the pressure of middle-class opinion led to the reforms of the older public schools and grammar schools by Arnold, the Arnoldians and others. In the second place, the popularity of the reformed schools led to the creation of a great many new schools in the 1840's and 1850's, largely fashioned on the Rugby model. It was natural enough that the powerful section of the community which called forth these schools should have some picture of the finished product which it hoped that they would turn out.

One of the best descriptions of this ideal of boyhood can be found in Reginald Farrar's life of his father, when he is writing of Dean Farrar's childhood in the 1840's at King William's, Isle of Man.

> I conjure up the picture of a happy and healthy schoolboy, of a bright and open countenance, with eager, well-opened eyes, clearcut features, and fine waving hair; gay and playful, yet tremendously in earnest; joining heartily in games, fond of bathing and swimming, but fondest of long rambles and scrambles along the cliffs and over the mountains, with his ear attuned to the voice of nature; remarkably well read for a schoolboy, and with his memory stored with treasures gathered from the best English poets; a good scholar . . . who had laid already the foundation of that habit of unflinching, unremitting industry which was one of the chief secrets of his success in life; a boy whose moral influence was always strenuously exerted on the side of all that is manly and honest; beyond all, a boy of stainless and virginal purity, who took for his motto the text: 'keep innocency and do the thing that is right, for that shall bring a man peace at the last'.[20]

This had been the child. The man was to become famous—among his other accomplishments—as the author of the best-selling novel of early Victorian school life, *Eric; or Little by Little*, written in 1858, and which in Farrar's own lifetime passed through thirty-six editions. The book, despite its enormous popularity, reflected more the sentiments of twenty years earlier than the moods and ideals of the 1850's. It looked back to a school wholly untouched by the spirit of Arnoldian reform, telling the story of the gradual descent into sin of the hero, Eric, a boy whose childhood had indeed been one of 'stainless and virginal purity' but whose flesh was weak and who succumbed to the various temptations that beset him, despite the efforts of one or two boys of saintly character, notably his friend Edwin, to save him. Eventually he runs away from school to escape expulsion for a crime which he did not commit, becomes a cabin boy, and returns home remorseful to die, repenting his past sins and lost opportunities. The atmosphere and sentiments would have appealed to Arnold as they surely did to George Cotton, the Arnoldian headmaster of Marlborough, to whom the book was dedicated. In the 1850's, however, Arnoldianism was showing signs of passing; and the reading public, whose picture of Rugby and its famous headmaster had been almost wholly coloured by Dean Stanley's *Life of Arnold*, written in 1844, had been presented in the year before *Eric* was published with a new schoolboy hero and a totally different account of Rugby life written by an 'old boy' of the school. The 'old boy' was Thomas Hughes; and the new schoolboy hero was Tom Brown.

It is in comparison with *Tom Brown's Schooldays* that Farrar's *Eric; or Little by Little* most appears an anachronism. The freshness and vigour of Tom Brown and his world made Eric look stuffy and absurd to the large class of people who were becoming dissatisfied with the ideals of godliness and good learning. Here was schoolboy life seen through the eyes of a boy—the sort of boy of whom any father might be proud—manly, honest, plucky, thoroughly sound at heart. He might prefer games to Latin verses, fisticuffs to preaching, but when it came to deciding between right and wrong he could be trusted to choose the proper path. Hughes was a perfectly honest writer. There is no insoluble dilemma in the fact that the Rugby described by Dean Stanley in the famous third chapter of his *Life of Arnold* bears little resemblance to the Rugby in which Tom Brown fought and played and cribbed and in which Flashman stalked the dormitories at night in search of victims for his torments. Hughes and

Brooke Foss Westcott, Bishop of Durham

Arthur Penrhyn Stanley

Stanley were totally different kinds of boy and lived entirely different ways of life at Rugby. The important fact to remember is that Stanley knew Arnold and Thomas Hughes did not. And this accounts for the curious circumstance that *Eric; or Little by Little*, although it makes no reference to Arnold or to Rugby, is a truer reflection of Arnold's ideals than Thomas Hughes's masterpiece which has done more than any other work to popularize Arnold and Rugby.

Both works became best-sellers. Naturally enough, opinions were sharply divided. When *Tom Brown* was published, Dean Stanley confessed that the picture of Rugby life which it portrayed was a complete revelation to him.[21] Westcott was horrified at the gross misrepresentation of Arnold's life and work.[22] Kingsley, on the other hand, saluted it with delight.[23] These three reactions reveal the two essential points. Firstly, *Tom Brown's Schooldays*, unlike *Eric*, looks to the future not to the past. By about 1870 Tom Brown had become a pattern for schoolboys and Arnold's teaching had given way to a new code in which manliness, animal spirits and prowess at games figured as the attributes most to be admired in a boy. Secondly, in any consideration of Arnold's ideals, the point must be stressed that Tom Brown was not the product which Arnold hoped to give to the world by virtue of what he preached and taught at Rugby. There would undoubtedly be Tom Browns; and he might be able to do something for them. There is no doubt, for instance, that some of Arnold's teaching left a very deep impression on Thomas Hughes; for to Arnold, and later to F. D. Maurice, Hughes owed the enthusiasm and courage which led him to give his wholehearted support to the Society for Promoting Working Men's Associations and, eventually, to the Working Men's College, of which he was a founder member. But Arnold's ideals were altogether loftier than this. He pointed to horizons which a Tom Brown could only dimly descry.

How, then, was the way to be made plain?

2

First of all there had to be purification. The six evils which Arnold described in his sermon as the chief causes of 'the profanation of the temple' had to be eradicated. It must be said at once that Rugby in 1828, when Arnold took command, was certainly not the sink of iniquity which one might suppose. Although numbers were low, Arnold's predecessor, Dr. Wooll, had been an efficient and respected headmaster and had in no way contributed to the falling away of support. Arnold was unable to find any explanation for the decline, and was pleasantly surprised to find few signs of unruliness in the first month of his new life.[1] Indeed the evidence would suggest that with the increase of numbers that followed Arnold's appointment (fairly well maintained until his death), so the problems of discipline increased and the evils which he sought to purge became much more marked than they had hitherto been. And it was not in Arnold's nature to let well alone. Although he wrote to J. T. Coleridge in August 1828 that 'you need not fear my reforming furiously; there, I think, I can assure you',[2] he could not easily sit back and view the workings of the machine without seeking somehow to set his own distinctive stamp on everything that came within his power to touch. 'My love for any place, or person, or institution, is exactly the measure of my desire to reform them', he once wrote to Stanley,[3] and no better description could there be than this of the restlessness and zeal which directed all his actions. It is difficult to resist the conclusion that sometimes he was urgent for the sake of being urgent and therefore created some of the troubles which he found so grievously hard to settle. Bad times were to come; and when Arnold denounced the six evils in his sermon he was confronting the Devil face to face.

The root of the trouble lay in the deeply respected tradition that boys at school should be left to govern themselves. Inside the classroom they might be drilled and driven and flogged: outside, they lived their own lives according to their own laws and standards. They might—and often did—choose jungle law; but provided that their follies did not lead to such wild excess that either the public in general or parents in particular felt obliged to demand magisterial intervention, the cruelties and injustices of boy life were studiously ignored. It was possible to defend such negligence on the grounds that the boys were learning the obligations and inconveniences of community life and that certain qualities of toughness and endurance were engendered by its rigours. Two important consequences came about. In the first place, masters and boys lived in a perpetual state of war, waged primarily on the issue of more privileges for the boys and less tyranny from the masters. Eton under Dr. Keate presented a good example of this: a curious mixture of autocracy and republicanism. In his particular sphere Keate was a merciless tyrant, possibly a well-meaning one for he would get the last ounce out of a boy in class if he could. In their particular domain, the boys formed a republic with their own code of laws and their own crude methods of punishment. Tyrant and republic co-existed in perpetual hostility, sometimes in a state of cold war, occasionally in open rebellion. At some schools, where the hostility was less marked, the tyrant had capitulated to the extent of conceding the most important of the republican demands—the legal right of self-government: a prefectorial system had been permitted, not of the Arnoldian type—a body of trusted lieutenants of the headmaster—but a régime of the most powerful members of the republic, who might make and execute its laws and enjoy the privilege of being served by fags.[4]

Secondly, the recognition of mob rule led to the acquiescence in mob values. How could the principles of godliness and good learning have any hope of surviving in a community ruled by jungle law? Work within the republic too often consisted in organised and ingenious cribbing; recreation was largely the baiting of the weak and the eccentric; conscience and the individual sense of decency and honour had to be subordinated to loyalty to the community, and thus one had to learn to lie boldly and never to betray any member of the group by sneaking into the enemy's camp.

To Arnold and to all like-minded reformers, this was the deadliest poison of all and led them frequently to despair.

That is properly a nursery of vice [Arnold told his Rugby congregation], where a boy unlearns the pure and honest principles which he may have received at home, and gets, in their stead, others which are utterly low, and base, and mischievous,—where he loses his modesty, his respect for truth, and his affectionateness, and becomes coarse, and false, and unfeeling. That, too, is a nursery of vice, and most fearfully so, where vice is bold, and forward, and presuming; and goodness is timid and shy, and existing as if by sufferance,—

where the good instead of setting the tone of society, and branding with disgrace those who disregard it, are themselves exposed to reproach for their goodness, and shrink before the open avowal of evil principles, which the bad are striving to make the law of the community.[5]

Arnold was not the first headmaster to attempt to end this warfare between masters and boys and to stifle the power of the mob, nor did he have the satisfaction of seeing his aims fulfilled. Thomas Hughes gives ample evidence of bullying and savagery and organised cribbing; and his testimony is corroborated by other Rugbeians who were at the school under Arnold.[6] It should never be supposed that Arnold found Rugby stinking and left it sweet. His own disillusionment and despair contradict such a view. 'It is quite surprising', he once wrote to a friend, 'to see the wickedness of young boys; or would be surprising, if I had not my own school experience and a good deal since to enlighten me.'[7] And again:

> It is quite awful to watch the strength of evil in such young minds, and how powerless is every effort against it. It would give the vainest man alive a very fair notion of his own insufficiency, to see how little he can do and how his most earnest addresses are as a cannon ball on a bolster.[8]

Sometimes he despaired of the whole system, especially when he came to consider the best form of education for his own sons.

> The difficulties of education stare me in the face whenever I look at my own four boys. I think by and by that I shall put them into the School here, but I shall do it with trembling. Experience seems to point out no one plan of education as decidedly the best. . . . Large private schools, I think, are the worst possible system: the choice lies between public schools, and an education whose character may be strictly private and domestic.[9]

However, within this system of public-school education his life's work had been fated to fall: despite its deficiencies, he was committed to do his utmost to make it holy.

Limited though his success may have been, he is to be admired both for the intensity of his effort and for the means he employed to attain his end. Briefly, these methods were: firstly, to assume autocratic control within the school by securing from the Trustees the assurance that the headmaster would have complete independence in all matters of school discipline and school routine; secondly, to raise the status of the assistant masters by paying them larger salaries and by associating them with him in the government of the school. While he was prepared to procure the dismissal of masters who were not willing to co-operate with him in giving whole-hearted service to the school, he did everything in his power to make them active partners in his projects, and, as Stanley observed, 'in matters of school discipline he seldom or never acted without consulting them'.[10] Thirdly, he aimed to make the school far more a corporate unit than it had hitherto been by abolishing 'dame's' houses and encouraging assistant masters to take boarding pupils over whom they were to exercise a general supervisory care, especially of a pastoral nature. Fourthly, he introduced the practice of superannuating boys who for various reasons were deriving no benefit from the school or who might be doing positive harm. In cases of grave misconduct he would resort to public expulsion. On the other hand, this device of periodic weeding of undesirable or unco-operative elements, although considered by some as grossly unfair and by some later reformers—Edward Thring for instance—as decidedly improper, meant that expulsions became rarer and the number of floggings was considerably reduced.

Arnold's most important measure, however, was the use he made of the prefectorial system. It was to the Sixth Form that he looked to set the moral tone of the school. They were to be his lieutenants, endowed with very considerable powers and privileges, receiving his complete confidence, in return for which they were to serve him with loyalty and obedience. There was to be an end to the war between autocracy and republicanism. Through the praepostors, his influence was to be diffused throughout the school and 'the lawless tyranny of physical strength'[11] put down. Here Arnold was devising nothing new; indeed, the temper of public criticism was in favour of abolishing or severely curtailing prefectorial powers at the public schools. What Arnold did was to take an existing institution and to divert it to his own ends. Of course the system could only work if trust were not abused; and in this belief that older boys could bear the weight of excessive moral responsibility lay the whole basis of Arnold's reforms. "You should feel", he once addressed his

Sixth Form, "like officers in the army or navy, where want of moral courage would, indeed, be thought cowardice."[12] And once, on one dreadful occasion before the whole school, he put the question to them all: "Is this a Christian school? I cannot remain here if all is to be carried on by constraint and force; if I am to be here as a gaoler, I will resign my office at once."[13]

This attitude is the essence of Arnoldianism. Thus Edward White Benson, on becoming headmaster of the new Wellington College, insisted that the school should open with a few older boys on the foundation so that he could begin as he intended to continue by basing the discipline on a small group of prefects bound to the headmaster by the ties of trust and responsibility. Similarly, George Cotton at Marlborough threatened to leave the school to flounder if the governors insisted that assistant masters should supervise the boys in their out-of-school activities. Either there would be prefects or there would be no public school.[14]

Moral purification, then, was to be secured by these measures. However earnestly Arnold might address his boys on the subject of sin, no lasting transformation could be wrought without the presence in the school of a number of boys whose lives were dedicated to fighting every manifestation of sinful conduct which they encountered. That Arnold was able to find such boys from time to time is well known. The schoolboy careers of Stanley, W. C. Lake, C. J. Vaughan and A. H. Clough have become famous. The extent to which these boys, and others similarly inspired at other schools, succeeded in achieving a moral reformation is not easy to assess. Against the testimony of schoolboy reminiscences recalling ugly practices in the dormitories, one has to weigh the numerous recorded instances of men whose schooldays provided the happiest memories of their lives and who received from their schoolmasters and the stimulating companionship of their fellows an inspiring influence which they never afterwards forgot. Even in the pre-Arnoldian days of the public schools, many boys left school with anything but bitter memories. Arnold, himself, was perfectly happy at Winchester; Pusey appears to have been content at Eton under Dr. Keate.[15] Charles Wordsworth and Manning at Harrow both looked back to their schooldays with some nostalgia, although both rather deplored the failure of their school to awaken any spiritual feelings within them.[16] More important is the evidence of rising public confidence in the schools after 1830. Mr. T. W. Bamford suggests that the marked increase in the number of entrants to Rugby during the years of Arnold's headmastership was not caused by the reputation of the school in academic circles.[17] On the other hand, the fact that the numbers in the school were rising, and rose even more markedly in the schools at which Arnold's disciples became headmasters (notably Harrow under C. J. Vaughan which rose from 69 in 1844 to 466 in 1859), undoubtedly suggests that the public believed that the schools were sufficiently safe in their moral standards for their sons to be entrusted to their care. The enormous effect of Stanley's biography in giving publicity to Arnold's life and work must, however, be taken into account here.

It is impossible, for instance, to write with any certainty on the prevalence of immorality in the schools at this period. Not surprisingly, the references made to it by contemporaries are so veiled and discreet that we cannot be sure of the nature of the offences apparently so grave. Even Arnold, usually extremely outspoken in references to sin in his sermons, speaks only of 'sensual wickedness, such as drunkenness and other things forbidden together with drunkenness in the scriptures'.[18] Dr. Mack states that the first overt mention of sex which he has found in his study of nineteenth-century public schools is in an article contributed to the *Quarterly Journal of Education* in January 1834, accusing the fagging system of encouraging older boys to teach sexual dirt to the younger, thus creating 'a prurient disposition'. Impurity naturally followed.[19] It has been suggested by Mr. G. F. Lamb that cases of sexual perversion were less common in an age when bullying and general hooliganism were rife, since privacy was seldom achieved and sadistic natures tended to find their outlet in other forms.[20] In *Eric*, however—a picture of life in a school without a prefectorial system of any kind—many are the hints of wicked deeds which delicacy forbids its author to describe. There is the famous passage, for instance, which relates Eric's first encounter with an indelicate expression, as he lies in bed listening to the other boys talking:

> The first time Eric heard indecent words in dormitory no. 7 he was shocked beyond bound or measure. Dark though it was, he felt himself blushing scarlet to the roots of his hair, and then growing

pale again, while a hot dew was left upon his forehead. . . . Now, Eric, now or never. Life and death, ruin and salvation, corruption and purity, are perhaps in the balance together, and the scale of your destiny may hang on a single word of yours. Speak out, boy! Tell these fellows that unseemly words wound your conscience. . . . Ah, Eric, Eric! How little we know the moments which decide the destinies of life. . . . Eric lay silent.[21]

Farrar concludes the chapter with a little moral exhortation:

Ah, young boys, if your eyes ever read these pages, pause and beware. The knowledge of evil is ruin, and the continuance in it is moral death.[22]

He then hastily drops the subject, his duty done, and turns to the more congenial task of describing illicit drinking sessions at the neighbouring tavern.

Arnold, who could be desperately severe with any offence involving a breach of trust, showed himself sympathetic and understanding in his dealings with boys guilty of immorality. Stanley writes: 'At times, on discovering cases of vice, he would, instead of treating them with contempt or extreme severity, tenderly allow the force of the temptation, and urge it upon them as a proof brought home to their own minds, how surely they must look for help out of themselves.'[23]

This, it should be remembered, was an era before the fetish for organised games. Yet the notion of the purgative effects of regulated rowdyism was gaining some adherents. One of the unsuccessful candidates for the post of first headmaster of Wellington, compelled by the Prince Consort in 1855 to submit an essay on his intended curriculum for the school, stated that 'on moral as well as sanitary grounds, I look upon the cricket field as next in importance to the schoolroom'.[24]

Benson seems to have been very much alive to the moral dangers arising from inadequate supervision. In a notebook which he kept for jotting down incidental thoughts and schemes relating to his plan of campaign for Wellington, he committed to paper a few considerations about immorality. He decided upon the cubicle system for the dormitories; he suggested various schemes for inspection:

Young boys to retire a certain time earlier than older ones. While they are undressing, steward and matron to walk up and down in the middle of the dormitories to report any boy who goes out of his own dormitory to another, and by the time that the candles are to be put out the prefects are to come up to bed, and preserve the same order of silence.

'The danger is in an evening,' he noted, '. . . also in afternoon when boys are tired of playing.' Then again: 'Doors of cubicles as at Eton to be incapable of fastening on inside, but may be locked on outside, every door to be commanded by a master key.' He even mused on the possibility of nailing a wire lattice flat over the top of each cubicle, but then wrote:

A vigilant inspection . . . sufficient to prevent evils of a gross nature is next to impossible, and much evil would be the result of such inspection. The best inspection will be the introspection of leading boys of high tone and character.[25]

In the prolific correspondence which has been preserved of Benson's mastership, only two cases of immorality are recorded. The first case—the sorry behaviour of a general's son who struck another boy between the legs—was little more than a peccadillo of a high-spirited but injudicious lad, and provides a good example of moral indignation carried to absurd extremes. The boy in question was locked in a bathroom and set to write lines while Benson got in touch with his family. There followed a tearful encounter, culminating in discreet removal.[26]

The second case concerned the sordid conduct of three foundationers who misbehaved with a serving maid during one of the school holidays,[27] the most interesting feature of which was the attitude of the intensely aristocratic Wellington governors who appeared to view with indifference—indeed amusement— the presence in the school of boys who had had carnal knowledge of a girl of fourteen: a nice indication that the oppressive moral code of the Victorian middle class had not penetrated the ranks of the aristocracy.

The case of the general's son occurred in 1861, two years after the opening of the college. Benson declared that the reason for his severity was the fact that it was the first instance of impurity that he had encountered at Wellington. The last offence occurred in 1872, a year before Benson left. Of course, arguments from silence are almost meaningless in cases of this nature, but the impression given from a study of the school records during these years suggests that cases of immorality were fairly rare in the period of Benson's mastership from 1859 to 1873. The later records suggest that the moral tone lowered somewhat during the next twenty years.[28] * This contention would contradict the educational theorists of that time who were advocating compulsory games and the cult of manliness as the most effective antidotes to adolescent sexual temptations.

Of all the schoolboy sins, lying was both the most common and the one visited with most severity by Arnold and like-minded moralists. Thomas Mozley, in his *Reminiscences of Oriel College and the Oxford Movement*, points out that 'in those days, probably even more than now, very few came out of a public school without learning the art of lying'.[29] Some undergraduates of his time rose above the common stock—the Wilberforce boys, for instance—whose evangelical upbringing had instilled in them a fierce regard for truth. Sometimes this led to embarrassment. Henry Wilberforce, Mozley tells us, on one occasion refused to accept an invitation to a wine party but chose to give no reason for his refusal since, had he done so, he would only have caused offence. The day after the party, he met his disappointed host in the covered passage leading from the Radcliffe Camera to the Schools' Quad.

> There was no escape. They came to a dead stand with their eyes fixed on one another. The other man waited for an explanation, and Henry had none to offer. Something, however, was expected, and there was nothing but the bare fact. He delivered it in naked form. '——I did not go to your wine party yesterday.' The man waited for the reason why, and said nothing. Henry, after a pause, could only repeat, 'I did not go to your wine party yesterday.' After another pause of helplessness on the one side and vain expectation on the other, he repeated a third time, 'I did not go to your wine party yesterday'; which said, both pursued their respective courses, and, it is needless to say, never recognised one another again.[30]

* The evidence for this rests mainly on entries in the Prefects' Books for the late 70's and early 80's, indicating a rather low moral tone; also the circumstances leading up to the hissing of Dr. Pollock at a school concert in 1895 suggest a similar conclusion.

The prevalence of falsehood was no doubt encouraged by the severe floggings meted out by a Dr. Keate and his like for even venial offences. Charles Kingsley saw this clearly enough when he wrote, 'the boy learns not to fear sin, but the *punishment* of it, and thus he learns to lie'.[31] * To Arnold, falsehood was the disease most likely to corrupt all his work. There grew up in the school, Stanley tells us, 'a general feeling that "it was a shame to tell Arnold a lie—he always believes one"'.[32] To be silent when duty compelled you to speak out boldly and tell the truth was bad enough. After all, George Hughes, Thomas's elder brother, was removed from Rugby for failing to report the names of some rowdy boys who had misbehaved in a Fifth of November rag.[33] But to persist in a lie to a master was heinous. One of the most unfortunate occurrences of Arnold's headmastership was the sad affair of young March, a boy who, in the course of one of Arnold's form reviews, told his headmaster that the passage which he had been called upon to construe had not been covered in his work. Consultation with the master who had taught March revealed that the boy was wrong.

> Arnold, [writes Mr. Bamford], already a terrifying enough figure, was faced with evil in its highest form—persistent telling of lies to authority, even after proof of guilt. He called the boy a liar, repeating 'Liar! Liar! Liar!' And still the lad protested his innocence.[34]

There followed a beating of eighteen strokes. A few days later it was discovered that the master concerned had made a mistake and that March had been speaking the truth all the time. Arnold's remorse was pitiful and complete. He made a public apology to the school. But the damage was done, the episode reached the ears of the Press, and Arnold was hounded by critics for several weeks.

It was in defence of truthfulness, then, that the advocates of 'godliness and good learning' most delighted to stand. It was the link which bound the two principles together. Truthfulness was as essential an attribute of godliness as the quest for truth was

---

* Kingsley, on a visit to Weybridge, filled up a questionnaire, which appeared in an autograph book, thus: 'The Virtue you most admire? TRUTH. The Vice to which you are most lenient? ALL EXCEPT LYING.'

the object of good learning.[35] To inculcate a love of truth was, then, the primary duty of the teacher. In their passionate conviction of the duty to extirpate falsehood, and the inclination towards falsehood, the Victorian moralists may seem at times brutal. Innumerable cautionary tales were manufactured for the edification of the young. For the liar no fate was too terrible. Even Eric, who—in his descent into sin—breaks most of the commandments, does not tell a lie. One boy in the story does, however, and one can sense almost a savage delight in the way in which Farrar describes his flogging and expulsion.[36]

All this was an essential part of the code of family ethics on which so many of the Victorians had been reared. A good example occurs in Purcell's *Life of Manning* where is recalled an occasion when Manning, at the age of four, stated untruthfully to his mother that he had seen a peacock while on a walk with his nurse, 'and my mother made me kneel down and beg God to forgive me for not speaking the truth'.[37] But at no period in the nineteenth century was the lesson taught with such force as in the thirties and forties when Arnold's influence was at its height. Nor did the lesson pass unheeded. Benson, at the age of eighteen, wrote to his friend J. B. Lightfoot, who had recently gone up to Cambridge, of an encounter between Prince Lee and a liar:

> On Tuesday, Elkington was brought before Mr. Lee for having told and persisted in a falsehood to Mr. Yates—and at half-past twelve Mr. Lee made Oh! such a speech to him and to the school. Truth was what he dwelt on as the foundation of all good—the contemplation of Truth—his own beloved Truth, and he spoke of how he had ever redeemed and would redeem to the last his pledge to extirpate falsehood, by God's help, from the school. If that fellow has not a heart of iron, he will be a changed being all his days. And then Mr. Lee said that as Elkington had been so severely dealt with in words his corporal punishment should be but light—and so he made it. Was it not nobly done?[38]

Twenty-five years later, Benson, himself a headmaster, had cause to take disciplinary action against liars.

> My dearest wife [he wrote to Mrs. Benson, who was on holiday in Germany], I returned to find hideously bad lying on the part of three boys who had misbehaved. I have sent two of them away. And yesterday the School lost their half-holiday, as notice had been

given some months ago that if any member of the school persisted in untruth they would all suffer. So we all turned in, all masters, all prefects, all boys, and by writing lines did penance—it's quite like the ancient and true principle of sackcloth and ashes—for two hours. Some people would say there was no justice in it, but vicarious suffering not only represents but *is* justice. . . . The effect on the school has apparently been excellent—all say so, even those who were against me. The boys look at me like angels and are better than ever. . . . I made the mathematical Sixth who had shown some levity a long speech and I never saw fellows so impressed.[39]

So the tradition passed on. Prince Lee had been with Arnold on the occasion of March's flogging; Benson had sat in Barry's great hall at King Edward's, Birmingham, while Lee inveighed against Elkington. Years later, Benson himself felt that he had done God's work in vindicating truth. 'As always in storms . . . my spirits rise, and I am *much better* for the difficulty.'[40] Righteousness had triumphed over sin. Indeed, as Benson wrote to Lightfoot, 'Was it not nobly done?'

3

The application of the doctrine of godliness and good learning to the upbringing of boys in the public schools did much to create that breed of diligent, earnest, intellectual eminent Victorian which has left its impress on almost every aspect of the age; admirable in its conscientiousness and moral fibre, slightly ridiculous perhaps to succeeding generations who have delighted in exposing the defects. There is no doubt that Arnold's methods are open to serious criticism.

There have been three main charges. Firstly—in the famous phrase of Francis Doyle—there was 'one qualification for a head-master which Keate possessed but Arnold did not—I mean the knowledge of God Almighty's intention that there should exist for a certain time, between childhood and manhood, the natural production known as a boy'.[1] This defect—the critics maintain—led Arnold to believe that the stage of childhood was inherently wicked and something to be outgrown as soon as possible. The only effective mode of dealing with children was to flog them; when, however, they were converted they received the immediate commission to strengthen their brethren. He therefore too readily equated boyish misdemeanours with grave moral sin and laid on boyish shoulders too heavy a burden of moral responsibility. The second charge follows from this: his products—those in whom he took pride as his products—became moral prigs and earned for their school at Oxford and in the Army, according to Charles Pearson, the reputation of being 'the disagreeable school'.[2] Thirdly, Arnold's teaching was so powerful that either he tended to mould his most receptive pupils in his own image, thereby stifling the free growth of their personalities, or, by encouraging them to pursue ideals impossibly high for persons of their age to attain, he sowed the seeds of later doubts and scepticism.

To accuse Arnold of not understanding boys might seem as presumptuous as to charge Shakespeare with failure to appreciate the English language. There were some boyish characteristics which attracted Arnold greatly: these were really characteristics of his own youth which he had never outgrown—enthusiasm and love of life, simplicity and directness, delight in physical activity. He loved the society of boys, especially older ones. Recalling his Laleham days, he wrote: 'I enjoyed, and do enjoy, the society of youths of seventeen or eighteen, for they are all alive in limbs and spirits at least, if not in mind, while in older persons the body and spirits become lazy and languid without the mind gaining any vigour to compensate for it.' And he gave this advice to his correspondent, who intended to become a private tutor:

> I should say, have your pupils a good deal with you, and be as familiar with them as you possibly can. I did this continually more and more before I left Laleham, going to bathe with them, leaping and all other gymnastic exercises within my capacity, and sometimes sailing or rowing with them. They I believe always liked it, and I enjoyed it myself like a boy, and found myself constantly the better for it.[3]

At Rugby it was somewhat different because it had to be. He could still say, 'I want absolute play like a boy',[4] but his official position prevented him from indulging in his fancies with too much abandonment. The younger boys often found him stiff and reserved; very probably they were right. Headmasters who have not appeared so to junior boys in a school are very rare.

Maybe the stiffness and aloofness went deeper than appearances. R. J. Campbell has suggested that 'he had too little humour to enable him to enter sympathetically into the workings of boyish nature';[5] Dr. Mack maintains that Arnold's uncompromising belief in the fallen nature of man coloured his whole attitude to the training of little boys, his theories on which 'show him in his most antipathetic and ludicrous light'.[6] Finally Mr. T. W. Bamford has revealed that Arnold was so unsympathetic to the very young that he was prepared to defeat the whole project of a Lower School to train the children of local parents up to the standard required for entrance into the Upper School, by deliberately appointing masters who were incapable of providing the necessary tuition.[7]

This last episode clearly shows that Arnold could be exceptionally ruthless—a defect common to many Victorian reformers. Prince Lee and E. W. Benson might well have done the same. It would, however, be rash to suppose that Arnold's attempts to suppress the Lower School were inspired by his loathing of little boys. It is much more likely that Arnold was striving to preserve the national character of Rugby and doing his utmost to prevent the school from being swamped by local children whose parents were claiming to benefit from Lawrence Sheriff's charity. For the moral health of the school—and this is what Arnold always put first in his work for Rugby—it was essential to keep numbers fairly low. The hopes of Wratislaw, the local solicitor who took proceedings against Arnold on this score, threatened to ruin everything for which Arnold had worked.

Equally rash is the conjecture—made by R. J. Campbell— that Arnold's treatment of the young derived from his belief in the Calvinist doctrine of original sin. Arnold's instructor was experience—not John Calvin. And experience had taught him that moral perfection was a goal not a starting-point. It was the duty of the parent and the schoolmaster to superintend the ethical training needed to raise the necessarily imperfect child to the stature of Christian manhood. Secondly, he appreciated that the home training of the child could—and often did—produce a high degree of purity and innocence. But inevitably, in the course of time, a child must become a member of a different society, and Arnold saw that it was in this transition from the family circle to the school community that the greatest trials of character had to be faced. That the child was still morally imperfect was evident from the fact that although he might achieve a high standard of honour and decency as an individual, in the society of other boys he invariably became vicious and indolent: he had yet to learn the most difficult of all virtues—that of moral courage. Thus, in a sermon, Arnold stressed this evil disposition —the working of the Devil in the crowd.

> You see a number of boys, who, while living at home, or by themselves, might go on very well, and think and act very rightly, yet, as soon as they mix with one another, and form one large body, the opinions and influence on that body shall be bad. Every boy brings some good with him, at least, from home, as well as some evil; and yet you see how very much more catching the evil is than the good, or else you would make one another better by mixing together; and if any single boy did anything wrong, it would be condemned by the general opinion of all the school. [8]

Stanley recalls how the sight of 'a knot of vicious or careless boys gathered together round the great school-house fire' would give Arnold great pain and anxiety. Moral childishness was 'the great curse of public schools', especially 'the spirit which was there encouraged of combination, of companionship, of excessive deference to the public opinion prevalent in the school'. [9]

In his published letter *On the Discipline of Public Schools*, Arnold defended his use of corporal punishment on the ground that it was not a degrading penalty for young boys in whom the sense of moral responsibility had not been fully developed, and then concluded with a description of the community-life of boys as being 'semi-barbarous' in character:

> The stress of this remark, however [he wrote], applies to a *society* in a low moral state, and not to an individual. Boys, in their own families, as the members of the natural and wholesome society of their father's household, may receive its lessons and catch its spirit, and learn at a very early age to estimate right and wrong truly. But a society formed exclusively of boys, that is, of elements each separately weak and imperfect, becomes more than an aggregate of their several defects: the amount of evil in the mass is more than the sum of the evil in the individuals; it is aggravated in its character, while the amount of good, on the

contrary, is less in the mass than in the individuals, and its effect greatly weakened.[10]

This, then, explains the severe judgement expressed in the famous letter to John Tucker:

> My object will be, if possible, to form Christian men, for Christian boys I can scarcely hope to make; I mean that, from the natural imperfect state of boyhood, they are not susceptible of Christian principles in their full development upon their practice, and I suspect that a low standard of morals in many respects must be tolerated amongst them, as it was on a larger scale in what I consider the boyhood of the human race.[11]

This letter was written as early as 1827, when Arnold had only his own school experience and his years at Laleham to guide him. The words may seem exceptionally hard. But Arnold, so often accused of being an idealist, was here being realistic; and his judgement was echoed subsequently by other experienced Victorian schoolmasters. Westcott, as an assistant master at Harrow, wrote to Hort in 1852: 'How much I should like to talk with you about boy-nature. Sometimes I am tempted to define a boy as "a being in whom the idea of honour exists only potentially". Truly one grows sad often at what experience teaches, and now I begin to understand Arnold's terrible words.'[12] Later, that most humane and sympathetic of Eton housemasters, Arthur Benson, wrote sadly in *The Upton Letters:*

> What an odd thing it is that boys are so delightful when they are alone, and so tiresome (not always) when they are together. They seem, in public, to want to show their worst side, to be ashamed of being supposed to be good, or interested, or thoughtful, or tender-hearted. They are so afraid of seeming better than they are, and pleased to appear worse than they are. . . . One sees instincts at their nakedest among boys.[13]

One could not say that the best of Arnold's pupils were 'afraid of seeming better than they were': hence the appearance of moral priggishness. The young Stanley, who for years after leaving Rugby was constantly comparing the excellence of his headmaster with the mediocrity of his new teachers and associates, must have been at times an irritating companion. And the letter which he addressed to Tait on the latter's appointment to the headmastership of Rugby after Arnold's death would certainly suggest that he had become over-serious to the extent of losing his sense of proportion:

> My dear Tait [he wrote], the awful intelligence of your election has just reached me . . . I have not heart to say more than that I conjure you by your friendship for me, your reverence for your great predecessor, your sense of the sacredness of your office, your devotion to Him whose work you are now more than ever called upon to do, to lay aside every thought for the present except that of repairing your deficiencies.[14]

A. H. Clough's letters to his younger brother George and to his former schoolfellow J. N. Simpkinson (at Cambridge) with their pious aspirations that 'a little leaven will leaven the whole lump'[15] and the implication that Clough, if he wins the Balliol scholarship, will thereby become God's gift to Oxford, make us sympathize with Pearson and others who had no wish to be elevated, and cause us to wonder how it was that W. G. Ward could say of Clough that he saw in him not the faintest trace of priggishness and self-sufficiency.[16] And was it desirable that Charles Vaughan and other Rugbeians at Cambridge should form 'a very nice little Rugby Debating Society here among ourselves'?[17]

On the other hand, Arnold was aware of the criticisms of his principles, especially his stress on moral courage as the first duty of man. "Can the change from childhood to manhood be hastened in the case of boys and young men," he once asked in a sermon, ". . . without exhausting prematurely the faculties either of body or mind?" Excess of study could both injure the health and exhaust the mind, he answered, but an attitude of adult thoughtfulness as opposed to childish carelessness could and should be acquired without any such effects.

> There may remain, however, a vague notion, that, generally, if what we mean by an early change from childishness to manliness be that we should become religious, then . . . it would destroy the natural liveliness and gaiety of youth, and by bringing on a premature seriousness of manner and language, would be unbecoming and ridiculous.

This notion, he thought, arose from a false conception of gaiety.

> If gaiety mean real happiness of mind, I do not believe that there is more of it in youth than in manhood. . . . There remains that

which strictly belongs to youth, partly physically—the lighter step and the lively movement of the growing and vigorous body; partly from circumstances, because a young person's parents or friends stand between him and many of the cares of life, and protect him from feeling them altogether; partly from the abundance of hope which belongs to the beginning of every thing, and which continually hinders the mind from dwelling on past pain. And I know not which of these causes of gaiety would be taken away or lessened by the earlier change from childhood to manhood.

To sinners, he continued, the thought of God might be fearful. They would be gayer without the reminder of the Day of Judgement.

But I suppose the point is, whether the thought of Him would cloud the gaiety of those who were striving to please Him. It would cloud it as much, and be just as unwelcome and no more, as will be the very actual presence of Our Lord to the righteous, when they shall see Him as He is. . . . When to natural cheerfulness and sanguineness, are added a consciousness of God's ever present care, and a knowledge of His rich promises, are we likely to be the more sad or the more unhappy?[18]

C. J. Vaughan, writing in later years, could see that he and his Rugby friends might at times have seemed absurd to their contemporaries whom they tried so hard to influence. But he thought that their lives were the richer for the efforts that they had made. His epitaph on Stanley was:

The influence of Arnold's character, at once so high above and so powerfully in contact, gave to this early period of his life a sort of fire of zeal (if I might so express it) at which Oxford undergraduates might afterwards smile, but which had in it the making of the future man, with that unresting energy, that forthright purpose, that restless attraction, that clean and pure soul.[19]

This is the real test of Arnold's success or failure. Did his pupils, when they went out into the world, live the Christian lives for which he had prepared them? For want of detailed knowledge, it is impossible to say. Although several of his pupils became eminent in later years, they were bound to be a tiny minority of the total number of boys whom Arnold attempted to bring up to godliness and good learning.

The main centre of Arnoldian influence—outside Rugby itself—was Oxford. Arnold was an Oxford figure; by far the majority of his assistant masters were drawn from the same university. In fact, all Dr. Wooll's assistants were from Oxford and when James Prince Lee was appointed by Arnold to an assistant-mastership in 1830, he was the first Cambridge man to join the Rugby staff for fifty years. Three other Cambridge appointments followed—G. E. L. Cotton in 1837, A. F. Merivale in 1838 and Charles Mayor in 1840.[20] All four men had been at Trinity. The statistics of university entrants from Rugby reveal the same bias. During the years of Arnold's headmastership, 627 Rugbeians proceeded to the universities, 404 to Oxford and 223 to Cambridge. The favoured Oxford colleges were Balliol (49), Brasenose (46), Christ Church (45), University (43), Exeter (41) and Oriel (39). Of the 223 Rugbeians at Cambridge, by far the majority went to Trinity. The figures are: Trinity— 119; St. John's—27; Christ's—15; Gonville and Caius—15; Emmanuel—10. The entries to other Cambridge colleges are all single figures.[21] Thus fair-sized colonies of Rugbeians could be found in the 1830's and 1840's at Trinity College, Cambridge, and at six Oxford colleges.

Two groups of disciples may be briefly considered. The first were Arnold's assistant masters. Of these, Bonamy Price was perhaps the one who knew Arnold the best. He had been a pupil at Laleham, had taken a double first at Worcester College, Oxford, and was Arnold's first academic appointment to the Rugby staff.* He did not become a headmaster (mainly because he was not ordained), remaining at the school until 1850. In 1873 he became Professor of Political Economy at Oxford. Three of Arnold's assistants obtained headmasterships—James Prince Lee at King Edward's, Birmingham, G. E. L. Cotton at Marlborough, and Herbert Hill at Warwick School. Lee was undoubtedly the one most influenced by Arnold, as the study of his career and of his pupils, which forms the subject of the next chapter, will seek to show. Cotton was perhaps the most original of all the Arnoldian headmasters, for his veneration for Arnold was balanced by considerable creative force, and, in the course of only six years

* John Sale, the writing-master, was the first appointment that Arnold was called upon to make.

as headmaster, he raised Marlborough from near bankruptcy and virtual anarchy to the position of a flourishing and important school. G. G. Bradley, a former pupil of Arnold and an assistant master under Tait and Goulburn, completed Cotton's work. It is fair to describe these men as Arnoldians, since their ideals and methods originated from a common source, yet the label should be applied guardedly. They were in no sense slavish imitators; indeed, Cotton and Bradley, faced with a very different situation from that which Arnold ever had to meet, introduced new elements into their scheme of school government—eventually leading to developments in the public-school system as a whole and the nature of its ideals—which Arnold would never have sanctioned. This change in the nature of educational ideals, however, is the subject of a later study.

Arnold's assistant masters have not received from historians the attention which has been directed to his pupils. Naturally those who came into closest contact with him and who were known to have been deeply influenced have excited most interest: A. P. Stanley, Dean of Westminster; Charles Vaughan, head-master of Harrow, Master of the Temple and Dean of Llandaff; W. C. Lake, Dean of Durham; Matthew Arnold, the doctor's eldest son; A. H. Clough, the poet. Recently, Miss Woodward has widened our knowledge of Arnold's pupils with detailed studies of J. P. Gell, a pioneer of education in Tasmania, and William Delafield Arnold, Matthew's younger brother, the author of the novel *Oakfield*, who in the course of his short life did much to lay the foundations of native education in the Punjab.[22] These intellectuals, however, were but a small pro-portion of the Rugbeians whom Arnold was in a position to influence. Very little is known about the more ordinary pupils, whom Dr. Mack describes as the 'private soldiers' in Arnold's army.[23] They have their occasional spokesmen in Thomas Hughes and Sir Alexander Arbuthnot, who both claimed to have been influenced deeply by Arnold, although—and this they did not see—not in the way which Arnold would have wished. The interesting link between the intellectuals and the muscular extroverts is W. C. Lake.

Until he entered the Sixth Form at Rugby, Lake belonged to the set of the 'bloods'. He was an accomplished athlete, indolent by nature, a boy like George Hughes who instead of giving his time to themes and verses would sit chatting round the fire with his friends and a few admiring fags, 'talking over football and cricket matches, and the Barley and Crick runs at hare and hounds'.[24] Then came the transformation: only a few words from Arnold were necessary to do the trick. "Now, Lake," he said, when the boy received his remove from the Fifth Form, "I know you can do well if you choose, and I shall expect you to do so." 'These few words', Lake wrote many years later, 'altered my whole character, intellectually, at all events.'[25] He became the intimate friend of Stanley and Vaughan, and together the three boys would walk and talk about deep subjects, comparing notes on Arnold's sayings and doings and sharing each other's hopes of the great work that confronted them in later life. Lake claimed to have known Arnold more intimately than the others, but threw off the influence more readily than they did when he was old enough to stand on his own feet. As an old man, he returned sentimentally to his earliest loves. He looked back wistfully to his boyhood days and came to the conclusion that 'it was the average idle boy, such as those whom *Tom Brown* describes, who were most improved, and more in their after-life than at school, by Arnold's training and example'. And he regretted turning his back on former friends:

> Nothing could be closer than the friendship of Stanley, Vaughan and myself; but to me it was the loss of what had been my earliest friends, the cricket-ground and football. These I gave up almost as a matter of course when I became an intimate friend of Stanley; and there were very few days when he, Charles Vaughan, and myself did not spend our spare hours in long walks and talks—a great mistake, and one which in after-life I have often bitterly regretted.[26]

We should not take too seriously the musings of an old man, at a time when muscular Christianity was all the rage, looking back at the lost opportunities of youth. Yet the critics of Arnold have frequently echoed Lake's sentiments. Arnold was so sure of the goal—the quest for Truth, the living of the Good Life— that although he might not have wished to make himself a Pope, and although he might have encouraged his pupils to think for themselves, he could not but inspire his pupils—boys at the most

58

impressionable stage of their lives—to follow in his wake. All this is true; but to represent this as a defect requires from the critics evidence that Arnold's pupils were led to postulate viewpoints that they could not wholeheartedly sustain or to mould their lives according to a pattern which was contrary to their natures. And here the evidence is weak. G. F. Bradby and R. J. Campbell have both pointed out that Arnold's pupils reflected in their lives 'a certain originality and independence of mind not very usual in the England of the period';[27] Dr. Mack observes that 'there were as many reactions to Arnold's teaching as there were individuals who felt its impact';[28] yet earlier he criticises Arnold for wanting 'his boys to subscribe emotionally and unthinkingly to the truth rather than to evolve their own scale of values, and to be boys of the right moral type rather than of diverse types'.[29]

If this last statement by Dr. Mack is a true representation of Arnold's wishes, then clearly he failed. Stanley and Vaughan, whom their examiners at school (Dr. Moberly and Christopher Wordsworth) described as 'magis pares quam similes',[30] turned their Arnoldianism into very different fields and each stressed a different aspect of Arnold's teaching. To Stanley, Arnold had given a love of learning and a hatred of the dogmatic pratings of the enemies of rational theology. So Stanley followed his master in introducing a note of sanity in the unedifying hysteria that greeted the publication of *Essays and Reviews*,[31] just as Arnold—twenty-four years earlier—had defended Dr. Hampden against the attacks of Newman and the other 'Oxford Malignants'. To Vaughan, Arnold had given an ideal of public-school education which he used as a model in his resuscitation of Harrow between 1844 and 1859. Lake experienced a sudden conversion in his youth and lived to regret it; Matthew Arnold began as a rebel and ended by writing 'Rugby Chapel'. He and his father shared almost exactly the same educational ideals but viewed them in different lights. In the words of Sir Joshua Fitch, the son saw them 'with the eyes of a poet and a philosopher, the other with those of an earnest Christian teacher and moralist'.[32] Clough was a visionary who was never able to reconcile his dreams with the world of reality; Gell and William Arnold both possessed considerable practical gifts and, if Gell was perhaps too disposed to test every measure by the degree in which it conformed to the fundamental truths which he had learnt at school, William Arnold allowed his own experience to lead him to an attitude of tolerance with regard to religious education which his father could never have endorsed.[33]

Yet, with all these divergences, these men had one thing in common—moral idealism. They judged men by what they were, not by what they had attained. Conduct—to them all—*was* three-fourths of life. And what more could—or should—a teacher hope to communicate to all his pupils? It might not be possible to make boys wise; but they should be taught to love and to respect wisdom. It was beyond anyone's powers to force people to be good; but it was wrong to fail to show that it was the duty of man to strive towards the good and that his true happiness lay in making the attempt. The realisation of this was the secret of Arnold's power as a teacher. As Bonamy Price put it: 'Every pupil was made to feel that there was a work for him to do—that his happiness as well as his duty lay in doing that work well.'[34]

Of course, teaching of this sort might occasionally misfire. As Miss Woodward has written: 'Arnold imbued his pupils with a zest for righteousness without imposing on their consciences burdens of detail, . . . to use the metaphor of "Rugby Chapel", he set them on the road to the City of God but furnished them with no precise itinerary.'[35]

A. H. Clough ultimately lost his way. He had felt—more keenly than any—that there was work for him to do, and as a boy he had plunged into the task of purifying his own particular world with all the ardour of a Crusader stirred into taking the Cross by the compelling exhortations of St. Bernard. Brain and energy were dissipated in endless petty combats with venial sins at a time when they should have been strengthened to prepare for the greater combat with more formidable foes than Rugby could provide. When faced with a direct frontal attack, Clough was piteously vulnerable. Enthusiasm had carried him further than his intellectual ability was able to comprehend. He was left with a vague awareness of the goal he should aspire to reach; but also a flagging will-power, caused by intellectual disillusionment, and uncertainty as to the means he should employ to attain the desirable end. Thus he experienced a sense of futile ineffectiveness, expressed memorably in the condemnation by the uncle of Dipsychus of the pious public-school boys who were 'full of the notion of the world being so wicked, and of their taking a higher line, as they call it. I only fear they'll never take any line at all.'[36]

Arnold was only partly to blame. Clough was forced into early maturity not by his headmaster but by the circumstances of his family. His parents were abroad; for years he had no home to go to in the holidays. As his wife pointed out in his *Memoir*: 'the self-reliance and self-adaptation which most men acquire in mature life were . . . forced upon him in his early youth'.[37] And the Clough that Oxford knew was not at all a man who had clearly been 'forced' at school or inspired to adopt an attitude of piety unnatural for his years. The futility which Lytton Strachey saw was not noticed by his brilliant Oxford contemporaries. Temple wrote of Clough that he was 'the ablest and greatest man I had ever come across',[38] * an opinion shared by many others who knew him well. It is sometimes forgotten that W. G. Ward's influence on Clough was quite as powerful as that of Thomas Arnold, and Ward later blamed himself entirely for Clough's disappointment in the Schools and subsequent disillusionment. If Clough had kept up his Rugby habits, all would have been well; he 'should have kept himself aloof from plunging prematurely into the theological controversies then so rife at Oxford,—I cannot to this day think of all this without a bitter pang of self-reproach'.[39]

4

Religious enthusiasm is commonly associated with a disregard for scholarship. Some reformers have felt that deep learning serves only to obscure the simple clarity of religious truth. Nothing, however, could be further from the minds of the group of moral reformers among whom Arnold stands out as the greatest and the most influential. To him and to the majority of the early Victorian intellectual class, godliness was virtually inseparable from good learning, the link between the two principles being,

* Tait recalled that Clough's paper on the character of Saul, written during the competition for the Balliol Fellowship 'was the best and most original thing he had ever known in any examination'.

as we have seen, the quest for truth. Good learning meant, naturally enough at this time, classical learning. Public schools, grammar schools and universities had been dominated for centuries by an exclusively classical curriculum. It was hardly possible that men who had risen to prominence within this educational structure and—more pertinently—through their ability to master its rigours, would countenance any other system than that from which they had themselves derived such profit. To be trained in 'modern' subjects, to acquire 'useful knowledge', a boy or a man would have to go to a private academy, as like as not a Dissenting Academy, where he might pay the penalty of being influenced by 'ungodly' principles. Was there anything wrong in this? Occasionally a dissentient voice was heard from within our group—F. W. Farrar,[1] for instance, or Frederick Temple—but such spokesmen represented only a very small minority.

This devotion to a classical curriculum has attracted almost as much criticism as the excessive emphasis on moral behaviour. Radical-minded contemporaries attacked the schools and universities for persisting in the worship of dead languages and in particular for the custom of emphasising the negative aspects of the study—grammar and syntax—and for encouraging boys to indulge in profitless occupations such as the writing of Latin verses.[2] Pupils who suffered from this experience have left their bitter reminiscences: boys, like Kinglake, who loved the classics but who were taught to hate them by the unimaginative and sometimes cruel methods of teaching them; or boys, like Charles Darwin, who just plainly hated the whole system as a waste of time. Mr. G. F. Lamb has made a compendium of these memories of dissatisfied pupils and comes to the conclusion that this 'long, unchallenged supremacy of the Classics in so many schools for so long a period' remains 'a fantastic feature of English education'.[3]

Change was in the air, however. The pressure was coming from below. Dr. Nicholas Hans's study of eighteenth-century education reveals that in a considerable number of schools of various types—private academies, technical academies, private classical schools—curricular reform was proceeding steadily. The pupils that they trained in modern subjects—mathematics, modern languages, history, mechanics, the elements of the natural sciences—were forming an increasing body of opposition to the older classical schools, some of which were bound by the terms of their endowments to a rigid classical curriculum, others being so tightly controlled by a clerical monopoly that all measures of curricular reform were strenuously resisted. A few of the older schools, such as Christ's Hospital and Manchester Grammar School, showed some disposition to move with the times.[4] But compared with what was taking place in the smaller private schools and academies, the reforms of a Samuel Butler or a Thomas Arnold appear negligible.

Yet it should not be supposed that, because the clerical advocates of godliness and good learning were jealous of the supremacy of the classics and resisted intrusions which nowadays are considered educational necessities, the system was moribund and failed to turn out educated men. The brilliant scholastic achievements of the Victorian intellectual class, exhibited in many fields, were founded largely on the excellent training provided by school and university; and what a later generation may have gained in width of curriculum has been won at the expense of that singular combination of severe linguistic discipline, cultural appreciation and philosophical training which had been the gift of a classical upbringing to such eminent scholars as Christopher Wordsworth, Westcott, Lightfoot and Hort.

Arnold certainly thrived on the classical training which he received at Winchester and appears to have loved his work. When he came himself to be a teacher of the classics, he communicated much of that delight and enthusiasm to his pupils. Samuel Butler and his successor, Benjamin Hall Kennedy, at Shrewsbury gained a greater reputation for their school in producing brilliant classical scholars, especially at Cambridge where, between 1841 and 1870, 37 Salopians obtained first classes in the Classical Tripos, including nine Senior Classics, twelve University Scholars and eight Chancellor's Medallists.[5] Lake suggests that Arnold's first four or five years at Rugby were less distinguished academically than the last years of Dr. Wooll, 'for Arnold (especially in versification) was not a finished scholar, and we had no honours, either at Oxford or Cambridge, to boast of in the way of scholarship till Stanley broke the spell by gaining the Balliol Scholarship in 1833'.[6] On the other hand, certain very significant changes both in curriculum and in teaching method took place in these years of Arnold's headmastership. Fortunately, in an article which Arnold contributed to the *Quarterly Journal of Education* in 1834, a description of these various changes has been preserved.

The weekly hours of work were as follows: On Mondays, Wednesdays and Fridays, there were two class periods in the mornings, from 7 to 8 a.m. and from 9.15 to 11. On these days there were also two afternoon periods between 2.15 and 5 p.m. On Tuesdays and Thursdays, the two morning periods were as on other days, but from 11 a.m. to 1 p.m. there was a two-hour composition period. Tuesdays, Thursdays and Saturdays were half-holidays. Saturday morning followed the same schedule with the exception that there was no composition period. This made a weekly total of twenty periods ranging from one to two hours' duration. Two of these periods were devoted to mathematics; two to modern languages; the remaining sixteen were used for classics, scripture and history.

The work in classics, scripture and history was so divided that by the end of each half year an equal number of periods had been spent on what Arnold described as 'language time' and 'history time'. This may give the immediate impression that classics and history were on an equal footing. In fact, a glance at the syllabus shows that this was not so. Much of the work in history entailed reading of classical authors—Xenophon, Tacitus, Livy, Herodotus and Thucydides. The study of scripture was in part linguistic (the New Testament in Greek) and also historical (biblical history). Teaching in classical literature, mathematics and French was carried out in special divisions—what would now be called 'sets'.

The syllabus was something of a masterpiece. In classics, the first form were introduced to Latin Grammar and Latin Delectus; Greek was begun in form three. Thence the various forms were taken through a comprehensive course of Greek and Latin authors, culminating in Virgil, Homer, portions of the works of the Greek tragedians, the private orations of Demosthenes, Cicero against Verres and Aristotle's *Ethics*, which were read in the sixth form. In mathematics, the syllabus was less enterprising. Beginning with elementary tables and the Rule of Three, it worked up to *Euclid Book VI*, simple and quadratic equations, plane trigonometry and conic sections. In French, the lower divisions worked mainly on grammar and exercises. Prose work was begun in the Removes; the reading consisted of La Fontaine, a Molière play and Pascal's *Pensées*, and, in the highest division, Guizot's *Histoire de la Révolution de l'Angleterre* (published 1826–7) and Mignet's *Histoire de la Révolution Française* (published 1824). In scripture, the syllabus covered a large portion of the Bible, the New Testament in Greek and a general course of biblical history. The most striking part of the syllabus, however, was the course in history. By the time a boy had finished his school career, having been in Arnold's Sixth, he would have studied Markham's two-volume *History of England*, the same author's companion volume on France, Hallam's *History of the Middle Ages*, Russell's *Modern Europe*, a history of Greece, the detailed geography of Italy and Germany, the physical and political geography of Europe, together with portions of Xenophon's *Anabasis*, Florus, Arrian, Paterculus, Herodotus, Livy, Tacitus and Thucydides. He would already have a general knowledge of biblical history from his scripture lessons and would have read the most recent studies in French on the English Civil War and the French Revolution.[7]

The classical bias is plain. Arnold would not have had it otherwise. In the course of the article from which these details are taken, Arnold defended at length his practice of making the classics the basis of the educational system. He was especially anxious to point out that such a basis was desirable only if the classical instruction were sensibly conducted.

A classical teacher should be fully acquainted with modern history and modern literature no less than with those of Greece and Rome. What is, or perhaps what used to be, called a mere scholar, cannot possibly communicate to his pupils the main advantages of a classical education. . . . The study of Greek and Latin considered as mere languages, is of importance mainly as it enables us to understand and employ well that language in which we commonly think, and speak, and write.[8]

Hence he drew a distinction between the laborious and profitless exercise of construing and the highly valuable work of translating into appropriately stylistic English—'Herodotus should be rendered in the style and language of the chroniclers, Thucydides in that of Bacon or Hooker, while Demosthenes, Cicero, Caesar, and Tacitus require a style completely modern';[9] hence he felt for some years a reluctance to encourage Latin and Greek verse composition.[10] The main aim of the teacher was to stimulate his pupils to acquire knowledge for themselves and to furnish the intellect 'with power to obtain and to profit by what it seeks for'.[11]

The publication of this curriculum undoubtedly made an impression. The Public School Commissioners of 1864 constantly referred back to Arnold and the Rugby curriculum as the recommended pattern for more conservative schools, especially Eton, where mathematics was still treated as an insignificant subject only to be taught by junior men who were not granted the status of an assistant master, and where French was taught purely as an 'optional extra'.[12] Prince Lee, a greater classical scholar than Arnold, certainly followed his example in using the classics to encourage wide reading of English literature and to stimulate interest in history, philosophy and culture. Benson, in preparing a curriculum for Wellington, drew upon his own school experiences and his knowledge of the way in which the Rugby system worked. He expected his pupils to read serious and difficult books and constantly exhorted them to apply what they had read to the consideration of wider issues.

Benson's lessons in Guizot's *History of Civilisation in Europe* illustrate this well. A pupil—the Rev. Walter Moyle—recalled them thus:

What we used to do was to prepare a certain amount one evening in the week and do it in class at first lesson next morning—that is, *viva voce*. In setting the lesson the Master would generally give us references to quite half a dozen other books—bearing on the passage to be prepared—and expected us to go to the school library and get these passages up. We read in this way, besides the Guizot, a good deal of the following books: Thierry's *Nouveaux Récits de l'histoire Romaine; Études de Littérature*, by Villemain, and also Duruy's *Histoire du Moyen Âge*. I used to *dread* these lessons, for in those days, at any rate, I knew hardly any French, and the learning even to translate several pages was in itself a prodigious labour. I have, after diligent search, found the following questions set by him on some part of the *History of Civilisation in Europe* . . .:

1. What does Guizot state as the chief moral results of the change in the condition of the Communes?
2. What was the prevalent feeling in the twelfth century, and later still of the mass of burgesses, with respect to their rights in the matter of government?
3. What is the origin of the desire for political power? Show that the causes were not at that time in existence.
4. Was the individual burgess-character devoid of enterprise?
5. Trace the history of municipalities under and after the Roman Empire, and
6. The relation of municipalities to seignorial government and the gradual attainment of sovereign power.[13]

This habit of demanding wide reading and the consideration of allied issues was made the subject of a parody by one of Benson's prefects.

1st lesson—Saturday.
The next two lines and a half in Guizot.
A small portion only is set because it is wished that the following illustrative points should be thoroughly got up—
1. The number of words and the number of letters in the passage set.
2. All other forms of meaning which the passage can be made to assume by the permutation of words and letters.
3. The weight and dimensions of the volume.
4. The manufacture of paper, and the various uses to which paper is applied.
5. The history of printing from the earliest times, with life of Caxton, and description of the modern process.
6. Memoir of Didier et Cie.
7. Lives of all the commentators on all the biographies of all the historians of the times referred to.
8. The continental Bradshaw.

N.B. Dr. Benson is positively resolved not to set any impositions, which he abhors, but if anyone fails to answer perfectly a single question, he will write out 5 times Dr. Benson's MS. notes on this passage, made at the age of six, and consisting of 20 closely written pages of foolscap 4to.[14]

The Wellington curriculum was very similar to the one devised by Arnold for Rugby. An unusual feature, however, was the inclusion of compulsory chemistry for all forms and compulsory French and German in most of the higher forms.[15] These novelties[16] * were introduced largely at the instigation of the Prince Consort, whose hopes for Wellington were that it should become a school of an entirely new type, breaking away from the traditional classical model and adopting in curriculum and discipline the best features of the German Higher Schools.[17] The evidence of school time-tables, however, is not entirely trustworthy. Under Benson, the chemistry instructor was a local Wokingham doctor, somewhat erratic in his attendance at the school, and the original apparatus appears to have been a box of sand and a poker.

The neglect of the natural sciences is the most lamentable feature of the public-school syllabus of this time. Arnold believed that the time-table would not accommodate any additional subjects; also he thought that the natural sciences were not suitable studies for boys. 'Physical science, if studied at all, seems too great to be studied.'[18] This did not, however, prevent him and many other great schoolmasters of this period from doing their utmost to encourage boys to regard the observation of the workings of nature and the search for an understanding of nature's laws as the most rewarding occupations of their leisure hours. It was all part of the restless and determined pursuit of knowledge which was one of the most characteristic features of the Victorian intellectual class. We should hesitate in accusing them of narrow-mindedness. This awareness that the whole of life consists in learning and that everything that comes from God, or from nature, or from man, both his brain and his hands, ministers to one's understanding is the secret behind their intellectual stature, their diligent lives and their sense of power.

Charles Kingsley delivered a lecture at Wellington in 1863 on the habit of observation. He recalled his childhood:

> When we were little and good, a long time ago, we used to have a jolly old book called *Evenings at Home*, in which was a great story called 'Eyes and no Eyes', and that story was of more use to me than any dozen other stories I have read.

* German was introduced by Arnold into the Rugby curriculum in 1835.

A regular old-fashioned formal story it is, but a right good one, and thus it begins:—

'Well, Robert, where have you been walking this afternoon?' said Mr. Andrews, to one of his pupils, at the close of a holiday. Oh, Robert had been to Broom Heath, and round to Campmount and, home through the meadows. But it was very dull, he hardly saw a single person. He had rather by half gone by the turnpike road.

'But where is William?'

Oh, William started with him, but he was so tedious, always stopping to look at this thing and that, that he would rather walk alone, and so went on.

Presently in comes Master William . . . terribly dirty and wet he is, but he never had such a pleasant walk in his life, and has brought home a handkerchief full of curiosities. He has got a piece of mistletoe, and wants to know what it is, and seen a woodpecker and a wheat-ear, and got strange flowers off the heath, and hunted a peewit because he thought its wing was broken, till of course it led him into a bog and wet he got; but he did not mind, for in the bog he fell in with an old man cutting turf, who told him all about turf-cutting, and gave him an adder; and then he went up a hill, and saw a grand prospect, and wanted to go again and make out the geography of the country by Carey's old county map—which was our only map in those days; and because the place was called Campmount, he looked for a Roman Camp and found one; and then he went to the ruin, and saw twenty things more, and so on, and so on, till he had brought home curiosities enough and thoughts enough to last him a week.

. . . And then it turns out that Master William has been over exactly the same ground as Master Robert, who saw nothing at all. Whereupon says Mr. Andrews . . . 'So it is. One man walks through the world with his eyes open, and another with them shut; and upon this difference depends all the superiority of knowledge which one acquires over the other. . . . Do you then, William, continue to make use of your eyes; and you, Robert, learn that eyes were given you to use.'

And when I read that story as a little boy, I said to myself, I *will* be Mr. Eyes; I will *not* be Mr. No Eyes, and Mr. Eyes I have tried to be ever since; and Mr. Eyes, I advise you, every one of you, to be, if you wish to be happy and successful. . . .[19]

Time and time again, in the biographies of the eminent Victorians, we meet this picture. In the *Life of Christopher Wordsworth*, Dean Burgon recollects that a walk with C.W. was a great treat; for he had inherited from his illustrious uncle an ardent love of nature, and took genuine delight in whatever natural objects met his eye. . . . I never before, or since, have known anyone who, like C.W., would expatiate on leaf and bud, fruit and flower, with a kind of rapture, inspired (as it would seem) by the most familiar furniture of a garden in early spring.[20]

Westcott, a generation younger than Wordsworth, was just the same. As a boy, he devoted most of his school holidays to walks. One of his companions has described the customary procedure:

We made an early start, and beguiled the way looking for special plants which his father asked for, or using and enjoying his keen observation and sense of natural beauty, as he pointed out to me some striking features in wood and field, 'the perfect beauty of the trees', and sometimes quoted lines of Wordsworth or other poets in illustration of his feelings or descriptive of the scene. Then when we reached the church, which was most likely the special object of our walk, he would sit down and sketch, and with a few rapid and suggestive touches, afterwards to be completed, strike off in perfect proportion the architectural character of the building.[21]

Mandell Creighton, a generation younger than Westcott, shared the same delights.

Long walks remained his favourite recreation. He explored every corner of the country round Durham, and began to take an interest in botany, making a collection of dried flowers which won the school prize. Though never in any sense a scientific botanist, this taste remained with him through life: he always noticed the flowers on his walks, and could unfailingly be appealed to for their names.[22]

The curriculum of the schools at this time and the stress laid on the educational aspect of leisure show that Victorian schoolmasters were confident that boys could be profitably driven to work far harder and that they could cope with reading far more difficult and rigorous than is nowadays generally thought desirable. What the records do not always tell us is how many boys proved incapable of standing the pace and endured in misery what their brighter companions pursued with joy. At Wellington under Benson, the battle between idealism on the one hand and dullness and apathy on the other was at times very keen. On the whole, the educational standard of the entrants was very low and Benson found it very hard to understand that inability and indolence do not necessarily spring from the same roots. He assumed at times that what a Verrall could do, all boys were capable of doing; and this assumption is perhaps the most vulnerable part of the system which these idealists were erecting. It led to ruthlessness at times; also a lack of sympathy for the weak and ungifted.

A letter written by Benson as a boy at King Edward's, Birmingham, to his grandmother gives some idea of the strain under which a conscientious boy could live; also it shows an enthusiasm for work which is ominous for his future Wellingtonian pupils who might not feel quite the same way:

I am about as uncomfortable as you can well imagine [he wrote]. Here I am sitting in a terribly cold room with a stone floor and without a fire, being examined in Mathematics. The only sound that I can hear is the scratching of quill pens on paper, with a deep drawn sigh occasionally. . . . We break up to-day week. . . . I am quite tired of this half-year, and shall be glad when the examination is over; it has been the hardest half-year I have ever had. I have not been in bed till after midnight for several weeks, frequently not before two o'clock, but I do not think hard work will ever kill me; it has done me no harm as yet, further than a headache now and then.[23]

The demands on the staff could be equally exacting. Arnold did much to raise the status of an assistant master in a public school. But he demanded not only devoted service to the school; he required also from his staff that they should remain intellectually alert and be active scholars—perhaps the most difficult of all resolutions for a hard-pressed schoolmaster to keep. Arnold deliberately took upon himself work requiring a high degree of scholarship in order to force his brain to be active. He refused to allow school commitments to prevent him travelling abroad in the vacations, so that he could gain new friends, enjoy new experiences and provide himself with fresh material for his teaching. "The more active my mind," he said, "the better it is for the school."[24] Benson, for the same reason, began his monumental study of Cyprian while Master of Wellington.

It follows that the assistant masters appointed during these years were of a very different type from those who came to the schools in the last decades of the nineteenth century. Many of them were fellows of colleges. At Wellington under Benson—a school which by the nature of its foundation had few scholastic pretensions—the staff of nine included three fellows of colleges, three wranglers, two firsts in classics and one first in modern history.[25] Salaries were high. In order to entice dons from the two universities, the schools were compelled to offer at least £200 p.a., the normal salary of a college fellow in the 1850's and 60's. Many were offered a good deal more than this. Benson's salary at Rugby, as an assistant to Dr. Goulburn in tutoring the Sixth, was over £900 p.a. He was still only in his twenties and while he was studying for the Trinity fellowship examination, his teaching programme was reduced to one hour a day, although he was expected to take private pupils most evenings.[26]

Mention has already been made of the distinguished scholars on the staff at Rugby in the 1850's. Harrow, during the same period, was equally impressive. Westcott was there, teaching a much heavier programme than Benson had had at Rugby and, in his spare time, examining at Cambridge for the 'Mays' in ecclesiastical history and producing a stream of important theological writings, including his *Introduction to the Study of the Gospels* and *The Gospel of the Resurrection*. With him were F. W. Farrar, Henry Nettleship, Bosworth Smith, the historian, John Farmer, the musician, and H. W. Watson, a distinguished mathematician and physicist.[27] For the boys who could appreciate it, there was an atmosphere of real scholarship in which they could grow up. All this talent was not wasted. Among Westcott's pupils in his last year at Harrow were Walter Leaf, Charles Gore, Sir Arthur Evans, G. H. Rendall (later headmaster of Charterhouse) and Frank Balfour. Four of these were among the school monitors who, in 1869, presented Westcott with an address to give him joy at Peterborough in which they expressed their great debt to him, saying:

> We feel heartily . . . the greatness of this boon. But at least through your influence some new hopes have been aroused, some new desires kindled, and some new thoughts engendered, which will in the appointed time bear fruit.[28]

Is it possible for us to feel anything of the thrill of these hopes and desires and thoughts which one day—'in the appointed time' —would bear fruit? Can we experience the enthusiasms which made them write what they wrote and do what they did? The era of godliness and good learning has not much meaning to us if we judge it by modern ways of thinking and the conventional standards of to-day. Viewed in this light, their curriculum may seem unenlightened and their preoccupation with religion and morals positively unhealthy; their discipline may seem brutal, their manners eccentric, their sentiments naïve. The pretentious disapproval expressed by one schoolboy of another schoolboy's lies to a master, the treatment of childishness as a manifestation of sin —these may make us feel very sorry for the boys who had to suffer such a humourless and arid childhood. Yet our sympathy may well be misdirected. After all, did not Stanley write of Arnold's great ideal of life, that he sought to achieve 'a close union of joyousness with seriousness'?[1]

Young Harry East, it may be recalled, teased his friend Tom Brown for puzzling so gravely over the behaviour of George Arthur, the delicate and gentle new boy whom Tom had been asked to protect.

'Tom,' [said he], 'blest if you ain't the best old fellow ever was—I do like to see you go into a thing. Hang it, I wish I could take things as you do—but I never can get higher than a joke. Everything's a joke. If I was going to be flogged next minute, I should be in a blue funk, but I couldn't help laughing at it for the life of me.'[2]

An Arnold or a Benson would have frowned at this. But the unaffected and whole-hearted enjoyment of life, derived not from the pursuit of frivolities but from the joy of conquest and attainment, the pleasure of intimate friendships and the satisfaction of doing good works, was something that they had felt and which they were constantly striving to communicate to their children and to their pupils. Archbishop Tait, in the memoir of his wife Catharine Spooner, described this spirit of Christian joyousness, which was always about her, thus:

There scarcely ever was anyone who so thoroughly enjoyed life. . . .
Indeed to her all life was happy. God gave her wonderfully good
health, and a buoyant, cheerful nature. She used to tell us that
when she was a young girl, she could not be prevented from
laughing to herself through mere joyousness of spirit. This went
with her through life.[3]

Later generations, in considering the atmosphere of early and
mid-Victorian family life, have found it difficult to forget the
fearful saga of the Fairchild family, in which domestic piety,
oppressive parental discipline and childish priggishness appear in
their most nauseating and loathsome form. And because common
features of the middle-class Victorian home have since disappeared—regular family prayers, family hymn-singing on
Sunday evenings, compulsory repetition of scriptural texts, the
excessive care that only what was moral and uplifting should be
permitted to reach the eyes and ears of children and servants—
it is tempting to suppose that those who were expected to submit
to these practices and conventions found them irksome and
oppressive. To read the letters of William Wilberforce to his son
Samuel, a century and a half after they were written, makes one
wonder how the boy could have endured the constant stream of
moral advice, sententious disapproval of trivial mistakes, and
pious exhortations, without becoming either a rebel or a prig.
At the age of twelve, he was told:

> I hope my dear Samuel remembers what I used to say to him of its
> not being enough to be good negatively, that is, not to be unkind,
> but that he tries to be kind positively. . . . How shocking must it
> appear to a Holy God, and to the Holy Spirit, for any one to grieve
> his Saviour by being *un*kind to others, who is himself continually
> receiving marks of such kindness from a gracious Providence. I
> hope you guard against wandering thoughts in prayer.[4]

The boy had been dilatory in writing home. When Samuel, at
the age of fifteen, had been beaten in a school examination, his
father pointed out:

> And to be honest with you, my very dear Boy, let me tell you that
> it appears to me very probable that the heavenly Shepherd may
> have designed by this incident to discover to you that you were
> too much under the influence of Emulation, and to impress you
> with a sense of the duty of rooting it out.[5]

When Samuel had reached the age of seventeen, his father began the practice of concluding his letters with the single word REMEMBER, written in large capitals,

> Charles I's last word . . . which may naturally be supposed to live in the recollection of the person addressed. My dearest Sam[1] well knows, therefore, what *my* REMEMBER means. *Remember* all a father's (let me say a Christian parent's) wishes and prayers for a dearly-loved child's temporal and eternal happiness, and endeavour to have them realised.[6] *

A young child, however, rarely resents what he has been brought up to respect as accepted and usual. He naturally supposes the pattern of his own family life to be the norm of behaviour and regards deviations from it as odd and eccentric. The fact that the routine of family life was ordered on the principles of Christian ethics and designed to promote Christian living did not necessarily involve such restriction of a child's natural inclinations that he was brought up in an atmosphere of gloom and oppression. In households of intense evangelical zeal—such as the family into which Samuel Butler was born—home might have been little better than a prison. On the other hand, to the children of Edward Stanley, brought up at Alderley Rectory, memories of happy childhood days had a quality of sweetness which the passage of time enhanced. Writing of the childhood of Leslie Stephen, Mr. Annan has observed:

> the pious air of an educated upper-middle class Evangelical family in the last century is breathed no more to-day. . . . The Stephen children led happy, gentle lives. Christianity flowed about them and they bathed in it. . . . The children were never troubled by the thought of their mother waiting for them to receive an 'illumination'. They learnt to pray at her knee, to join every morning and evening in family prayers, and to read the Bible as the best of all story books. The children believed that Jesus lived because their parents talked to Him each day; and their conviction that Jesus was journeying through the world, but always at hand, was extraordinarily vivid—as if another member of the family were living under the same roof.[7]

* Westcott, when writing from Cambridge to his future wife, regularly employed the same device, the intention being that 'we might, each time this word comes before our eyes, offer a prayer more particularly each for the other'. A. Westcott, *Life of Westcott,* I.65.

One of the best pictures of life in a Christian household in the 1850's emerges from the memoir written by Catharine Tait of her five little daughters who all died from scarlet fever in the space of six weeks during 1856, when their father, the future Archbishop, was Dean of Carlisle. Catharine Tait wrote this heart-rending account of the tragedy shortly after her children had been taken from her, and subsequently addressed it to her only son—Craufurd—expressing the wish that he should publish it, in the hope that 'it may speak a word of comfort to those upon whom a similar burden is laid, and who are feeling that it is too heavy for them to bear'.[8] The extract quoted here describes the life of the Tait household at Carlisle before the disaster occurred.

Each morning, a quarter before eight, Craufurd * and Chatty † used first to come to me, learn their verses of a Hymn and Psalm, and then say their prayers. Chatty generally left after that, though, when she liked, she used to stay for the others. Frances ‡ used to come to say her little verse and her sweet prayer; then, with a merry bound, would she kiss her mother, and run off to breakfast, for which she was always in a hurry. She was the most artless, innocent babe, and would say in a voice we hear now, 'Forgive me all my dear sins.' She never lived, sweet lamb, to understand what sin was. . . . At that time Chatty was learning the Morning Hymn in which this verse occurred

> 'Saviour, to thy cottage home
> Once the daylight used to come
> Thou hast oft-time seen it break
> Brightly o'er that Easter lake.'

Each time when she came to that verse, she, 'my heavenly child', as I used to call her, would stop, and with her sweet finger point to a picture (on the other side of my bed) of our Saviour's childhood, and say, 'That is the cottage home, Mamma.' She knows more about it now, sweet lamb, than we do. Catty § and May ‖ used generally to stay in their own room at this time and say their

* Craufurd Tait, the Taits' only son, was born 22 June 1849.

† Charlotte Tait, their third daughter, was born 7 September 1850.

‡ Frances Alice Marion Tait, their fourth daughter, was born 29 June 1852.

§ Catharine Anne Tait, their eldest daughter, was born 16 March 1846.

‖ Mary Susan Tait, their second daughter, was born 20 June 1847.

prayers together, learn their Hymn and Psalm, then come to me to say them. After this they used with Craufurd to read a portion of the Bible, then I said a short prayer with them, and they went to their breakfast. We had prayers about nine, and papa used to question them on what he had read, to which they used to reply very nicely. The three eldest then went into the schoolroom for an hour. Chatty, Frances, and Susan¶ used to be our sweet and merry companions at breakfast. When they became, as they often did, too noisy, clinging Chatty would beg to stay, ever longing to be near her mother, and boisterous little Frances would ask for her bit of bread and honey, and be off to fill the nursery with her merry laugh and play. Susan, my lovely baby, used always to stay till the church-bell began.

On Wednesdays, Fridays and Saints' Days, also on every birth-day, any that liked used to accompany us to the Cathedral. I always found two, more frequently four, ready when I came down. On other days they used to play in the garden and Abbey grounds, and what a merry party always came round to claim a kiss when we came out of church. It was my busy time, and I could not stay much with them then, as I had either home business to do, or school, infirmary, workhouse, or poor to attend to. We had days and times for each, and these sweet girls used to think how they would love to help when they grew older; in many ways they did help me already.

Saturday was their own day. I used to spend from half-past eleven or twelve in the schoolroom, hear all the lessons of the week, question closely on history, which I had read on purpose (it was wonderful how much they knew), look over all exercises, copies, etc., and hear the music learned in the week. Great was the delight these Saturdays gave them, and who can tell the joy they were to their mother? Chatty was my own little pupil till December . . . and after reading, etc., and work with me, she would creep into the schoolroom with her sweet, pleased look, and there she also has left her unfinished copy-book. . . .

Sundays were days of great happiness with them. They would often, before we were up, come in, the five together, with their bright, happy Sunday look, take their place beside us, and chant with clear voice, 'This is the day the Lord has made', etc., then say all together a Sunday hymn, 'Put the spade and wheel away', then the 122nd Psalm, 'I was glad when they said', etc. After their

¶ Susan Elizabeth Campbell Tait, their fifth daughter, was born 1 August 1854.

prayers I would explain the Gospel or Epistle to the three eldest. At family prayers, we sang a Hymn; they always had the books ready, and I had looked forward to my dear Catty and May, when Spring came, playing the Hymn for us to sing to. They could already play several, and I was anxious that they should in this be able to take my place.

When we went to breakfast, Catty and May, in turns, would conduct a Sunday School of all the rest. They used to arrange it in beautiful order—in summer, when warm enough, in the garden, or when this could not be, up the little steps leading to their father's dressing-room; and we, from our room, would hear their sweet voices singing Hymn after Hymn and chanting Psalms. They then said Hymns and Psalms they knew, and Catty would always have some nice book ready to read which the little ones could follow. We had either the school or teachers to attend to at this time, so that I could not be with them. When we returned, the four were ready for church.

After church they dined at our luncheon, and dear little Frances was always of the Sunday party. When I had time, I heard them say their catechism, and at two went for a class at the night-school, and coming back would be greeted by five bright faces ready to take their places beside me at church. After church, for an hour and a half, unless when at tea, they were with us; this was the longed-for time. The little ones saw Sunday pictures, and then we read some book—*The Pilgrim's Progress* last summer; we sat all together in the Abbey, outside the Deanery door, to read it, and people who came to walk there used to look with pleasure at that happy company. I can see little Chatty's look of delight as she ran for the big book, and found the place. After our return from Ireland we read the *Infant Pilgrim's Progress*, and had begun *Naomi* by Mrs. Webb. . . . After dinner was their time with their Father; each one in turn would climb on his knee and say the Hymn and Psalm they had learned for Sunday. When the little ones were gone to bed, the elder children would sing Hymns and chant Psalms till their bed-time came.[9]

Now these were perfectly normal children living perfectly happy lives in circumstances that to-day would be considered unendurable. Vitality—gusto—spontaneity—laughter; none of these were lacking in their lives. There was, it is true, for the child, the schoolboy, even the undergraduate, more direction from above than would be countenanced to-day. Every opportunity was taken to divert the need for enjoyment and relaxation into instructive and edifying channels.

Mention has already been made of the Victorian concept of leisure, the fable of 'Eyes and No Eyes', the educational value of long walks and the study of nature. The influence of home training in this respect, strengthened by precepts learnt at school, often lasted a lifetime. Encouraged to read serious and difficult books at a tender age, taught to abhor light reading and novels as inducements to mental languor, the young Victorian was soon brought to realise that the world he lived in was beset with serious problems, in the solving of which he might be called to play an active part. He must learn to appreciate its culture, best acquired by mastering early a few essential techniques. He must be able to sketch and to paint, to read music, to write verses, to train his memory by constant essays in repetition. But above all he must learn to love knowledge. As a child he would be expected to make his contribution to the family scrapbook, and was himself encouraged to keep commonplace books and a diary, and to develop the ability to communicate his discoveries and thoughts by means of letter writing. As he grew older, it became almost instinctive to observe persons and places with a keen and critical eye, to make handy digests of books read and sermons heard, to record everything that might prove of value for some future occasion.

Edward White Benson was a typical product of such training. Amongst his private papers, preserved in Trinity College Library, is a collection of commonplace books and diaries, dating back to his schoolboy days. One book is entitled *Tomoi Atomoi*, a collection of anecdotes, ideas, thoughts and derivations; another is called *Mirabilia Testimonia*, being a notebook of dreams, strange coincidences and unusual occurrences. There are two volumes of *Contexanda*, containing useful extracts from books and poems, and another volume, entitled *Philocalia*, bearing the sub-title 'Goodly Sayings and Sentences as well heard as read and anecdotes'.[10] At Wellington College there has been preserved an enormous scrapbook, compiled by Benson during his Mastership, containing not only newspaper cuttings, illustrations, letters and personal mementoes but also minute notes and studies of the symbolism employed in the carvings, mosaics and windows of the college chapel, built by Gilbert Scott in 1863.

Benson was incapable of wasting time. It was his practice to read the Greek Testament while shaving. He walked or rode daily, but seldom without either a book to read or a companion to talk to. When he relaxed in the evening, he would spend the time in earnest discussion with friends or in playing intellectual games, such as the impromptu compilation of Latin verses ('Latin verses—the sweetest and prettiest things in the world',[11] he used to say), or in teaching his wife German. It should never be supposed that the preoccupation with spiritual matters and with organised religion disposed these people to renounce the world and to ignore temporal concerns. Nothing could be further from the truth. The passion for knowledge was inspired by the hope and conviction that knowledge was supremely worth while: that in the possession of wisdom lay the promise of a better world as well as the certainty of a better understanding of God's revelation and His purpose in creating man.

Filled with this conviction, the mid-Victorian schoolmaster of the stamp of Arnold, or Benson, or Prince Lee, was not inclined to allow his pupils to be regimented into the playing of organised games. If a boy was to learn the educational value of leisure, he had to be provided with sufficient time and freedom to pursue his particular bent. Although *Tom Brown's Schooldays* is one of the earliest examples of the delight in athleticism, the ideal there expressed is not that of Arnold but of Thomas Hughes. That Old Brooke's words after the great School House match ('I know I'd sooner win two School-house matches running than get the Balliol Scholarship any day')[12] were received by 'frantic cheers' shows indeed that the majority of boys in the 1830's at Rugby were more at one with Thomas Hughes than with their head-master. And Arnold tolerated this state of things—even gave Old Brooke the opportunity of saying that he approved of it ('Didn't you see him out to-day for half an hour watching us?')—[13] mainly because he believed that boys should be left to choose their own forms of recreation in their out-of-school hours and that it was better that the high-spirited 'bloods' should indulge their love of dangerous living in playing football rather than worrying the neighbourhood with poaching and rowdyism.

Some schools, Harrow notably in the realm of cricket and Winchester somewhat later through the influence of the old-

Harrovian Charles Wordsworth, were taking competitive games-playing seriously in the early decades of the century. But it was not really until the 1860's and 70's that schoolmasters began to give their official encouragement to organised games and to see in them a great force in 'character-building'.

Before these decades any organisation that there was in school-boy games tended to be left to the boys themselves. If they wished to engage a professional to coach them at their cricket, they were permitted to do so on the understanding that he was their employee. Certainly at Wellington under Benson the financing of the games and the payment of the professional were the res-ponsibilities of a boys' committee presided over by the head of the school. The Master conducted an annual audit of the accounts.[14] Very little official interest was taken in school matches; the 'bloods'—Tom Brown's 'kings of the close'—were given no privileged status by the authorities. It is interesting to note that on the occasion of the annual steeplechase at Welling-ton, inaugurated by Charles Kingsley, Benson could write to Elizabeth Wordsworth: 'The boys are all out in Blackwater Meadows running or watching Kingsley's Steeplechase.'[15] It did not occur to him that it was his duty to watch too. Twenty years later, few headmasters would have dared to spend such an after-noon writing letters.

Because of this lack of regimentation in out-of-school hours, the activities chosen by the boys of this period were both more childish and more adult than those of later generations. Certainly they were more natural. In the public school of the late nineteenth century, small boys of twelve and young men of nineteen spent most of their leisure hours doing the same thing—playing at various levels of skill the game of the season. Earlier, small boys were not frowned upon for being childish nor were maturer minds subjected to undue victimisation for preferring walks and talks to rougher pursuits. One of the most popular pastimes in the schools of the first half of the nineteenth century was little more than a primitive version of 'cowboys and indians'—the game described by Thomas Hughes as 'mud-patties'.[16] An imaginary fort was set up on some eminence and defended by a team of boys, while the opposing side tried to pull the members of the garrison down to the bottom of the hill. Arnold, apparently, delighted in this game at Winchester.[17] At Wellington, in Benson's time, the siege of Cock-a-Dobby (usually known as the Hill of Bashan) was the most favoured occupation on a snowy afternoon. We hear also of marbles, quoits and hop-scotch as being popular schoolboy games.[18] In a memoir of Wellington in the 1860's, written by Henry Richards in his ninetieth year, the writer recalls his predilection for outdoor pursuits, but the activities which he describes are birds'-nesting, expeditions in search of lobster-moth caterpillars and stag-beetles, walks to Caesar's Camp, sailing toy boats on the lakes and going into the woods for picnics.[19] Mr. Peter Green, writing of Kenneth Grahame's schooldays at St. Edward's in the late 1860's paints a very similar picture.[20]

Even in the Rugby of Tom Brown the pressure to participate in team games seems to have been a good deal less strong than it was to become. A. P. Stanley, admittedly an exceptional boy, was not molested for his lack of interest in physical pursuits. He played at Rugby football only when he felt that his duty as a praepostor required him to do so.[21] Lake, as has been seen earlier, abandoned games-playing on entering the Sixth Form; and an eccentric boy like Martin, 'the old Madman', was able to spend hours on end birds'-nesting with his climbing-irons, pecking-bag 'and pockets and hat full of pill-boxes, cotton-wool, and other etceteras'[22] while still a fag.

A memoir of Uppingham in the 1840's—before the coming of Thring—reveals an even greater degree of freedom enjoyed by the boys. The author, the Rev. T. G. Bonney, writes:

> We spent more time in country walks than many school-boys, going in pairs. On half-holidays we had a 'calling-over' but the headmaster readily gave leave of absence to the older boys. . . . The result of our freedom was that several of us took an interest in natural history: some collected birds' eggs; a few, like myself, looked after fossils . . . Churches or other buildings in neighbouring villages often had features of interest . . . and I have several sketches taken in these rambles.[23]

If young boys behaved like the children that they were, many of the older boys naturally tended to develop adult enthusiasms. Arnold's interest in political events while a boy at Winchester may seem pure precociousness. On the other hand, it was by no means exceptional. In a period before the minds of schoolboys became almost totally obsessed with school and house loyalties, youthful enthusiasm and the urge to succeed could find expression in other ways than the collecting of trophies and the winning of matches. For the pupils of the advocates of 'godliness and good learning' were nothing if not spirited. There was so much to be excited about: the future was full of promise. After all, the exhilaration which accompanied the advent of the railways and the certainty of advances in material progress beyond the most sanguine expectations of their fathers was as yet barely touched by the nagging anxiety and disillusionment which their children's children would come to feel. To many of the more intelligent boys of the middle years of the nineteenth century, the dramatic religious movements of their time and the doctrinal and ceremonial squabbles which accompanied them seemed immediately important. Despite Arnold's care that his pupils should not become indoctrinated with his very individual views on church organisation and the relations of church and state, there is no doubt that they eagerly devoured his controversial publications.[24] Benson and his contemporaries at King Edward's, Birmingham, could not but be affected by the presence in their city of one of the greatest religious controversialists of all time. The excitement, the sense of guilt, the spiritual thrill of seeing Newman in his pulpit were emotions which a later generation of schoolboys might find difficult to share.[25] But so it was. And the mention of Newman brings to mind that striking dictum in the *Apologia* which has a truly authentic ring when one sets it beside the circumstances of his time: 'Deliverance is wrought, not by the many but by the few, not by bodies but by persons.'[26] Perhaps less well known is a similar remark by Kingsley, for once in agreement with his great adversary: 'It is not the many who reform the world, but the few, who rise superior to that public opinion which crucified our Lord many years ago.'[27]

Inseparable from this ardent craving for activity was the tendency to emotionalism and to passionate friendship. The doctrine of the stiff-upper-lip was no part of the public-school code of the Arnoldian period. This gradually came in with the manliness cult of the 1870's and 80's. For it would never have done for Empire builders and games players to exhibit their emotions. A boy must not cry as he walks from the crease, bowled out for a duck; he must never show temper with the referee. Temper was certainly regarded as a defect in this earlier period. Benson, for instance, suffered agonies of remorse on the many occasions when he displayed it. But tears were usual, the expected consequence of reproof. There was not a dry eye in the Wellington chapel when Benson preached his farewell sermon. Headmaster and assistant masters occasionally wept together in the course of a difference of opinion.[28]

And the word 'love' was more frequently on their lips, used with real sincerity. The association between master and pupil seems to have often been very intimate, admitting of expressions of emotion on both sides. This is curious, in a way, because the points of contact between staff and boys were narrower then than they have since become. When schoolmasters tended to become overgrown versions of their pupils and began to take an active interest in games and boyish pursuits, they seem to have been no longer hated with the old vehemence and, also, no longer 'loved'. Doubtless the trend of school stories, begun by Anstey's *Vice Versa* and Kipling's *Stalky and Co*—the tendency to regard schoolmasters as either well-meaning nincompoops or pompous hypocrites—has done something to lower the prestige of the profession generally, so that the poor old 'usher' has become too unimportant to be regarded with strong emotions at all.

Charles Kingsley, meeting his old headmaster (Derwent-Coleridge) many years after he had left Helston Grammar School, flung his arms about his neck, exclaiming 'Oh! my dear old master! my dear old master!'[29] Henry Richards, compiling his memoir of Wellington College seventy years after he had left, wrote:

> The master I loved far the most was Eve.*. . . He was very good to us all. Once he went away to take some high degree in scholarship, and when we came back he was completely tired out and looked very white and all dark round his eyes, and we tried to do everything we could for him and did errands for him.[30]

The same was often true of the relationship between tutor and pupil at the universities. The historian of Lincoln College,

* Mr. H. W. Eve, subsequently headmaster of University College School.

Mr. V. H. H. Green, has commented on this feature of Oxford life in the middle of the century, quoting a letter from one of Mark Pattison's pupils written to his tutor after he had gone down:

> You don't know how I your old undergraduate pupil regard you. . . . I believe that under God (and in that name lies the whole secret) there is scarcely any person that on all the earth could fetch me off my perch; but this I feel—have always felt—since I knew you—feel now . . . that if you ceased to regard me the thermometer of my self-respect would go down at once to something a good deal under freezing point. . . . Towards you the old feeling of reverence is as strong as ever. If you asserted that black was white I verily believe I should nod a ready assent.[31]

The writer suggests that the bond which united teacher and pupil into a sacred intimacy was essentially the name of God. This explains much, but by no means all. It fails, for instance, to account for William Cory. The author of the Eton Boating Song, the poet of *Ionica*, William Cory Johnson (as he was known to Etonians) is a figure gloriously unique among the ranks of Victorian schoolmasters. He was of the same generation as Benson and Westcott and, like most of his contemporaries at Cambridge, was an admirer of Arnold.[32] * Yet it would be wholly misleading to describe him as an advocate of 'godliness and good learning'. Later we may see in Cory some affinities with the school of the 'muscular Christians', but strong as these were it would be impossible to represent him even as a sleeping partner in the firm of Charles Kingsley and Thomas Hughes.

The truth is that William Cory belonged heart and soul to Eton; and Eton, of all the old-established public schools in the nineteenth century, showed herself most jealous of her traditions and least receptive of outside reforming influences. Hawtrey, with the assistance of the Provost, Dr. Hodgson, strove to sweeten the atmosphere of Eton after the long rule of Dr. Keate, but the methods which he used were his own, and in two important

---

* Letter dated February 1843: 'I have been reading lately Arnold's and Manning's Sermons—both in very different kinds and degrees, with high admiration, amounting to love for the men, and no little advantage in comparing the two.' In a letter to H. O. Sturgis about Carlyle, he writes (1881): 'No book of his has done so much good as Keble's *Christian Year*, Stanley's *Life of Arnold*, . . ., etc., . . .'

respects Eton was kept pure of what the school regarded as the taint of Arnoldianism. Firstly, the religious spirit was much less influential there than elsewhere—a phenomenon of which Cory did not entirely approve;[33] and secondly, the prefectorial system was kept at bay by the retention of the tutorial system, the workings of which have been described by Cory's latest biographer as follows:

> At Eton a boy passes through division after division under various masters, but he has normally one tutor from the day he arrives as a small boy of any age from nine (in the old days) to fourteen, till the day he leaves. His tutor supervises every detail of his life at school, studies his character closely, quickens his mind to natural effort, helps him to mental courage and mental soberness, to self-knowledge (here I quote William Cory), and he is, or should be, his best friend. This indeed can be a momentous relationship—or it can be nothing.[34]

To William Cory it was everything. This was the element in which he worked, enabling him to convert the relationship between master and pupil from one of natural enmity into a kind of romance. For did ever a master love his pupils with less reserve than Cory? His most famous poem—*Heraclitus*—captures the sentiment exactly:

> They told me, Heraclitus, they told me you were dead,
> They brought me bitter news to hear and bitter tears to shed.
> I wept, as I remembered, how often you and I
> Had tired the sun with talking and sent him down the sky.

So, in his journal, a characteristic entry evokes the same image:

> July 1868. I wish to remember my day on the river, St. Barnabas, with Montagu Butler, . . . my wonderful poetical evening at Marlow and Harleyford, moonlight and reflected Venus, . . my fourteen mile walk with F. Wood across the Park on a Sunday evening, my moonlight strolls with him in the playing fields.[35]

He was by nature a lover of youth. Thus in *Academus*, he opens his heart:

> I'll borrow life, and not grow old;
> And nightingales and trees
> Shall keep me, though the veins be cold
> As young as Sophocles.

> And when I may no longer live,
> They'll say, who know the truth,
> He gave whate'er he had to give
> To freedom and to youth.

A profound classical scholar, he loved his Plato. One hardly needs the testimony of his journal to see the yearning for Platonic relationships:

> Feb. 1864. Item, my favourite bit of Plato, where Theodorus introduces to Socrates the teachable, quick, even minded Theaetates, the ideal listener, telling Socrates that the boy is like him in having a snub nose and ugly eyes, but speaking with motherly joy of his sweet nature.[36]

Such relationships could be misunderstood. In his *Vale* for Frederick Wood (*An Epoch in a Sweet Life*), he concludes:

> We trifled, toiled and feasted, far apart
> From churls, who wondered what our friendship meant;
> And in that long retirement heart to heart
> Drew closer, and our natures were content.

In 1872 Cory was compelled by Dr. Hornby to leave Eton; not for any very good reason save that it was dangerous for a schoolmaster to allow his emotions to carry him so far that they were capable of being misunderstood. But the age of emotionalism was passing, even though Cory in his poetry struck a note which has a timeless appeal. Percy Lubbock summed it up most felicitously when he wrote of him:

> A man of bold reason who wasn't afraid of poetry, a romantic lover of youth who was all too sharply aware that youth can't stay, can't wait to be adored: so that he couldn't bemuse himself in a mere haze of dreams, he couldn't blind his fancy: this man voiced the thought of all those, they must be many, who have felt of the reward of the schoolmaster that it is bitterly mixed. To give so much and to get so much, to give with mind and heart and to get so much in return to fill them both—and then to lose so much, to be always losing it: it is the schoolmaster's portion, who stays behind while youth that is life and work to him is always in flight.[37]

Cory put good learning before godliness; and before both he put the desirability of achieving perfect sympathy between the

87

teacher and those whom he taught. He was remarkably successful. Out of sixty boys of his fifth form division, eighteen took first-
class degrees at Oxford or Cambridge.[38] More satisfying to him
was their enduring affection. Charles Wood, later Lord Halifax;
Reginald Brett, later Viscount Esher; Sidney Herbert, Francis
Elliott; many more besides; they corresponded, frequently
visited him and brought him joy mingled with sadness. Some of
the sentiments which he expressed in his teaching—fierce
patriotism, love of physical activity—might give him a modern
look, but in temperament, especially his unashamed emotionalism, he was essentially mid-Victorian.

His most recent biographer warns us against reading too much
into this emotionalism and yearning for passionate friendship:

> William matched a diamond-sparkling intellect with the soft
> emotionalism of the age he lived in. Then a letter could be headed
> 'Beloved' and mean less than 'Darling' does now. Ecstatic souls
> laid themselves bare in the pretty, mauve penny post. There was
> little reserve.[39]

We cannot separate the ideals of godliness and good learning
from the spirit of the age in which they were supreme: the spirit
supplying the passion, the intensity, the rapture of love and the
bitterness of hate which we meet at every turn. In the long run,
they perished together, killed by the same foe. Of the revelations
that were to come from the pens of Freud and Havelock Ellis,
these generations were blissfully unaware. No exception was
taken to boys linking arms[40] * or to men occasionally showing
deep affection by embraces. When Christopher Wordsworth said
good-bye to Benson, his former Chancellor, after the frequent
visits of the Benson family to Riseholme, he 'used to kiss his
cheek, even on the crowded platform of Lincoln station, and give
him a solemn blessing with uplifted hand'.[41]

There is really nothing odd about the attitude of these early
and mid-Victorians to friendship save in comparison with later
standards of outward conduct. To be openly affectionate, to use
excessive terms of endearment were the natural corollaries of a

* Cory noted that in a bookshop at Rugby he had seen '3 schoolboys
leave the shop arm-in-arm; nearly all the Rugby boys go arm-in-arm
and just as often threes as twos'.

concept of friendship such as described by J. T. Coleridge in writing of his youthful association with Arnold:

> That is the season when natures soft and pliant grow together, each becoming part of the other and coloured by it; thus to become one in heart with the good, and generous, and devout, is, by God's grace, to become, in measure, good, and generous, and devout.[42]

To men whose learning had been almost exclusively classical, such a concept was very familiar. They knew their Plato; had certainly read the *Phaedrus* and the *Symposium*; they had very likely construed the *Satires* of Horace and read of the meeting with Virgil, the concourse of 'souls such that never earth bore fairer, to whom none could be more devoted than I. What embraces, what joy was there! In my senses, there's nothing I'd compare to a friend's good company.'[43]

6

In an unpublished sermon, written in the 1870's when canon of Peterborough, Brooke Foss Westcott considered some of the blessings which his generation had received, asking himself whether these gifts had been put to good use; whether he and his contemporaries were passing to their heirs and successors something of endurable value, which one day might win the respect of posterity.

> We, too, are ancestors [he wrote], and we are constrained to ask what is the inheritance which we are preparing for future generations? For what will our descendants bless us? Will they be able to say, when they look at the work which we have wrought in our brief time of toil, at the words which we have coined or brought into currency, at the spirit which we have cherished: 'They gave us of their best—their best in execution and their best in thought: they embodied splendid truths in simple forms and made them accessible to all: they kept down the hasty and tumultuous passions which an age of change is too apt to engender: thus they have made sacrifice easier for us; they have made wisdom more prevailing; they have made holiness more supreme; and for all this, and for the innumerable pains of which we know not, we bless their memory.[1]

What an epitaph for these giants! Characteristically, Westcott wrote these words in no spirit of complacency. They were to be uttered as a challenge—a call to action, an invocation to hear and receive the teaching of the gospel of work. Man's life on earth was indeed a 'brief time of toil'; the inspiration behind that incessant labour was faith. 'Faith', he once said, 'is a power for life and not a thesis which can be maintained successfully.'[2]

The key word perhaps is 'power'. It was the sense of power which underlay the solid achievements of the Victorians and sustained their efforts to add to what they had achieved. In part it rested on the consciousness of a sound economy and commercial and industrial supremacy; equally, it sprang from an educational and religious training which had as its end not simply the communication of knowledge, but the quickening of intellectual, moral and spiritual life. Such a training (again the phrase is Westcott's) enabled them 'to take possession of the wealth for which we were made as men'.[3]

Jowett, Sir Geoffrey Faber tells us, had no patience with idlers. "You are a fool," he once said to a rich young idler, "you must be sick of idling. It is too late for you to do much. But the class matters nothing. What does matter is the sense of power which comes from steady working."[4] In this phrase 'the sense of power' the virtues and the defects of the system may be found. It could lead to ruthlessness, excessive dogmatism, rigorous living unsoftened by the graces of humour and tranquillity. On the other hand, certain facets of the wielding of power it could triumphantly withstand. Samuel Wilberforce, in a famous speech urging the Government to throw open the Civil Service of India to the universities, expressed admirably how the pride of a power-conscious nation could be tempered by a sense of vocation.

> It was not much in the habit of the British people, even at home, to raise magnificent structures as emblems of their power and greatness. It was rather their vocation—and he thought it a higher one —to leave as the impress of their intercourse with inferior nations, marks of moral teaching and religious training, to have made a nation of children see what it was to be men.[5]

The spectacle of a Victorian bishop assuming the role of a Pericles may seem both amusing and irritating to modern eyes. Perhaps, after all, it would have been better to leave the nation of children alone. But we should take care lest we ascribe to these high-minded idealists the cant, hypocrisy and desire for ruthless exploitation which sometimes lay behind the pretentious assumptions of late Victorian imperialism. There is no reason whatever to doubt the sincerity of Wilberforce's mission. The sense of power and the sense of vocation were to him virtually the same. To possess power and to lack the will to use it for the betterment of mankind was to squander the blessings of God.

And when Wilberforce called his generation a nation of men, he gave them no more than was their due. The contrast between 'men' and 'children' was exactly the distinction which Arnold was wont to make in his Rugby sermons. To be a man was not necessarily to be a fine muscular specimen who could outfight and outplay all his foreign foes and rivals. To be a man meant to be adult in mind and ideals; to have the courage and the will, in fact, to adhere to a philosophy of life such as that described by Westcott in a letter, written in 1849, to his future wife:

You have often heard my views of life, yet hear them once again . . . To live is not to be gay or idle or restless. Frivolity, inactivity, and aimlessness seem equally remote from the true idea of living. I should say that we live only so far as we cultivate all our faculties, and improve all our advantages for God's glory. The means of living then will be our own endowments, whether of talent or influence; the aim of living, the good of man; the motive of living, the love of God.[6]

The Idealist: James Prince Lee

James Prince Lee, headmaster of King Edward's, Birmingham, and first Bishop of Manchester is that rarity among eminent Victorians—a celebrity whose praises were unsung. In searching for material on his life, we look in vain for 'those two fat volumes with which it is our custom to commemorate the dead'.[1] The little we may easily find out about Lee both suggests a reason for the omission and excites our curiosity to know more. Lee left very little manuscript material for a biographer to work on, and, immediately after his death, no obvious biographer could be found to work on what little there was. He had no sons; his elder daughter was estranged from him; his other daughter was probably reluctant to take upon herself a task which would have inevitably involved dealing with the distressing domestic situation which had brought the estrangement about. Of his many devoted pupils, some were too busy to undertake the necessary research, others were too devoted to be capable of viewing dispassionately the failures of Lee's unhappy years as Bishop of Manchester. Thus the material on Lee's career that is available to the general reader is very slender—a memorial sermon by Benson, edited with reminiscences of former pupils by J. F. Wickenden;[2] a published address by Westcott on the occasion of the opening of the Grammar School for Girls at Camp Hill, Birmingham, in 1893;[3] and, finally, a somewhat meagre and guarded account of his career by C. W. Sutton in the *Dictionary of National Biography*.[4]

An isolated reference here and there to Lee's work and influence may greet us while reading other biographies or contemporary works; enough to show that Lee's personal influence was such that he could excite extremes of love and hate from those with whom he came in contact. There is, for instance, the passage in Arthur Benson's *Life* of his father, where he recalls Benson's deep attachment to Lee:

My father's reverence for Lee was reverence as for a character almost divine: I shall never forget how in 1877, in Cornwall, when we were being entertained by a leading clergyman of the diocese, our host said to my father genially at dinner, 'By the way, Bishop, you were under Lee at Birmingham, were you not?' 'Yes, indeed', said my father, all in a glow. Then followed a highly disparaging criticism. There was a silence, and my father grew quite white—then he said to his host, 'You can hardly expect me to agree to that, when I owe to him all that I was or am or ever shall be.' Our host tried to qualify the expression: but my father was completely upset, and hardly said a word for the rest of the evening. As we went to bed he said to me, 'Lee was the greatest man I have ever come within the influence of—the greatest and the best—you see how people are misunderstood.' [5]

Could this really be the same man as the subject of a cruel lampoon which appeared in the *Manchester Examiner and Times* shortly after Lee's death, and which was subsequently reprinted in *Notes and Queries?* The author, who signed himself 'Southern-Wood', was a prominent Manchester antiquary called James Crossley, a man who evidently must have nourished a hatred for Lee unusual even for that outspoken and emotional age. The lampoon is in the form of an epitaph:

Here lies a Right Reverend Father in God,
Who ne'er spoiled his children by sparing the rod,
Who took not his pattern from Him who, when living,
Was merciful, large-hearted, meek and forgiving;
But, preferring in strife to work out his salvation,
Made quarrels and scolding his Christian vocation;
And, in mind of the pedagogue's narrowest span,
Held the birch the sole nostrum for governing man.
Would you edit a book without learning or brains?
You have only to study his 'Barrow's Remains'.
Are you seeking your posthumous venom to spill?
You cannot do better than copy his will. [6]

What does it all mean? If possible, the riddle must be solved.

2

James Prince Lee was born in London on 28 July 1804. His father, Stephen Lee, was then Secretary of the Royal Society, a position which he occupied for sixteen years—a man of substance, descended from a family of wealthy merchants who had trading connections with the Levant. Through his mother, James was related to the distinguished classical antiquary and topographer, Colonel William Martin Leake, and he appears to have shown from a very early age an enthusiasm for the same fields of study, having an eager and inquiring mind and a passionate interest in nature and all scientific pursuits. This was not altogether surprising in view of the academic background of his home at Somerset Place and the frequent meetings there of distinguished scientists and philosophers.

At the age of nine the boy entered St. Paul's (24 August 1813), then ruled by that most staunch defender of the classical curriculum, Dr. Sleath. He was there for ten years, rising to the position of Head of the School. His contemporaries regarded him as uncommonly well read and stood somewhat in awe of his remarkable general knowledge. Maltby, later Bishop of Durham, who frequently examined at St. Paul's, wrote later of Lee's work there:

> Our attention was very early drawn to the manner in which Mr. Lee appeared to excel his contemporaries in habits of industry, evinced by superior soundness and extent of knowledge. Each succeeding year, while he remained at school, we had fresh reason to admire his unabated diligence: and consequent progress as well in the knowledge of books as in accuracy and beauty of composition.[1]

In October 1824 Lee went up to Trinity College, Cambridge, as a Campden Exhibitioner. He became Scholar of Trinity in 1827, Craven Scholar in the same year, and was prevented from becoming Senior Classic only through ill health which compelled him to take his degree without competing for honours. In October 1829 he was elected Fellow of Trinity. Very little has been recorded of his undergraduate career, but he appears to have made a very deep impression on both his colleagues and his pupils in his year as a don and tutor. He began work on the Isaac Barrow manuscripts in the Trinity Library. His pupils testified to his 'general knowledge of modern and foreign literature, science and discoveries . . . combined with . . . first-rate scholarship'.[2] Gerald Wellesley, one of these pupils, subsequently wrote of him:

He was considered the finest classical Tutor in the College. . . . I was much impressed with the purity of his life. His health was very bad even then—his face pallid, with restless, roving eyes. But I had conceived a great affection for him.[3]

The testimonial which the Master and Fellows of Trinity later wrote for him when he applied for the headmastership of King Edward's School is a most remarkable document.

Mr. Lee [they wrote], was generally considered one of the most distinguished classical scholars ever known in the University; and as a private tutor he was equally remarkable for the great range of his knowledge, for his clearness and precision in teaching, and for the deep and active interest which he always took in the welfare and success of his pupils.[4]

In 1830, the year in which he married Susannah Penrice, he received an offer from Arnold of an assistant mastership at Rugby, with the special duty of taking charge of the Fifth Form, the form next below Arnold's own. His coming broke the long succession of exclusively Oxford appointments to the Rugby staff, and there is no doubt that Arnold viewed this as one of the most important steps of his headmastership.

We have got a Cambridge man [he wrote to George Cornish in August of that year], a Fellow of Trinity, who was most highly recommended to me as a new master; and I hope we shall pull hard and all together during the next half-year: there is plenty to be done, I can assure you.[5]

Lee's acceptance of Arnold's offer was the turning-point in his career. He was in his twenty-seventh year. In physical appearance he was unprepossessing—small of stature, with a pale and angular face, set usually in a stern and purposeful expression: a precise man, both in manner and speech, with expressive eyes that glittered when he was pleased and flashed menacingly when confronted with an offender, so that they seemed to pierce the toughest armour of excuses in their determination to reach the heart of truth. Yet he was of a nervous disposition, and the precision and economy of movement which he affected were a defensive covering to hide an acutely sensitive temperament and a restless, emotional spirit. When he was sure of himself, his voice was clear and decisive, firm and controlled; when he was nervous and conscious of the presence of unfriendly critics, his articulation became slurred and hesitant. Occasionally his emotions broke loose from the barriers which he had contrived and revealed depths of fury which would surprise those who thought they knew him well; at other times, the hard features would dissolve into paroxysms of grief.

Lee was dogged by ill health all his life. The nature of his trouble is not certain. It appears that he suffered greatly from neuralgia, for which he had often to dose himself with laudanum to deaden the pain;[6] also he was periodically afflicted with acute inflammation of the eyes.[7] Benson, in his memorial sermon, spoke of his great suffering: "Some of us have seen him suffer, and hardly known that he did suffer: have known him forget the acute pain of the most sensitive of organs, while, in a shaded room, he would rivet the attention of his young listeners hour after hour."[8] He had a dread of sympathy, a horror of being dependent on others. Much of his terseness of manner, his stern demeanour in public and before strangers, may be explained by the superhuman efforts he made to conceal his physical discomfort.

He served eight years at Rugby, during which time he drew nearer and nearer to Arnold, whom he greatly admired. It was from Arnold that he derived the passionate love of truth, which became the most infectious quality of his teaching at Birmingham; he even developed some of Arnold's mannerisms, gestures and expressions. Lightfoot recalled his lessons on Butler's *Analogy* with the First Class at King Edward's, how

> when, leaning back in his chair and folding his gown about him, he would break off at some idea suggested by the text, and pour forth an uninterrupted flood of eloquence for $\frac{1}{2}$ an hour or more, the thought keeping pace with the expression all the while, and the whole marked by a sustained elevation of tone which entranced even the idlest and most careless of us.[9]

And undoubtedly he followed Arnold in attempting to form a *corps d'élite* of the boys in his boarding-house and in his own form on whom the whole tone of the school should depend.[10] Benson, writing to his uncle—William Jackson—from school in 1846, informed him that he had been reading Arnold's *Life and Letters*, and the more I hear of him, the greater does my admiration of him become. He certainly was, according to my ideas, if I may so far presume, a great, good man. . . . He seems to me to have been equally estimable in every way: perhaps I like him the more, from the many points of resemblance which exist between him and Mr. Lee.[11]

Yet, according to Westcott's testimony, Lee and Arnold did not always see eye to eye. In 1865 Westcott visited Lee at Manchester, and his old headmaster 'discoursed with much energy of Dr. Arnold, and was intensely angry with *Tom Brown*, which he declared utterly misrepresented Arnold's mode of dealing with boys'. In a letter to Benson, after his visit, Westcott recalled that 'sometimes he spoke of Arnold, and vaguely of differences between himself and A., which seem to have been great. "The letters", he said, "which bore witness to them I burned a short time since."'[12]

Indeed, Lee's pupils, comparing the headmaster they knew with the Arnold they had read about, were wont to give the palm to Lee. He was the 'very greatest of teachers', Benson declared in a speech before the boys of his old school in 1883,

For after having read the lives and seen the systems and studied the methods of, I think I may say, nearly all great masters, I still do maintain that James Prince Lee was *Magister Unicus*. You know the greatness of the spirit which Arnold breathed into all schools. All that spirit breathed in him: and beyond it there were many, many points in which I say he was *Magister Unicus*.[13]

In May 1838 Lee sent in his application for the post of headmaster of King Edward's, Birmingham, shortly to be vacated by Dr. Jeune who had been elevated to the Deanery of Jersey. Among the thirty-one testimonials which Lee submitted to the governors, Arnold's letter in his favour probably created the greatest impression:

It is difficult for me to wish him success [Arnold wrote], because it would be next to impossible for me to supply his place adequately at Rugby. . . . His general reputation in the School may be best estimated from this fact, that the number of his private pupils has always far surpassed that of the pupils of any other Master: and in the choice of a private Tutor the views of the boys are influenced solely by the character for scholarship and attention to his pupils which a Master bears generally in the School.

Of the excellence of Mr. Lee's scholarship, indeed, I feel it almost presumptuous in me to speak, because it is much superior to my own. I feel sure, indeed, that there is no man employed in education in England at this moment, whether at the Universities or elsewhere, who can in this respect surpass Mr. Lee.

His acquirements, however, are very far from being confined to classical scholarship. His knowledge is very extensive and accurate, and the mass of information of all kinds which he is able to impart to his pupils is really extraordinary.

His activity of body and mind is unwearied: his interest in his profession intense: and his manner with boys is at once firm and courteous. They would never, I think, put him in a passion,—they would find him always kind; but they would know that he would always be minded.

In pecuniary matters, Mr. Lee's public spirit and liberality are quite noble. In every transaction of this sort he has uniformly shown a gentlemanly and munificent spirit, which I hold to be no unimportant quality in the Head of a great public institution.

In his religious instruction and care of the boys in his own house, Mr. Lee has been zealous and judicious. He is an earnest and sincere Minister of the Church of England, with nothing of any party tendency whatever.

Finally, Mr. Lee has had experience in public education for some years:—he has been thoroughly tried,—and I am in a condition to pronounce on the result of that trial. I know, from eight years' close observation, that he is most admirably qualified in all respects for the situation of Head Master of a Public School.[14]

Lee was one of three applicants nominated to the short list of candidates. The others were the Rev. Richard Michell, Fellow and Tutor of Lincoln College, Oxford, the avowed enemy of Mark Pattison in the great rectorial election of 1851 and subsequently Professor of Logic and Principal of Hertford, and the Rev. Thomas William Peile, Senior Fellow and Tutor in the University of Durham.[15] Lee was unanimously elected to the post on 21 May 1838.*

* Compare T. W. Hutton, *King Edward's School, Birmingham, 1552–1952* (Oxford 1952), 85, n.1, where appears the suggestion that Lee obtained his election by only one vote, a rumour originating from an allegation by Mr. Thomas Gutteridge. The Governors' Order Book, 368, records that the appointment was unanimous.

Arnold, who regretted losing him, was confident that Lee had found his true calling. A year after Lee had left Rugby, he wrote to Archdeacon Hare: 'You would rejoice in the good that Lee is doing at Birmingham; I do not think there is, in all England, a man more exactly in his place than he is now.'[16] Lee's letter of farewell to Arnold deserves to be quoted in full:

My dear Dr. Arnold, I have written my letter of resignation to Lord Denbigh. There remains for me one other duty before I close my connection with Rugby School. It is to return you my most grateful thanks for all that, under God, you for the last eight years have done for me and mine. For your invariable kindness, courtesy and liberality, for the information and advice I have gained from you, and the advancement and support you extended to me in the School I, from my heart, most sincerely thank you. But for what I feel especially I have derived from you, a knowledge of higher aims and a desire to aim at a simpler, truer course of life and thought, I cannot thank you merely as for an advantage gained, for I feel at the same time at once the privilege it gives and the responsibility which it entails on me.

But it is your best thanks that you have my assurance of my humble hope and wish, that what you have taught I may be aided to persist in, and that though distant we may still be fellow-labourers till at last we meet for ever.

Forgive my troubling you with these expressions of my feelings. You do not want them, but it is a relief and a pleasure to me to give vent to them. I shall indeed be sorry if you do not allow me in any opportunity to show my sense of what I owe you by any service to you or your children. That God may bless you, dear Mrs. Arnold and them, is the earnest wish both of myself and of my wife.

Believe me ever with sincerest esteem and respect, your deeply obliged and affectionate friend,

James Prince Lee.[17]

3

King Edward's School, Birmingham, had been founded in 1552 by royal charter, establishing a free grammar school 'for the educacion intruccion and institucion of children and younge men in Grammar forever to endure',[1] endowed with part of the lands previously belonging to the Gild of the Holy Cross. These lands ensured future prosperity, for although the 120 acres of school estate were then outside the town of Birmingham, the subsequent growth of the town into a city brought a vast yield to the endowment in the course of time. The estate covered what now is the very heart of the city—New Street, Bull Street, Moor Street, Dale End, Edgbaston Street, Spiceal Street, Digbeth and the Bull Ring.[2] As the school expanded, so the site of the buildings changed. In 1832, Charles Barry was commissioned to build magnificent new premises in New Street. What the governors had intended, and what Barry had produced plans for, was not entirely realised, owing to an important change of policy inaugurated by the headmaster of the time—Dr. Francis Jeune. When Jeune took up his appointment in 1834, he was confronted with a school which had lamentably declined in numbers and where the discipline had become lax and inefficient. Although Jeune was headmaster for only four years, and although he was only twenty-eight when he was appointed, he achieved something of a transformation. A strict disciplinarian, he restored respect for authority by means of exceptional severity, and, having enlightened views on curricular reform, he persuaded the governors to make a radical alteration in the structure of the school. Previously the governors had intended that the Grammar School of King Edward's foundation should be housed in the building which Barry was in the course of erecting. The 'School of Arts' or the English School, in which modern subjects were taught to boys who were not aiming to proceed to the universities, was to be housed in a separate building elsewhere. Jeune, however, sensibly pointed out that the number of boys in the Grammar School was too small to fill Barry's new building and that the two schools should therefore be combined, that they should occupy the same premises and 'that the Headmaster should take a real interest in the work of what now would be called a Modern Side, while at the same time he fostered in the Grammar School History, Ancient, Modern and Scriptural, Moral Philosophy and Political Economy'.[3]

The governors approved these proposals; changes in Barry's original plans were called for. The launching of the new constitution of the school and the official opening of Barry's building took place in the same year—1838. In the spring of that year

Jeune announced his resignation. Thus it was that Prince Lee was called upon to execute a new plan for the ordering of the school which his predecessor had devised and to take up his duties at the moment when the school moved into their new premises.

A word must be said about Barry's New Street building—in many ways an architectural masterpiece—the scene of Lee's scholastic triumphs. It stands no more to-day, having been pulled down in 1935, when the expansion of the school and the unsuitability of the building to provide for twentieth-century educational needs necessitated the moving of the school to a new site in Edgbaston. It was a massive Gothic structure with a street frontage of 174 feet, a height of 60 feet and a depth—from front to rear—of 125 feet. Its external appearance, Westcott observed in an article which he wrote for the first number of the *King Edward's Magazine*, resembled strikingly the chapel of King's College, Cambridge.[4] The most impressive feature inside the building was the Big School, or, as it was then called, the Grammar School. In this enormous room—102 feet long, 35 feet wide and 45 feet in height—the various classes were collectively housed. At one end, beneath a gallery, stood the great desk for the headmaster, probably designed by Pugin, who was at that time in Barry's employment. Over it was inscribed the single word 'Sapientia', and around it, occupying three sides of a square, was a low, railed desk at which Lee's pupils would sit —literally—at the feet of wisdom. At the other end of the room was a similar desk, with a canopy of open tracery, for the second master.[5]

The taking of classes in a single great hall was a very common feature in schools at that time. We know that Benson as a small boy used to watch with awe from one of the lower forms in the body of Barry's Big School, the little group of devoted pupils round Lee's desk, among them Brooke Foss Westcott 'leaning his head on his hand, the only boy who was permitted this luxury'.[6]

This, then, was Lee's inheritance. He appears to have had a capable and loyal staff, and certainly an excellent second master in the Rev. Sidney Gedge, whom Benson greatly liked ('I like him even better than Mr. Moyle', he wrote to his uncle in 1843, 'and nearly as well as Mr. Lee'.)[7] Lee reported to the governors at the end of his first year as headmaster:

The chief difficulty under which I at present labour in the Classical School regards my own classes and those of the Second Master. The admirable training of my predecessor has left me little, if anything, to wish as regards the upper boys. But the serious difficulty attending the raising the school when rapidly increasing in numbers, from a low to a high standard of scholarship, has caused necessarily a portion of the school to be advanced at a rate quicker than allowed time for sound grounding in first principles, and the time necessarily deducted from the Classical Instruction of the Upper Boys by the introduction of mathematical lessons for four hours each week and French and Drawing lessons for two hours each, much increases the difficulty as regards the present set of boys. This however will I trust in time be remedied by the promotion of boys more completely grounded from the lower classes. From the monthly examinations of each class which I have established I find the most beneficial results arise. Independent of the stimulus to exertion given the boys as well as watchfulness to the masters, I find the personal knowledge thus acquired of every boy most useful in forming character and maintaining discipline. The same may be applied to the Reports of Conduct and Improvement which are issued at the end of each half year. . . .

The moral state of the School I am happy to add is much improved. Falsehood which at one time prevailed to a great extent, has much diminished. The number of boys punished severely for serious offences amounted in the first half year 1839 to 30. In the second half year it was reduced to 19. Of the latter, one was publicly expelled and eight others compelled to be privately withdrawn. This severity will not seem extravagant when the great difficulty is taken into consideration of reducing into discipline upwards of 200 boys many of them unused to all restraint, taken at once into a newly opened school where there was no routine established for them to fall into, as was the case in the important experiment of opening the new Department in 1838. . . .[8]

Lee was faced with very different circumstances from those which confronted Arnold in 1828. Even had he been disposed to import Rugby traditions and Arnoldian methods, he would have had to adapt and modify them very considerably to suit the special conditions of a large local grammar school. Birmingham was fast becoming the industrial capital of the Midlands, a great centre of the hardware industry, surrounded by coal and iron fields, with railway and water communications with London, Liverpool,

Bristol and Hull. The boys largely sprang from a different class and a different home-background from those who patronised Rugby. Also the school was primarily a day-school, having provision for only a very small number of boarders. The headmaster was responsible for both the Grammar School and the English School and, besides that, was expected to superintend certain additional local schools which had been established as the value of the endowment increased. As Lee explained in a letter to G. E. Anson in December 1843, in reply to some queries raised by the Prince Consort shortly before a royal visit to Birmingham:

> In 1831 an Act of Parliament was obtained by the Governors enabling them to extend the subjects taught in the school, and to establish additional schools. . . . In July 1838, on my election to the Head-Mastership, I found the Classical School then containing about 220 boys (now 235, its number as limited), and two elementary schools just opened, one for boys and one for girls, containing about 136 each. In 1839 I opened the English School with 215 boys, and in the same year two additional elementary schools for boys, holding together about 350, and one for 136 girls, were commenced. The whole seven schools are wholly under my superintendance.[9]

Lee, unlike Arnold, was unable to exercise a profound religious influence over the school as a whole. He might certainly do so over the individual boys in his own boarding-house and the members of his First Class. But in any arrangement for the religious instruction of all the boys in the school, he had to take into account the presence of a number of children from dissenting families, Wesleyans, Unitarians and Independents, and also some Roman Catholics and Jews. All classes were given regular 'Religious Instruction'; the school day began and concluded with prayers.

> The principle I avow, and endeavour to carry out is this [he explained to Anson]. We are a Church of England school, our Doctrine, Discipline, Tenets and Teaching are those of the Church of England, and these we profess and seek to practise. But we do not compel the attendance of the Dissenter at our direct Religious Teaching, we allow him to absent himself if he asks leave, and lay on him the responsibility of so doing. I offer Religious Instruction, if they will not take it, I cannot help it.[10]

Although the age of entry to the universities was commonly lower than it is to-day, the majority of the boys even in the Classical School did not proceed to the universities. Between 1835 and 1857, 49 Edwardians went up to Oxford and 78 to Cambridge. A good many of the boys in the Classical School left before they reached the standard that would give them the privilege of sitting at the feet of 'Sapientia'.

Lee's astonishing academic successes during his headmastership of only nine and a half years are, therefore, all the more remarkable. Before Lee's time, the reputation of the school had been greatly enhanced at the universities by such scholars as William Linwood at Oxford (Student of Christ Church; Hertford, Ireland and Craven Scholar in 1836 and Boden Sanskrit Scholar in 1839), and Charles Rann Kennedy at Trinity College, Cambridge (Senior Classic, Senior Bell Scholar and Pitt Scholar, Porson Prizeman and Browne's Medallist for Greek and Latin Ode). Lee's successes, however, were unique, and justified the superlatives with which Arnold and others described his classical scholarship when he applied for the headmastership in 1838.

The best of Lee's pupils went to Cambridge. The honours won by his pupils at Oxford were not especially impressive—three Lusby scholarships at Magdalen and four college fellowships (including a fellowship at All Souls won by James Octavius Ryder). The Cambridge honours were as follows:

First Class in the Classical Tripos

1844.	Henry Keary, Trinity.	3rd aeq.
1845.	Hubert Ashton Holden, Trinity.	SENIOR aeq.
1845.	Frederick Rendall, Trinity.	SENIOR aeq.
1845.	Thomas Cox, St. John's.	5th.
1847.	Charles Evans, Trinity.	SENIOR aeq.
1847.	John Smythe Purton, St. Catharine's.	8th.
1848.	Brooke Foss Westcott, Trinity.	SENIOR aeq.
1850.	Henry Chance, Trinity.	16th.
1851.	Joseph Barber Lightfoot, Trinity.	SENIOR.
1851.	Christopher Blick Hutchinson, St. John's.	6th.
1852.	Edward White Benson, Trinity.	8th.
1852.	James Thomas Pearse, Trinity.	9th aeq.
1852.	Arthur Ayres Ellis, Trinity.	9th aeq.

Five of these scholars were Chancellor's Medallists: Rendall, Charles Evans, Lightfoot and Benson, winning the Senior Medal, Westcott taking the second Medal in 1848. In addition Keary was Bell Scholar in 1841, Holden was Senior Bell Scholar in 1842, Charles Evans won the Craven Scholarship in 1846 and J. T. Pearse became Bell Scholar in 1849. Westcott won almost every honour that was offered. He was Battie Scholar in 1846, Browne's Medallist for Greek Ode in 1846 and 1847, Norrisian Prizeman in 1850 and won the Members' Latin Essay Prize in 1847 and 1849. Benson gained this last honour in 1851.[11] Lee had the additional satisfaction of seeing eight of his former pupils gaining Fellowships at Trinity. These were: Keary (1845), Rendall (1846), Holden (1847), Evans (1848), Westcott (1849), Lightfoot (1852), Benson (1853) and Ellis (1854).[12]

4

How did he do it? Fortunately, Lee's pupils have left on record descriptions of his teaching.

Some things never grow old [said Westcott on one occasion]. His presence, his voice, his manner, his expression have lost nothing of their vivid power in half a century. I can recall, as if it were from a lesson of yesterday, the richness and force of the illustrations by which he brought home to us a battle piece of Thucydides, with a landscape of Virgil, or a sketch of Tacitus; the eloquence with which he discoursed on problems of life and thought suggested by some favourite passages in Butler's *Analogy*; the depths which he opened to us in the inexhaustible fulness of the Apostolic words; the appeals which he made to our higher instincts, revealing us to ourselves, in crises of our school history or in the history of the nation. We might be able to follow him or not, we might as we grew older agree with particular opinions which he expressed or not; but we were stirred in our work, we felt a little more the claims of duty, the pricelessness of opportunity, the meaning of life. And when I reflect now on all that he did and suggested in the light of my own experience as a teacher, I seem to be able to discern something of my master's secret, the secret in due measure of every teacher's influence. He claimed us from the first as his fellow workers. He made us feel that in all learning we must be active and not receptive only. . . . He encouraged us to collect, to examine, to arrange facts which lay within the range of our own reading for his use in dealing

105

with some larger problem. In this way we gained little by little a direct acquaintance with the instruments and methods of criticism, and came to know something of confident delight in using them. There was, we rejoiced to discover, a little thing which we could do, a service which we could render, an offering which we could make towards the fulness of the work on which we were engaged.[1]

We may recall Bonamy Price's description of the enthusiasm of Arnold's pupils at Laleham. Lee assumed that all those around him were as eager to learn and as determined to reach the truth as he was himself. He never pretended that the way was easy. He never talked down. Thus when Lee greeted a boy after the holidays, he welcomed him excitedly with, 'Well, what have you read? What have you seen?'[2] He threw open his magnificent library to the boys to encourage them to gain familiarity with original sources of criticism and history. In the days when young classicists had to find their way through texts without commentaries and were expected to work on the Greek Testament without the aid of Tischendorf,[3] access to a library which contained volumes of facsimiles and texts of the Fathers was of immeasurable benefit to a boy who had sufficient training to be able to use them.

And Lee's method of training in linguistic discipline was second to none at that time. He combined a remarkable width of vision with 'the severest discipline of verbal criticism'.[4] Arthur Benson has written of the effect of this training on his father and his fellow pupils. In the first place, Lee encouraged repetition of classical texts. He had himself a phenomenal memory, seldom used a book in class and was capable of repeating page after page of Thucydides without a mistake. 'The consequence of this was that all his scholars who resolved to be not only like but exactly like him, learnt immense portions of the classics by heart.'[5] Benson, even in later life, could still repeat continuously five or six books of Virgil. Westcott's feats were even more amazing. His dearest schoolboy friend, T. M. Whithard, recalled how Lee gave permission to his form to do voluntary repetition in the holidays and how Westcott chose to recite by heart 2,600 lines of Virgil and 500 of Homer. On another occasion he recited faultlessly the whole of Cicero's second Catiline oration, which he had chosen himself to learn during the school holidays.[6]

Lee's pupils were also taught to make very close analyses of words and to detect—almost by instinct—their shades of meaning. Arthur Benson suggests that Lee exaggerated the importance of this technique of verbal study, while admitting that the exercise greatly appealed to his pupils who retained the habit all their lives. It led Benson to develop a somewhat 'crabbed and bewildering' English style, encouraging him 'to pack the sense of a sentence into an epithet' and giving him 'a curious love for strained and fanciful words'.[7] A. W. Verrall, who received his classical training from Benson, noted this also. He felt that his master was 'too much of the grammarian and verbalist. There was handed down to us . . . a certain imaginary translation by him from the *Georgics,* beginning *"Continuo*—From the first *and all along—in silvis*—in the *wild* woods—none of your trim groves!"* and so on.'[8] Westcott, too, has been criticised for his over-ingenious interpretation of the precise meanings of words. To an evangelist who once asked him whether he was saved, he is reputed to have replied: 'Do you mean σωθείς, σωζόμενος or σεσωσμένος?'[9] Lightfoot, perhaps the greatest textual critic and commentator of them all, subsequently wrote of this characteristic of his old master: 'His teaching was most irregular in one respect, and yet rigorously exact in another; irregular in form, but strict in enforcing habits of precise observation and analysis. There was a singular absence of special rules, but a constant recurrence to broad principles.'[10] What might have seemed to have been weakness, he observed, was in reality the strength of his teaching. Like Arnold, Lee insisted on his pupils being well read. He gave no instruction in English literature and English language: he assumed that he did not need to. His pupils were expected to interpret the language of every author not only with reference to other writings from the same pen, but also by drawing comparisons with other works of literature, history or poetry, of which he expected a very wide range of knowledge.

Lee, indeed, was the least narrow of classical scholars. His remarkable general knowledge—especially in the fields of topography, art and science—had been noted by schoolfellows, his companions at the university and by his colleagues on the Rugby staff. This enthusiasm for wide learning was felt keenly by his pupils. On one of their three half-holidays in the week, they were often sent out to do some practical surveying. Armed with sextants and theodolites, a team of boys would invade one of the town's subscription gardens to make a joint survey of a stretch of water and the surrounding woods. Often senior boys would be encouraged to attend lectures in the city on art, archaeology or physics.[11] Some of his innovations in the school curriculum were regarded as rash and idealistic. For instance, he was the first schoolmaster to use Butler's *Analogy* as a class-book for boys. Lightfoot's striking testimony to the value of these lessons is sufficient to justify his decision. 'I have sometimes thought', Lightfoot wrote in later life, 'that if I were allowed to live an hour of my past life over again, I would choose a Butler lesson under Lee.'[12]

The consummation of all Lee's teaching, however, came in the lessons on the Greek Testament. 'For all his reading', Canon Wickenden later wrote, 'he might, more truly than almost any man, be called a man *unius libri*. The New Testament in Greek was his one book.'[13] It seemed to those who watched him—glowing with delight as he opened the text—almost as if he thought in Greek. (Certainly it was known that he made—what was to him—the wearisome study of mathematics a pleasure by reading Euclid in the original.[14]) "Read nothing with the Epistles but the Epistles," he would say. "Look out every word in Schmidt's Concordance, and see how St. Paul uses it in other places, and especially what words he couples with it."[15] The class would be taken through St. John's Gospel, St. Luke, the Epistle to the Romans and then—his special delight—the Epistle to the Philippians. Benson recalled how his pupils would tensely await the hours devoted to the Epistle to the Hebrews:

> There the uncreate majesty of the Son of God, there His suffering love, there His priestly intercession, were realised for them with a truth, a present might, which even for boys gave to our life its true interpretation, and slew all low ambition.[16]

Now this was no mere admiration or respect felt by boys who realised that they were experiencing great teaching. It was something immeasurably more powerful: inspiration, adoration—a unique experience. Where did the secret lie? It may be, as Westcott said, that the boys were made to feel that they were fellow workers. But it was surely the consciousness of the end that they had before them that so enthralled them. This end was no immediate honour that might come their way—success in an examination, a fresh trophy for the school. Somehow Lee contrived to lift his pupils above such thoughts, enabling them to gain a glimpse of something infinitely more precious; to his pupils it seemed that they stood on the very threshold of Truth. Only one who felt it can describe it.

Never less and seldom more than twenty-five boys were at one time under his influence as his own proud scholars at the head of his school [Benson said in his memorial sermon]. For about ten years at Birmingham they came to him and left him in even flow; their intercourse with him was hourly, and their loyalty absolute. The love of him was always at the height; they were bound together by it then and ever since: it was the perfectness of affection for him which has made so many of them seek his own profession. And how was it established? Whatever gentleness, whatever courtesy, whatever strictest honour he showed to the greatest, were paid to these boys in fullest measure, and on them he lavished all his stores; for them he took the poets, Latin and Greek, and read them like no pedant, he wrought out with exquisite taste and truth the pictures that were in words, and more, the touch of feelings, the pathos, the moral greatness, but above all things, again and again let me say it, the very *truth*. . . . For them the life of Athens was lived over again. . . . The chief power lay in the method: it was not so much the teaching he infused or the ardour he aroused, as the truth-seeking spirit he created, in those who were worthy.

But there was a greater than Athens—the Heavenly City:

There was one set of lessons which seemed to make even his others colourless. At a time when the highest honours of his university were falling to him over again through his pupils, he ever said that the study of the Greek Testament was that which he prized for them beyond every study and every honour. . . . To open before them a true method of study, a living study of that book, which even as boys they might begin and as men continue without ever having to look back on one misdirected effort—this was his grand aim in the formation of their plans, and even then the immediate teaching was full of fruit.[17]

The boys, then, of Prince Lee's First Class were quite as much under the spell of their headmaster and quite as distinct a coterie from the other boys in the school, as were Stanley, Clough and Lake and others of Arnold's Sixth Form. There was 'a tremendous seriousness, an intense enjoyment of work, and an extraordinary enthusiasm for virtue'[18] common to both groups. It is perhaps significant that whereas the majority of Arnold's pupils—and certainly those whom he most keenly influenced—went to Oxford, there to form a group dedicated to godliness and good learning, all Prince Lee's most prominent pupils went to Trinity College, Cambridge, where they dedicated their lives to the same ideals. Westcott wrote, in later life, of his friendship with Benson and Lightfoot at Trinity: 'It would be difficult to find a parallel to such a fellowship. . . . We "saw visions" as is the privilege of young men, which, if their fulfilment lingered, still coloured all our later years.' Gradually the realisation of what was needed came upon them, and, in the 1860's, all three had resolved to devote their lives to supplying that need: 'One conclusion was pressed upon us with overwhelming force, that there was no effective spiritual power in England able to bring the Faith into living contact with all the forms of human activity and thought.'[19] The institutions which most needed spiritual resuscitation were the universities and the cathedrals. Westcott and Lightfoot, after occupying chairs of Divinity at Cambridge and earning a reputation as two of the most eminent of Anglican theologians, both ended their lives as bishops, Westcott succeeding his dearest friend at Durham on Lightfoot's death in December 1889. By that time, the youngest of the trio—Edward White Benson—was Archbishop of Canterbury. Lee, who lived to see 'his favourite pupil' and son-in-law—Charles Evans—occupying 'Sapientia',* was denied the satisfaction of knowing how fully his hopes for his pupils were to be realised.

Exceptional boys, they became exceptional men. It is not always so. Certainly both Westcott and Benson were inclined to precociousness before ever they came under Lee's influence. Arthur Benson has pictured the young Westcott as 'hot-tempered, laborious, high-minded. He never played games, he detested sport, he kept himself from other boys. He took a vivid interest in social questions, and was a convinced Chartist.'[20] This does

* Charles Evans became headmaster of King Edward's in 1862. The post had been offered to Benson.

not bring out the kindness of his nature which was very marked
even as a boy. He was brought up in ways of strict frugality at
home, taught to despise luxury and frivolity. At once he per-
ceived a kindred spirit in Prince Lee. Like Clough at Rugby, he
started a school magazine, the main purpose of which was to sing
the praises of his headmaster. All the characteristics of the ideal
of boyhood in the age of godliness and good learning are displayed
in Westcott's school career: the passionate friendship with Thomas
Middlemore Whithard, nearly four years younger than himself;
the intensity of purpose which marked his approach to work and
leisure. In his spare time he would work at scientific pursuits,
attending lectures at the Mechanics' Institute, experimenting
with his galvanic battery, manufacturing gun cotton and making
sketches of the animals in Wombwell's travelling menagerie.
He worried greatly over the social problems and political events
of his time. He was convinced that 'virtus in agendo constat'.

This serious approach to life never left him. The letters which
he wrote from Cambridge to Mary Whithard, his future wife,
must rank as some of the most extraordinary love-letters ever
penned.

> You ask me, my dearest Mary [one letter begins], how you can
> keep the Fast of Lent. I do not think I can give you more advice
> than I did in my last note. You will, I have no doubt, have the
> opportunity of denying yourself often, and embrace it; and if you
> have any time for retirement and meditation, do not devote it to
> more trifling purposes.[21]

Another letter opens:

> As I generally do before writing my note to you, my dearest
> Mary, I have been reading Keble for the day, and though I do not
> recollect noticing the hymn particularly before, it now seems to
> me one of the most beautiful; and especially does it apply to those
> feelings which I have often described to you: that general sorrow
> and despair which we feel when we look at the state of things
> around us and try to picture the results which soon must burst
> upon our Church and country.[22]

Mary was expected to enter into all his enthusiasms and loves.
A letter dated 18 October 1847 opens with ecstatic excitement:

> My dearest Mary—First of all I must tell you of an event at which
> you will rejoice for our Church's sake—Mr. Lee is the new Bishop

111

of Manchester! . . . 'Remember', Marie. I sincerely rejoice at it
for the good he will do; much as Birmingham will suffer.[23]

Benson's boyhood was very similar, although he was much
more interested in ecclesiastical events than Westcott had been
at that age. When he was only fourteen, he converted a little
room in a disused factory, once owned by his father, into an
Oratory, appropriately furnished and decorated by himself, and
said there daily the Canonical Hours. He was passionately interested in liturgical history, an enthusiasm aroused by his uncle
—Christopher Sidgwick—not by Lee who remained all his life
indifferent to liturgical questions.[24] At the same time he was
avidly studying the *Tracts for the Times* in the Birmingham
Free Library. He was an indefatigable reader: by the time he
went up to Cambridge, he had read, in his private work, the
whole of Livy, Herodotus and Thucydides. He was reputed to
have been able to recite almost the whole of the Psalter by heart,
and was considered an authority on the ecclesiastical questions of
the hour. Canon C. B. Hutchinson recalled a walk with Benson
and Lightfoot from Birmingham to Coventry, stopping on the
way to examine churches,

> and I remember that as we walked there he gave us a clear account
> of the arguments on either side, in Cardinal Wiseman's Con-
> troversy with Dr. Turton, the Bishop of Ely; and on our way back
> he cheered our flagging spirits and put fresh springiness into our
> tired legs by his graphic stories, or vigorous recitations. And so,
> instead of dropping on the road, we accomplished our 40 miles'
> walk, and reached home quite lively.[25]

Benson's greatest friend at King Edward's was J. B. Lightfoot.
Lee undoubtedly encouraged intimate friendships among his
pupils, appreciating the stimulus to activity and intellectual
emulation which can so often arise from the union of fertile
minds at an age when boundless enthusiasm and the urge to
reform the world are natural feelings. Fortunately copies, made
subsequently by Arthur Benson, of many of the letters which
passed between these two particular friends in their last years at
King Edward's and the early part of their undergraduate careers
have been preserved in the Trinity College Library. These
illustrate admirably the excitement of intellectual discovery, the

common interest of the two boys in all that was happening within the Church, their enthusiasms and delights, and, above all, their intense devotion to 'Mr. Lee'.

The moods vary from frivolous banter to deep and earnest discussions of doctrinal questions and the purpose of life. Writing from Liverpool during the school holidays, at the age of sixteen, Lightfoot has this to say:

> My dear Benson, I am glad to hear that you are so jolly. . . . Liverpool is really a lovely place and only lacks your angelic self to make it a complete Paradise. Paradises, however, do not seem to be good places for reading either Classics or Mathematics in, for I have not done anything worth mentioning since I came here. By the bye I have got a nice equation for you to try your experienced hand at:
>
> $$x^2 + y = 7$$
> $$x + y^2 = 11$$
>
> I intend to bother Abbott* with it next half year. . . . What did James tell you to read these holidays? *Agamemnon* of Aeschylus? perhaps the *Thesmophoriazusae* or those other two plays of Aristophanes—was it so? . . . I think I shall be back in Birmingham in about a week. . . . And now believe me, Much respected Sir, your very obedient pupil (*in arte remigandi*),
>
> Jas. B. Lightfoot.[26]

Returned to Birmingham, he writes again:

> By the bye if you remember Mr. Lee said he should like to see some of our letters. Should I show him yours? It is certainly well worth perusing. . . . Your suppositions are far from being right, when you imagine that I am 'sweating my eyes out'. The fact is that I find my vows and determinations after reading so many Greek plays these holidays, all turn out to be of the genus pie-crust, viz: made to be broken. . . . The school, that infinite source of gratification to all the lovers of learning (and among those not the least to the gentleman who with his usual modesty styles himself 'the ever glorious incomparable E. W. Benson Esquire') will be opened on the 19th of this month.[27]

We can discover exactly what work the two boys were doing that following half-year from a letter written by Benson to his uncle:

> Mr. Lee has made us work very hard this half year, we have had Soph: *Antigone*, Eurip: *Orestes*, the last book of Herodotus, the

* The Rev. John Abbott, mathematical master at King Edward's.

third book of Thucydides, which, by the way, is the most difficult book I ever read, the third book of Horace's *Odes*, and the third *Georgic*, the second book of the 2nd action *against Verres*, and we are just going to begin the *Menexenus* of Plato, which we are to finish within a fortnight; besides our other work. At home I have read Aristoph: *Ranae* and 6 books of the *Odyssey*. . . . Mr. Lee pays much more attention to boys who are going to Cambridge, than to those for Oxford as most of our masters, as well as himself, are Cam: men. I should like to read a great deal next holidays, but I have no one to read with except school-fellows and one can't help talking to them, at least I have found it so before. . . . I forgot to mention in my list of school work, voluntary translations of *Anacreon* into English verse . . . (and Paley's *Evidences*).[28]

Occasionally Lee felt compelled to call a halt to holiday work if he thought that his pupils were doing too much.

I saw Mr. Lee on Monday in Union Passage [Benson wrote to Lightfoot in April 1846], and he told me to read no more during the last two or three days—a proposal in which I very contentedly acquiesced. I spent the whole of Wednesday at Wickenden's . . . and we walked and talked and were very jolly. He has been very industrious and—not read all Xenophon—but he has brought home some very nice sketches, and some really very fine rubbings of sepulchral brasses which latter I was helping him to ink and mount.[29]

In October 1847 Lightfoot left Birmingham for Cambridge, a year in advance of his friend. The tone of the letters becomes more serious and intense. Benson, although still only a schoolboy of seventeen, wrote to Lightfoot in July of that year:

All my old friends in ideas, etc., are coming over again and puzzling me sadly. You may imagine the difficulties I feel when it is assumed as a matter of course, and a ground to argue upon, that Dr. Arnold was a good man indeed but holding very mistaken and dangerous opinions. '*Nulla salus extra ecclesiam*' is the prime feeling: and love for the Church (i.e. of England) is what children are to be specially and above all things taught. But they now go a step further than I ever heard before. You must know that the Roman Church may be a true Church in Italy, but in England it is not only in error, but in heresy and schismatical. . . . It is as if Christ had come down from Heaven as some great teacher to found a Society which should have power to save of itself all who belonged to it, and as if He had then gone away again; the Atonement and Mediation of Christ seem to be very little thought of in reality of feeling, however much they may be acknowledged in doctrine.

He then went on to discuss the Latin version of the Athanasian Creed.[30]

A few months later, he began a letter to Lightfoot:

You really quite alarmed me by your paragraph on the 14th Century. Dear me, do you take me for a Papist? But if you will read the last few pages of Waddington's first volume, and Guizot as he is there quoted, you will see that there was something else than Church Music and Gothic Architecture which the *Church* of the Middle Ages did for mankind. Don't you think a very noble essay might be written comparing Heathen and Christian *Philosophy*? I do not think it could be dangerous to look at our faith in that light—and it would show how mean a thing is humanity raising itself to its greatest heights, as compared with humanity raised by God above itself.

He then launched into a lengthy comparison of the doctrines of Socrates and the doctrines taught by St. Paul.[31]

At this time Lightfoot was full of ideas of forming a small society dedicated to holy living. Benson was excited at the proposal. He thought it

advisable that we should meet and have together a peculiar Service, and declare solemnly to each other, before God Almighty, what our intentions and resolutions are, . . . still these vows must not be perpetual—and a certain form must be agreed upon by which they may be renounced—and all must be secret, we must observe strict silence, except to one another.

He discussed the nature of the Baptismal vows.

The noblest object of all is one which few have as yet aimed at. The Kingdom of God was for the *Poor*. Oh! let the *Poor* have the Gospel preached unto them. Let us league with all our souls and hearts, and powers of mind and body, that it may be no more God's witness against us, 'My people perish for lack of knowledge.'

Let us determine while our hearts are still warm, and unchilled by the lessons of the world, to teach the *Poor*. . . . And again to promote the Spiritual Unity of the Church, even if the outward union may be difficult or even impossible to affect, should be our constant endeavour. All these things are noble objects to live for, to study for, to write for, to pray for, to die for. . . . We may begin this work now. . . . Should we . . . be ever able to co-operate as Clergymen in the same Parish Church, our united efforts might be productive of good by writing, if God will bless us, and our labours among the people would prevent our Christianity from becoming solely theoretic; and all pleasant and lovely things might be done in the Service of His House.[32]

Lightfoot, meanwhile, had come under the influence of Westcott at Trinity.

The object of my greatest admiration is Westcott [he wrote to Benson in March 1848]. I shall not attempt to tell you all his good qualities, for that would not be possible, but imagine to yourself one of the most gentlemanly, quietest, humblest, and most conscientious of mankind! (to say nothing of cleverness) and you have my opinion of him.[33]

The letters that follow are concerned primarily with a discussion of the rival merits of the evangelical and tractarian systems; culminating in a most moving description by Benson of a sermon by Newman on the Parable of the Sower, which he had heard one Sunday evening during Lent. It is difficult to realise that the writer of these words was only eighteen:

Such a style of preaching I never heard before, never hope again to hear. Yet it reminded me very forcibly of Arnold, and his appearance was exceedingly interesting; he was very much emaciated, and when he began his voice was very feeble, and he spoke with great difficulty, nay sometimes he gasped for breath; but his voice was very sweet, rather like Westcott's though. But oh, Lightfoot, never you turn Romanist if you are to have a face like that—it was awful—the terrible lines deeply ploughed all over his face, and the craft that sat upon his retreating forehead and sunken eyes.

He recalled Izaak Walton's description of Hooker and then outlined the substance of the sermon. He continued:

Then if you had seen how his eye glistened and his whole face glowed, as he turned round to the Altar, lifting his Priest's cap, and bowing low, while he pronounced His name, and with such a voice—you could not but have felt your heart yearn towards him, and when you observed what a thrill ran through the congregation, you must have said, 'Surely if there be a man whom God has raised up in this generation with more than common powers to glorify His Name, this man is he'—but how was it spoiled when he linked in 'the Name of the Holy Mother of God'; when he joined together 'Jesu! Maria!' How painful was it to think that he had been once an English Churchman; and yet how can we wonder at the change when we think of the thousands of prayers offered up abroad and at home, in Church and in Chamber, that Newman might be converted? I am very much inclined to that opinion of Pusey's which I well remember laughing at, that he was removed from us for that we valued him not as we should have done, and were unworthy of him. How sincerely do I hope that it may be as Pusey also said, 'That he was only labouring in another portion of the Lord's Vineyard'; yet to my mind it is difficult, nay impossible, to conceive that he has not sinned the sin of those who have left their first love. *Ora pro Jacobo* (sic) *Henrico Newman.*[34]

For the moment the account of this astonishing correspondence must rest here. Perhaps the most remarkable letters in the collection are those written about Lee on the announcement of his elevation to the see of Manchester. These will be considered in their place. The extracts already quoted reveal plainly the intensity of the spiritual influence which Lee exercised over his pupils, and also the fact that this influence was not exerted in such a way as to drive them away from doctrines which their master did not himself accept. Lee could never have written as Benson did of Newman. His hatred of Tractarianism was not communicated to his pupils. He taught them a sense of values, an attitude to life, a goal to be attained. In all things, their duty was 'to carry all our independence, all our diligence, all our love of truth, back to one source, to one judgement . . . to attain to the measure of the standard of Christ'.[35] But, as Westcott pointed out, this never involved the acceptance of definite opinions. 'We were almost forced to be independent.'[36]

Thus in the nine and a half years of his headmastership, Lee was rewarded by phenomenal academic success and a devotion from his pupils that can scarcely have a parallel. His relations with his Governing Body appear to have been good. There is no hint in the school records of outstanding difficulties with his staff or of severe disciplinary troubles within the school. He had made an excellent impression on the Prince Consort who had visited the school during a royal visit to Birmingham. High preferment was certain to come. His pupils expected it as his due, dreading the day, however, when Lee should be called to other work.

Towards the end of 1845, however, the sky darkened. Into Prince Lee's life entered the ominous figure of Thomas Gutteridge.

5

Thomas Gutteridge was a prominent local surgeon, known well to the municipal authorities as an outspoken critic on any question which involved the expenditure of public funds and as a fearless champion of what he maintained to be his rights. He had been Professor of Anatomy to the Society of Arts, and, in the 1840's, had established himself in a practice in Colmore Row. Lee, who by nature of his office was drawn into local politics and administration, was bound sooner or later to cross his path. The occasion of their first encounter came in September 1844 at the annual general meeting of the governors and subscribers of the Birmingham General Hospital.

Earlier in the year, Gutteridge had published certain allegations of corruption against the administrators of the hospital, maintaining that their recent appointments of surgeons to the hospital had been governed by corrupt interests and that in consequence the patients had suffered from the criminal negligence of men incompetent to carry out their duties.[1] It is relevant to point out that Gutteridge was one of the disappointed candidates for the post most recently filled.[2] At the annual general meeting, Gutteridge, supported by another surgeon—Mr. J. J. Ledsam—demanded a public inquiry into these allegations by an impartial tribunal. In particular, the two malcontents attacked a Dr. Blakiston for criminal negligence, accusing him of having 'wilfully and improperly administered an undue quantity of prussic acid to a patient, under which he died'.[3]

Lee was a member of the Board of Governors of the General Hospital; one of the surgeons whom Gutteridge attacked had been his own medical attendant and had by skilful and timely treatment of an eye complaint cured him of an affliction that might have resulted in the loss of his sight.[4] He therefore felt it his duty to defend the hospital against Gutteridge's allegations. "I have come down here," he stated at the meeting, "prepared wholly and entirely to resist anything like inquiry by a Committee . . . on grounds which I believe would be taken to insult your medical officers in the grossest manner."[5] He maintained that every charge against Blakiston was utterly unfounded, inviting the complainants to substantiate their imputations then and there. Gutteridge and Ledsam refused this invitation on the ground that the Governing Body of the hospital was not an impartial tribunal.

There—for a few months—the matter rested. But Lee had made a dangerous enemy. Unknown to him, Gutteridge now prepared to switch his attack from the hospital to King Edward's School, in particular to the Secretary to the Governors and the Headmaster. In 1845, Gutteridge fired his first salvo. This was a pamphlet in the form of a letter to Lord Calthorpe, alleging corruption and abuses both at the General Hospital and at King Edward's School;[6] and this was followed in the next year by two more pamphlets—one addressed to the Bishop of Worcester as Visitor of the School and President of the Hospital (alleging 'corruptions and abuses and Clerical delinquency'[7]), the other publishing a report of the proceedings of a public meeting held in the Town Hall in which Gutteridge addressed a large assembly, demanding a general inquiry into the abuses of public charities within the city.[8]

The charges in these pamphlets against the school secretary— John Welchman Whateley—need not concern us here. They were similar in substance to the attack on the administrators of the hospital—accusations of procuring appointments for unqualified men on payments of money, unlawfully retaining public money and receiving enormous sums for professional services over and above his fixed annual stipend.[9] The attack on Lee, however, was more bitter and more serious.

Gutteridge's description of Lee's attempt to refute his charges against the Birmingham Hospital shows how deeply the affair had rankled. In his objections at the public meeting, Lee exhibited 'in his demeanour the coarse and vulgar brow-beating of a low bred Old Bailey pleader'.[10] Subsequently, Gutteridge alleged, he had caused the report of that meeting to be falsified. This came ill, he went on, from a person manifestly unsuitable to occupy an important public post. In the first place, Lee had procured his election to the headmastership by unfair means. He canvassed among the governors for support, contrary to the

119

rules relating to such appointments, and so contrived to gain election by one vote, ousting 'a gentleman at once his superior in scholastic attainment, in the opinion of the best judges, and far too honourable to seek by forbidden means the post to which his less scrupulous rival thus unjustly attained'.[11] And what a discredit he was to the school!—Gutteridge continued.

> He not only brought with him the reputation of a restless and implacable disturber of the peace of every institution with which he connected himself; but he disclosed qualities so odious as to render him an itinerant pest—an universal torment. He eagerly sought to connect himself with every public establishment here whether of charity, literature, or science; and almost everywhere, by exhibiting a most officious, insolent, and domineering behaviour and an intriguing and ill-natured disposition * which dishonoured his character as a clergyman, he insulted and disgusted the most respectable and respected supporters of our public institutions; and further pursued with spite and bitterness many, *even in the persons of their children*, who dared to act with independence and spirit so far as to resist his intrusive and offensive advances.[12]

Then came the specific charges. Firstly, Lee had visited a youth, who was dying at the Blue Coat Charity School, in a state of such intoxication that the headmaster of the school felt himself bound to report the scandal to his Committee. Secondly, Lee— in an attempt to avenge himself against the headmaster who had reported him—'with unheard-of indecency, . . . attempted to control the Headmaster in matters relating to his own proper authority . . . for no assignable reason but that his drunkenness had been witnessed by him'. Further, he attempted to procure his dismissal in the hope that his report of Lee's scandalous condition would appear to be 'the spiteful calumnies of a discarded servant'.[13]

The third allegation was that Lee, on one occasion, officiated at divine service in Bishop Ryder's Church, Birmingham, in a state of intoxication 'greatly to the disgust of those who witnessed an exhibition so scandalous to his clerical character'.[14] Finally, it was alleged that he, as headmaster, treated with exceptional cruelty an under-master who complained of the inadequacy of his stipend. The headmaster was reputed to have said to him:

* According to Gutteridge, his maxim was, "If a man cross my path, I'll crush him."

"How many curates, think you, in England, have so much as £160 a year?" (the sum complained of). To which the under-master replied: "Oh! If that is the scale, how many *rectors* in England, think you, have three thousand?" ('the amount of the headmaster's yearly receipts', noted Gutteridge, '—nineteen times that of the Under Master's stipend'). Because of this, Gutteridge maintained, Lee 'became this man's persecutor and oppressor' and earned for himself at Oxford such a low reputation that it was generally determined 'to forbear to enter into any competition for a mastership under such a ruthless chief'.[15]

All these offences, stated Gutteridge, compelled him 'to denounce him most emphatically to his face, for conduct which I designated, as I deemed it,—DIABOLICAL'.[16] At the meeting held in the Birmingham Town Hall, Gutteridge described Lee as

the most troublesome neighbour any of us ever had. [He had] secured and accumulated upon himself a degree of odium such as I have never known before in the case of any individual having the character of a clergyman of the Church of England and having the care of the education of youth.[17]

He demanded that Lee should be dismissed from his position and exhorted the Bishop of Worcester to take disciplinary action. 'Act as a Bishop or cease to be one. . . . Do your duty or resign your office.'[18]

It seems incredible to us that Lee could have endured this attack upon his personal character and integrity for nearly three years without taking any step to silence his persecutor, beyond calling a meeting of his friends to counsel him as to the best means of vindicating his reputation. While suffering horribly, he endeavoured to ignore everything that was said or written against him; even allowing Gutteridge triumphantly to declare that the silence of his adversary demonstrated the truth of all the allegations.[19] *

In October 1847, while Gutteridge and his friends were still clamouring for Lee's degradation, Lord John Russell recommended

* Report of *The Queen* v. *Thomas Gutteridge.* Gutteridge pointed out, 'Mr. Lee has not rebutted any of the allegations brought against him, and has given no satisfactory reason why the matter has been allowed to sleep for 3 years.' Lord Chief Justice Denman said on this point: "His forbearance towards him by whom he has been calumniated is thrown in his face as a reproach. I am quite satisfied that he was right."

121

his name to the Queen as the most suitable appointment to the newly-created see of Manchester. The effect of the announcement of this news on Gutteridge may be imagined. He became almost hysterical in his determination to bring disgrace upon Lee before it was too late. Copies of his letters to Lord Calthorpe and to the Bishop of Worcester, and of his address at the public meeting of May 1846, were reprinted in a single volume and dispatched to the members of the episcopal bench and to the Dean and Chapter of Manchester. The scurrilous documents were introduced by the Pauline text:

> This is a true saying: if a man desire the office of a bishop, he desireth a good work. A bishop then must be blameless, the husband of one wife, vigilant, sober, of good behaviour, given to hospitality, apt to teach: not given to wine, no striker, not greedy of filthy lucre: but patient, not a brawler, not covetous; one that ruleth well his own house, having his children in subjection with all gravity. . . . Moreover he must have a good report of them which are without (1 Tim. iii. 1–7).*

In the face of this new onslaught and the avowed intention of Gutteridge to interpose objections both at the Archbishop's confirmation of the election and at the consecration ceremony, some action had to be taken. Gutteridge subsequently maintained that Lord John Russell himself came down to Birmingham to impress upon Lee the necessity of answering the charges made against him.[20] On 2 November 1847 a huge meeting was held in the Birmingham Town Hall, presided over by the Bishop of Worcester and attended by the two members of Parliament for Birmingham, the Mayor and the main civic dignitaries and representatives of 'church, chapel and synagogue' to declare their confidence in Lee's fitness to discharge the responsibilities of his new office, and to draw up a testimonial to mark their respect and esteem both for his work at Birmingham and for the excellence of his private character.[21] A week later a correspondent in *Aris's Birmingham Gazette*—Dr. J. E. N. Molesworth—exhorted Lee to take Thomas Gutteridge into court 'not only for the honour and character of the Church; but also for your own future peace and usefulness'. This provoked Lee into writing a stinging reply:

* T. Gutteridge, *Three Pamphlets, containing the charges of immorality publicly brought against J. P. Lee, etc.* (Birmingham 1847), 5.

It is, in my mind, more than questionable how far the absence of an offensive spirit, which you claim for yourself, might not have led you in the first instance to inquire privately . . . of myself, before you made my conduct, sanctioned and supported by such authority as it has been, the subject of newspaper comment. To have addressed me previously to publishing, would have been as easy, to say the least, as to have done so now. . . . . I have taken the earliest opportunity to submit the case to the present Law Officers of the Crown. By their advice I shall act irrespective of individual criticism or newspaper objectors.[22]

Lee's legal advisors recommended applying for a criminal information against Gutteridge in the Court of Queen's Bench with the intention of obtaining a Rule *nisi* imposing absolute restraint upon his persecutor from uttering and publishing further libels on his character. The case (*The Queen* v. *Thomas Gutteridge*) was heard in Queen's Bench before Lord Chief Justice Denman and Justices Coleridge and Erle. The Attorney-General filed the criminal information on 16 November, and Gutteridge was summoned to show cause why the Rule should not be imposed on Wednesday, 24 November. He was not legally represented and addressed the court himself for four hours. Against thirty-four affidavits on Lee's behalf which had been put before the court, Gutteridge was unable—according to his testimony, unwilling—to produce a single one. He said: "that he had not come there to put affidavit against affidavit: after having made a statement upon his honour, he should regard it as a public indecency to make an affidavit in support of it". He confined his remarks to attempts to discredit the affidavits of his opponent and to far-fetched arguments based on their silence on certain particulars. He cut rather a pathetic figure in court. The allegations of drunkenness rested on Lee's unusual behaviour in two instances—the visit to the dying youth at the Blue Coat School and the occasion on which he took the service at Bishop Ryder's Church. An affidavit from the Bishop of Worcester stating that he had already made inquiries into the truth of these two charges and that he had come to the conclusion that they were utterly unfounded; affidavits from other persons who had witnessed Lee on these occasions and who strongly denied that his condition was as Gutteridge had chosen to describe it; affidavits from medical men to prove that Lee could never have taken alcohol in excess and explaining why it was sometimes necessary for him to take doses of laudanum to kill internal pains: all these made Gutteridge's uncorroborated assertions appear malicious and wholly unconvincing. After informing the Attorney-General that there was no need for him to reply to the defendant, Denman had this to say:

> The total omission of all pretence on his (Gutteridge's) part to state that he believed these charges to be true, convinces me beyond all question that his charges are utterly false. The gentleman has stated that this must lead to a further inquiry. First, I should say that this Reverend gentleman has long lain under the charge, dormant and indifferent. Does he believe, does anybody believe, that charges can be preferred against any man in an eminent situation . . . without costing him sleepless nights and miserable days? And a dart thrown by the most malignant hand may be a torment to his heart, may visit his fireside, may haunt him in the execution of his public duty, and may make him insensible to anything upon such an occasion but the question whether he owes it to his character to vindicate himself by some public proceeding. He knows by whom he is surrounded—he knows with whom he lives—he knows that there are persons who form a true and responsible opinion of his character; and that, if all these persons are perfectly satisfied there is not the least ground for any one of the charges, and that all the charges are traced to a feeling in the mind of him who makes them, disgraceful only to himself, why should he come into a Court of Justice, and why should he apply to vindicate his character, which has maintained itself unsullied notwithstanding the malignity of the imputations cast upon it?
>
> . . . When I see so plainly the motive of this long address to the Court, and the feeling which actuates the mind of him who makes it, I feel it to be a duty to the Rev. gentleman who comes before this Court for protection, to tell him that, as far as my opinion can give him protection, he has it in the fullest degree; that his character appears, from its unvindicated purity, only so much the brighter because these charges have been made. It is to prevent, as far as I can, that perversion of the public mind, which certainly was the object of Mr. Gutteridge's long address, that I have framed this opinion.[23]

Gutteridge maintained years later—after Lee was dead—that he had been the victim of a conspiracy. There had been 'a monstrous perversion of official propriety'; the Lord Chief Justice of England showed 'gross partiality' and acted like 'a reckless and lawless political partisan, capricious, if not venal, as a Turkish Cadi'.[24] At any rate, he comforted himself that his attack upon Lee had succeeded in estranging him from the Court, for 'he ceased to be a guest at Windsor Castle'; the Prince Consort decided to go no further with his intention of making Lee the guardian of the Prince of Wales's education.[25]

There are no grounds whatever for believing Gutteridge to have been maligned. His pamphlets attacking Lee were a tissue of lies. The affidavits produced in court told the true story of what had happened in the Blue Coat School and at Bishop Ryder's Church. Gutteridge's other allegations do not stand the test of facts. Lee was not elected headmaster by a single vote[26]; the lowest salary of any assistant master in orders at the school was £200 p.a., not £160 as Gutteridge asserted; Lee's own salary was not £3000 p.a. He received a fixed stipend of £400 p.a. to which were added capitation fees amounting to about £700 p.a. and which did not vary from year to year beyond about £5 or £10 more or less than that figure.[27] The truth is that Gutteridge was a born scandal-monger who never bothered to verify the gossip which he collected. Nor did his contest with Lee cause him to mend his ways. In the early 1850's he was attacking the Birmingham General Hospital again;[28] a few years later he appears to have been more peacefully employed in launching a Lithotomy Fund to enable him 'to accomplish his scheme of promulgating his peculiar Operation for the Cure of Stone in the Bladder'.[29] In the 1860's he dared to cross swords with Dr. Ullathorne, the Roman Catholic Bishop of Birmingham, and Dr. Newman. The story—a significant one for estimating Gutteridge's reliability as a witness of truth—is told in a pamphlet entitled *The Alleged 'Nunnery Scandal' at Birmingham*.

Gutteridge appealed publicly to Newman in 1867 to refute the following case of debauchery which was alleged to have taken place in a neighbouring convent. A girl had been committed to the convent by her father in order to protect her from a liaison of which he strongly disapproved. When the father subsequently paid a visit to his daughter, he was told that he could not see her because she was 'under holy vows'. A year after her admission to the convent, he was permitted to take his daughter away, and while they were driving home from the convent in a cab, the girl gave birth to a child. She had manifestly been 'debauched by the Father Confessor'.

Dr. Ullathorne thought it desirable that a committee of magistrates should investigate this allegation. Their report showed that not only was the statement 'untrue and without foundation in fact in any one of its details', but that Gutteridge had picked up the gossip from a seamstress of nineteen, engaged by his family, and had made no attempt whatever to verify any of the facts.[30] The *Daily Post* commented pertinently:

> Poor Mr. Gutteridge! He has at last been induced to expose his 'little secret' to enquiry; and has promptly and most effectually had the bottom kicked out of it. Nothing remains but a clumsy imposture and a shattered reputation. . . . We need not, however, trouble ourselves about Mr. Gutteridge. He belongs after all, to a large class of vulgar gossips—greedy recipients and eager retailers of any scandal, true or false, that may happen to come in their way.[31]

This unhappy episode in Prince Lee's life has been told at length because it provides a clue both to the understanding of his character and to the explanation of his failures as a bishop. If Gutteridge's allegations against Lee were false, at least his almost frenzied hatred of his opponent was sincere. That this was something more than fury levelled at a man who had ridiculed him on a public platform is suggested by the fact that Lee was to make similar enemies, quite as outspoken as Gutteridge had been, when he went to Manchester. Gutteridge had written of Lee's demeanour when upbraiding him in public as 'coarse and vulgar'. Even a friendly critic at Manchester had to regret Lee's 'propensity . . . of haranguing on a platform . . . the lowest of all acquirements'. As a bishop, Lee should have abstained from 'the vulgar plaudits of the platform'.[32] We may recall the words from the cruel lampoon of James Crossley: 'Who took not his pattern from Him who, when living, was merciful, large-hearted, meek and forgiving: but preferring in strife to work out his salvation, made quarrels and scolding his Christian vocation'.

His ill health must be remembered; often making him testy and apparently aloof. His attempt to hide his feelings would lead on one occasion to exaggerated reserve and on another to a triumphant breaching of the barrier by his emotions and consequently an unedifying display of temper, in which Lee would say very much more than he intended. A public manner which impresses schoolboys may easily irritate adults; and even great schoolmasters are not always at their best in a society where they are liable to be effectively contradicted. Benson was very like his master in this respect. He had been so accustomed to dominate any society in which he lived that he came to dread—as Archbishop—the occasions when he had to speak in the House of Lords. He was so afraid of losing his temper in the face of opposition that he often became hesitant and indecisive.[33] It is significant that Lee never attended the House of Lords and very rarely appeared in Convocation.[34] Also he strenuously resisted any attempt to introduce diocesan conferences. The Chancellor of the diocese, in commenting on Bishop Fraser's encouragement of free discussion by the clergy of all matters affecting the diocese, wrote of Lee: 'Meetings of the clergy in the way of synods or conferences had been extremely distasteful to Bishop Lee. When they met for the election of proctors for convocation, he never would permit any discussion, and would never consent to hold diocesan conferences'.[35]

Again, throughout his career Lee appears to have left the impression upon his contemporaries of an astonishing omniscience. By the end of his life he was a Fellow of the Geographical Society, the Theological Society, the Royal Botanical Society, the Cambridge Philosophical Society, the Manchester Literary and Philosophical Society and the Archeological Institute of Rome. This extraordinary range of interests allied to his profound classical learning made him a teacher of unique power. He was entirely in his element in the company of eminent intellectuals, delighting in the evenings he would spend at Sir William Fairburn's house at Ardwick, Manchester, in the midst of a group that might contain such figures as the Chevalier Bunsen, Sir David Brewster, Lord Derby, Lord Brougham, Lord Shaftesbury and Mrs. Gaskell.[36]

But a man who expected to be listened to with respect by adoring pupils and who could stand in his own right as the peer of eminent specialists in many spheres might well assume, albeit unconsciously, a somewhat domineering manner in the local

societies to whom he gave his active support. Officers of local
societies, whose position has been for long unquestioned and un-
contested, and local antiquaries, who somewhat naturally assume
that their knowledge of their local history is superior to that of
any outsider, do not always take kindly to the patronage of such
a man as this. Gutteridge, it may be recalled, described Lee as
"an itinerant pest. . . . He eagerly sought to connect himself
with every public establishment here whether of charity, literature and science." He went on to speak of him "exhibiting a most
officious, insolent, and domineering behaviour."*

One would be tempted to dismiss this comment along with the
other of Gutteridge's scurrilous allegations were it not for the
fact that later troubles at Manchester strangely confirm the
existence of a similar type of resentment. Soon after Lee arrived
at Manchester, he fell foul of two prominent laymen of the city,
whose dislike of the Bishop and whose attempts to discredit everything he said and did came to be as strong and as injurious as ever
those of Thomas Gutteridge had been. One was James Crossley
of Booth Street, Piccadilly, a Fellow of the Society of Antiquaries
and later President of the Chetham Society in Manchester.†
The other was Samuel Crompton, a grandson of the famous
inventor, a prominent local doctor, Secretary of the Manchester
Medical Society and a member of the Manchester Literary and
Philosophical Society.‡

Crossley we have met before as the author of the satirical
epitaph on Prince Lee which appeared in the local papers shortly
after Lee's death. As an antiquary of considerable local standing
he was sure to make the acquaintance of the new bishop who,
as soon as he arrived in Manchester, began to amass a vast library
of works dealing with Lancashire antiquities and the history of
the diocese and county palatine.[37] The initial cause of the
estrangement is uncertain; probably—as the lampoon would
suggest—Lee threatened to oust Crossley from his position as an

* Above p. 120.

† There is a large collection of Crossley's letters in the Chetham
Library, Manchester; also an excellent portrait of him as President.

‡ I am very grateful to Miss Hilda Lofthouse of Chetham's Library
for supplying me with much information about Samuel Crompton and
his career as a local doctor and antiquary.

acknowledged local expert by tactless intrusion and a dogmatic, domineering manner. At any rate, Crossley relentlessly laboured to discredit Lee's reputation as a scholar. The occasion of Crossley's triumph was the discovery that Lee's only published work of scholarship—a collection of sermons and writings of Isaac Barrow[38]—contained a number of unfortunate blunders, the most signal of which was the ascription to Barrow of sermons which manifestly belonged to a different period and style.[39]* Crossley himself was something of an expert on Isaac Barrow and he gave vent to his delight in a witty poem—quite as cruel as his satirical epitaph—which was published in *Notes and Queries:*

> Good reader, would you wish to see
> The only work of Bishop Lee?
> Then take a walk to Chetham's College
> And you may soon enlarge your knowledge:
> But look not for profound discerning,
> For genius, talent, taste or learning;
> His single duty was to edit
> And do the subject no discredit.
> The work imposed on him was small,
> But there was nothing done at all;
> What need be written was not long,
> But all that he *did* write was wrong.
> Pray read it, and you'll find with wonder
> The whole is one egregious blunder,
> And that of Barrow's style or metal
> He knew no more than does a kettle:
> In fact to him, whate'er the name,
> All styles and dictions were the same.
> Much, therefore, to his friends' distress
> His book dropp'd stillborn from the press;
> He lost his chances of being famous

* Dr. Whewell, who produced an edition of Barrow's mathematical works in 1860, and the Rev. A. Napier, who edited the theological works in nine volumes in 1859, both came to the conclusion that the sermons published by Lee were not Barrow's.

As author on the banks of Camus,
And pierced by satire's trenchant arrow
He loathes the very name of Barrow.

Moral

Take warning then from Bishop Lee
All you who editors would be
Before you've learned your A B C.[40]

Seven months after Lee's death, Crossley was still on the prowl for Barrow material which might further damage the late Bishop's academic reputation. Samuel Crompton, his friend and accomplice in the baiting of Lee, wrote to Crossley from Cambridge in July 1870. He had been on a visit to Trinity, and while there he looked in at the Library and at

> the Barrows—I fished out very speedily the MS in which you take so much interest and made a tracing of a line or two to give you an idea of the handwriting (see Preface to MS Vol of Napier's Barrow). The *attan* printed by the learned Rt. Rev. Dr. Lee *atten*, is perfectly plain. I forgot, however, hang it to look at the passage about the 'curs'. How vexing.[41]

Crompton had his own reasons for disliking Lee. In two pamphlets published in 1862 and 1863 he accused the Bishop of sharp practice in his administration as President of the two public charities known as the Manchester Deaf and Dumb School and Hearnshaw's Asylum for the Blind (Crompton was then surgeon to the Blind Asylum). Crompton maintained that although the charities had been provided with a chaplain (by the name of Thomas Buckley), no spiritual instruction had been given to the inmates of the institutions for some three years; that Buckley had been drawing an income of £500 for doing virtually nothing; that the Bishop, as President, had allowed the chapel of the institutions to be alienated from the charities and conveyed into his own patronage as Bishop of Manchester; and that the Bishop —with the patronage now in his hands—had duly installed Buckley as the incumbent. Although Lee denied that he had any official cognisance of this transaction, Crompton accused him of malversation of public funds and demanded that the charities be reinstated in their rights at the Bishop's own personal expense.[42]

There is no doubt that Crompton and Crossley were both behind this attempt to stain Lee's character with imputations of dishonesty and negligence. On the copy of the printed letter addressed to Lee which has been preserved in the Manchester Central Library, a covering note in Crompton's hand is attached. It is addressed to Crossley and reads as follows: 'Everything goes well in the Blind Asylum affair. Mr. Philips is in earnest; and so, I believe, are others.'

If Crompton and Crossley were hoping to bring about a public inquiry or to force Lee into a court of law, they were unsuccessful. As Lee had refused to answer Gutteridge's allegations, so he ignored this. That was his way. On another occasion, he wrote to one of his rural deans, Canon F. R. Raines, with reference to some offensive complaint made against him by one of his diocesan clergy, 'I shall take no notice of it, which will be the severest punishment I can inflict.'[43] This sentence explains a great deal.

Although Lee lived at a time when the publication of vituperative pamphlets was an everyday occurrence—caused partly by the cheapening of the printing processes[44] and partly by the common reluctance to invoke the protection of the laws of libel—he seems to have been particularly unfortunate in the number of such bitter attacks which he provoked. His refusal to reply to them only served to make his critics more strident and more determined to compel him to offer explanations. His natural disposition to conceal his emotions and to refrain from lowering his dignity by explaining his conduct to people whose concern for the public welfare was merely a cloak for their improper desire to embarrass authority gave him more and more the popular reputation of arrogance and disdain. He never forgot Gutteridge. If a man could so misinterpret high-minded actions, his mind must be perverted to the extent of rendering him incapable of appreciating any explanation. Such an adversary was beneath his contempt. Unfortunately, however, Lee in later life began to suppose that all his critics were of the same genus. The more he was misunderstood, the more he contented himself with the thought that such people were evilly-disposed towards him and did not want to understand. Thus, whenever he sensed a lack of sympathy, he revealed a face of granite; only to those who loved him and who trusted without question the motive behind his acts, did he show the warmth and affection which had once made him a schoolmaster acclaimed by his devoted pupils as their 'king of men'.[45]

6

Lee's pupils knew very little of the agonies which their master endured from Gutteridge's attacks until the late summer of 1847. Benson wrote to Lightfoot early in September of that year:

> Monday was a holiday. Mr. Lee went to Worcester to be installed as Canon of the Cathedral, and I hope now he is a great gun elect he'll go off at Mr. Gutteridge. Isn't it jolly? I use the word with satisfaction now Lee can't hear me. Twig—don't you?[1]

A month later there were greater tidings to recount:

Here then beginneth

KING EDWARD'S HERALD
Thursday the 14th of October 1847.

Mr. Lee and Mr. Abbott together gave us a lecture on the Pendulum from eleven o'clock to half-past twelve in the Lecture Room. A few minutes before the half hour Mr. Lee said, 'While you are here I may as well give you the subject for your copy— Latin Verse, isn't it?—take for your motto 'Inventas aut qui vitam excoluere per artes', and you may treat it in any way you like— and as I shall not be able to be with you tomorrow—(I am called away unexpectedly) I will set you some work to do on paper. That will do for the present'—and so upstairs we went, and Mr. Lee followed us and gave us the fifth book of Tacitus' *Histories*. "Only 26 Chapters, you see, you'll finish it easily. . . ."

Next day (Friday) all that was known about him was that he was in London—not a soul, either boy or master, knew what he was gone for. Many were the odd surmises as to what could have taken him away so suddenly. *Saturday*—when we came into school Mr. Lee was sitting back in his seat; he looked very pale—and certainly I thought looked at me in a very peculiar manner as I passed beside him—indeed all thought that there was something unusual in his manner. When he began to read prayers he read with difficulty, and was evidently much affected by something or other, for the corners of his mouth were working strangely. . . .

James Prince Lee, from the portrait at King Edward's School,
Birmingham

'Sapientia', Prince Lee's desk in Barry's 'Grammar School',
New Street, Birmingham

We soon after went up with Davison's Chapter on the union of
free-will in man with Divine fore-knowledge. Mr. Lee gave us
one of the fairest pieces of his own eloquence that I ever heard. . . .
[His] eyes filled with tears, he seemed almost choked, and he leant
on his desk—and after repeated attempts, and with great difficulty,
he said, "This is an awful subject, and one which is peculiarly
interesting to me at this time." After a short time he went on—
you know we have all seen him several times moved to tears, but
I never saw him so much moved as then. . . .

On Sunday evening I went to my uncle's to meet Mama who
had been nursing him; and to take her to Church. Mr. Hodgson
[the surgeon] had seen her and told her that Mr. Lee was appointed
Bishop of Manchester. When I knew it so for certain I was thunder-
struck. I could have done anything—I could have laughed or cried
or danced or sung or anything in the world but stand still and think
—it was positively dreadful. Here was all cleared up and in such
a manner. I really was so selfish that I did not feel glad a bit till I
had walked two or three hundred yards—and then I thought how
very wrongly I was doing—yet I could not help it, and my eyes
filled with tears once or twice during the evening service.

On Wednesday the boys of the first two classes met to consider
a testimonial for Lee. Benson was charged with the writing of a
circular to raise subscriptions.

You can have little idea how I felt in setting about it. It seemed
such a privilege and honour to be actually setting down on paper
what one thought of Mr. Lee, and something that should be read
by 500 boys about him, and how all would hate me if I did not praise
him enough—and then the fear of overdoing it—and then the
feeling that I *could not* possibly write down why I loved him, and
why we ought all to love him—it was the strangest mixture of
feelings I ever felt.[2]

The Circular to Edwardians at Cambridge was sent out on
29 October. Benson related the latest news of Lee's doings and
the threats of Mr. Gutteridge.

On Saturday we said to Mr. Lee one more lesson of Davison—
the last, I fear. Should it prove to be so, I shall always remember
that I myself said to him the last lesson which he ever heard in
that happy place, and that as he was going out of school, at half-past
twelve, the last words which he said to anyone there, were said to
me. . . . Mr. Lee has been spending 3 days with the Queen at

Windsor, he returns to-night. Is not everything most perfectly rejoicing? How well he is now meeting the reward of all his labours. Little did he think of all this when he used to lie awake at night, as he told us, going over all Clarke's book, in his head, and getting up to light his candle and seek out the passage, if he forgot any parts of the argument. Glorious Mr. Lee.

. . . But now for that infamous Gutteridge. I met him in the street the other day. Oh! how I clenched my fists, and I said to him something that would give you no very exalted idea of my wisdom if I told it to you. But I could not help it. The dog, for whom hanging is too good, was dressed very handsomely as I ever saw him in the days of his best practice. It is clearer every day that he is upheld by a party; . . . there must be a horrid system at work somewhere. . . . Now it is rumoured that G. intends to denounce Mr. Lee, by all the foul means which he deserves himself, and so put the finishing touches to his malice. What is to be done? It really is maddening to think the contemptible snail can do so much damage. He must be beaten into a mummy, or bruised so that he won't be able to stir for 6 months, or pounded in a mortar—that's perfectly clear. What *can* we do? [3]

Then, when the circular had been sent out, Benson wrote to Lightfoot in acute depression:

You have no idea of the sort of void that the thought of his going seems to make in my mind—What will become of me, I know not. . . .

He took consolation only in 'the thought that I spoke of Him . . . in a way which his best lovers approved'. [4]

Lee was consecrated Bishop of Manchester on 23 January 1848 at Whitehall—Westminster Abbey was closed for repairs—the Archbishop of York and the Bishops of Worcester and Chester officiating. On 11 February he was enthroned in the Cathedral Church (previously the Collegiate Church of St. Mary, St. George and St. Denys) at Manchester. Lightfoot wrote of it to Benson:

By the way an omen! a good omen! a very noble omen!

When, as the Right Reverend the Bishop of the lately created Diocese of Manchester was appointed to be enthroned upon Friday the 11th day of February last; the last day of the ceremony being now come, the morning was fair and the sky serene yet somewhat overcast withal. Ten thousand people were abroad that day, and flags were flying over all the city—and the people that were gathered in the Cathedral for to behold the first Bishop of their See, though they had a fair view of him as he passed along with his clergy and as he sate within the altar rails, yet did the dimness of the air prevent that he should be well seen over all the space of the Church until in the same moment wherein the Dean did seat him in the Episcopal Throne, the sun burst forth from behind a cloud as though the windows of the Church shone full upon his person. This being a very fair omen upon such a memorable occasion was so remarked by the most that were there present—and for the truth thereof the narrator will himself vouch, being related to him with much more circumstance of the same by the daughter of the noble prelate (herself being an eyewitness) whom God preserve. Amen.[5]

7

The clergy and people of Lancashire viewed Lee's elevation somewhat less romantically. They seemed at first to be more conscious of his disabilities than of his qualities: he had had no parochial experience; he was a nominee of the Prince Consort whose favour he had courted by praising his views on education; he was too much of a disciplinarian and a scholar to adapt himself to new circumstances which would above all require tact, flexibility and a readiness to mingle with his flock.[1] Outside Lancashire, the general impression was that Lord John Russell had conformed to his habit of elevating unsuitable men to the episcopacy. This was especially felt by the High Church party. Wilberforce wrote later to Cavendish and Gladstone complaining of Russell's 'miserable episcopal appointments',[2] and Hook was so disgusted that he recommended that a special ecclesiastical body should be set up to advise the Prime Minister on episcopal appointments.[3] That there was little popular clamour to respond to Gutteridge's mischievous pamphlets was mainly due to the fact that the appointment of Dr. Hampden to the Bishopric of Hereford closely followed the announcement of Lee's promotion and the objections to Lee were drowned in the ensuing tumult.[4]

Lee arrived, worn out from his contest with Gutteridge, to be met with a cold reception. The prospects before him were truly formidable. The diocese consisted of the four deaneries of

Amounderness, Blackburn, Manchester and Leyland in addition
to several parishes in the deaneries of Warrington, Kendal and
Kirkby Lonsdale. These were administered by the two arch-
deaconries of Manchester and Lancaster.[5] Although the area of
the dioceses was not especially large, the population was densely
packed in a few great centres. There was a desperate shortage of
churches; only 284 to serve a population of 1,123,000 people.
Also the population was growing enormously, especially in the
mining and manufacturing districts. In the next forty years the
population was to be doubled in size, half of this number living
within the city of Manchester itself.[6] Clearly one of Lee's first
tasks was to sponsor a scheme for church building throughout the
diocese and to appeal for lay support in the financing of such an
enterprise.

Even Lee's enemies recognised that he was a brilliant adminis-
trator. He corresponded regularly with the upper clergy of the
diocese, especially with the rural deans, with whom he was
usually on excellent terms. He would attend the Diocesan
Registry in St. James's Square daily, and was so punctual in his
arrival in his coach-and-four that it became a saying within the
city that Manchester men would set their watches by his daily
coming and going.[7] He never took a holiday. By the end of his
episcopate in 1869 he had consecrated 110 new churches, caused
20 existing churches to be rebuilt, and had formed within the
diocese 163 new parishes and ecclesiastical districts.[8] He was
equally assiduous in his efforts to ensure that these new churches
became effective spiritual centres of the districts in which they
were erected. Each new church was provided with its day-school;
the Bishop saw to it that the supply of clergy did not fail—he
ordained 471 priests and 522 deacons in his episcopate of twenty-
two years;[9] he held confirmation services with unusual frequency,
even though his physical disabilities made lengthy ceremonial
occasions agonising to him.[10]

Unfortunately a dispute over the provision and endowment of
churches within the city of Manchester broke out in the first year
of Lee's episcopate and led to the almost total estrangement
between the Bishop and the Dean and Chapter of the Cathedral.
The dispute arose from an attempt by the Manchester Church
Reform Association to prove that the whole of the property of the

Chapter was really parish property and that the Dean and Canons were not dignitaries in the ecclesiastical meaning of the term, but had 'cure of souls'. The Association accordingly petitioned Parliament for the right to appropriate the Chapter revenues, thus 'seeking to restore the religious benefactions of a past age to the purposes to which they were originally dedicated'.[11] The dispute promoted a bitter pamphlet warfare, in which absurd charges were flung at both sides—the Cathedral Chapter was accused of complicity with the Chartists and of conspiring to violate the law of the land.[12] A settlement much to the disadvantage of the Chapter was achieved by the Manchester Parish Division Act, whereupon the disappointed party put much of the blame on Lee's shoulders, and for many years after this dispute the Bishop was very rarely seen in the Cathedral. In 1854 he had cause to rebuke the Chapter severely for giving incorrect written replies to questions submitted by the Cathedral Commission. 'I omit to dwell on minor inaccuracies and mis-statements, less injurious in themselves, but discreditable in a document forwarded to a Royal Commission', he wrote to the Dean and Chapter, '——it is enough for me to show that I have not lightly, or without examination, found fault with them'. He concluded:

Nothing will give me greater pleasure than to recall any statement, or correct any representation I have made, when such is proved to be erroneous. But until such proof is given, I must repeat my conviction, that 'it is impossible, on a perusal of the Answers, not to be struck with the numerous and repeated mis-statements, misquotations, and perversions of sure facts, as well as the suppression of others, on the part of the framer of the replies'.[13]

Lee delivered his first Charge in November 1851. In this he clearly revealed his attachment to the Establishment and his mistrust of the Tractarians. Services were to be conducted in such a way that they were clearly intelligible to all the worshippers: 'the people, and not the Clergy only, constitute the Church';[14] great care should be taken to avoid undue decoration and ceremonial. 'The very name "Altar" she (the Church) has wisely rejected for the "Holy Table", as tending to countenance the notion of a reiterated sacrifice.' The church 'would have the house of God a fit place for the preaching of His pure word, and administration of His holy sacraments, simple, chaste, elegant in purity of style and fitness of decoration'.[15]

He firmly expressed his approval of the jurisdiction of the State in the Gorham Judgement, declaring the decision of the Judicial Committee of the Privy Council to be in accordance with 'the true and scriptural doctrines of the Church of England. . . . I cannot but express my thankfulness at the decision which was pronounced, as well as my approbation of the tribunal to which the cause was ultimately submitted.'[16] It was therefore the duty of the clergy

> to abstain from all which may tend to bring the Church into collision with the State or set up an *imperium in imperio*, to strive earnestly and faithfully to bring the State into closer union with the Church, by seeking to render the spirit of its institutions, public, private, and social, in all respects more Christian.[17]

He followed this Arnoldian aspiration with something even more reminiscent of his master: 'Education, to be useful to the individual educated . . . cannot exist without religious instruction'.[18] He advocated an extension of the principle which operated at King Edward's, Birmingham, whereby Dissenters were given instruction at a Church of England school but permitted to absent themselves from the periods devoted to religious teaching. He concluded by warmly approving the efforts to draw closer to 'our foreign Protestant brethren'[19] (a clear reference to the work of the Chevalier Bunsen and the project of the Jerusalem Bishopric) and by launching into a vehement attack on 'the unwarrantable aggression of the Court of Rome', exhorting his clergy to resist all attempts to introduce Roman novelties—especially the 'disgusting' practice of the Confessional—and reminding them that 'the minister is made for the people, not the people for the minister'.[20]

Lee adhered strongly to these principles throughout his episcopate. His fear of the advances made by the Roman Church and of the influence of Roman doctrine and ceremonial on the High Church party is expressed most forcefully in a letter he addressed to Canon Raines and the incumbent and parishioners of Milnrow in November 1850, in response to a petition deploring the recent examples of papal aggression. 'I hope', he said, 'you will not fail to make your representations to the legislature and state your firm determination to support Her Majesty's advisors in such steps as may expel in future these attacks.'

As for the Catholics in England—

> We are bound to watch them jealously and from time to time to raise a warning voice, should aggression without or treachery within purpose to injure or assail the rich inheritance we have so long enjoyed, and which we hope to transmit unimpaired to our posterity for ever. . . .

The Roman Church stood for 'the usurpation of temporal authority. Every country in Europe has more or less successfully resisted this: will England alone submit to it? Never.'[21]

Lee's churchmanship, then, was Low with some inclination towards the Broad.[22] Wilberforce noted that he was favourable to Dr. Hampden, being one of the two bishops (the other was Edward Denison, Bishop of Salisbury) who sent away candidates for orders who could not show certificates of attendance at Hampden's Divinity lectures.[23] On the other hand, Lee was vehement in his denunciation of *Essays and Reviews*, published in February 1860. Westcott was horrified at his old master's attitude, and Benson declared that he was 'ready to die with shame at seeing J. P. Manchester's name among those impotent rowing Prelates. Fancy Arnold's name there if you can.'[24]

Both the Bishop and his Registrar (Mr. T. D. Ryder) commented on different occasions on the relative absence of party spirit among the diocesan clergy.[25] Ritualism had not gained much ground. We may suspect that Lee's constant vigilance and autocratic manner did much to keep it in check. He used his rural deans to keep him informed. The correspondence with Canon Raines supplies evidence of this. As soon as a rumour of trouble reached the Bishop's ears, the rural dean was commissioned to make a full inquiry and to report back to the Bishop. One day it might be the suggestion of some impropriety between an incumbent and one of his Sunday School class;[26] another day, a 'detestable novelty' required investigation:

> My attention has been drawn by the Churchwardens of Norden to a wooden cross lately placed on the Communion Table. Will you

have the goodness to report on it as Rural Dean, and state whether
it is moveable or not, and also whether it comes under the class of
Ornament allowed in the Privy Council's Judgement in the
Knightsbridge case?[27]

There is no doubt that this vigilance was often bitterly
resented. One of the first disputes in which Lee was engaged
concerned certain rubrical changes introduced by the Rev. James
Irvine (Vicar of Leigh) and the Rev. J. R. Alsop (Perpetual Curate
of Westhoughton) which became the subject of a compendious
pamphlet. The two incumbents accused the Bishop of using spies
and informers and of obliging them to adhere to his rulings by
refusing to recommend grants to their churches from the
Additional Curates' Aid Society. A letter from the Vicar of Leigh
described Lee's behaviour as utterly 'dishonourable'. He 'tried to
frighten me into the making of unlawful and most unreasonable
concessions. . . . The atrocity of such a procedure only falls short
of that of the Popish Inquisition'.[28] Lee's reply was cold and
disdainful:

> Reverend Sir. I have to acknowledge the receipt of your letter. I
> have neither time nor inclination to undertake the, I fear, needless
> task of commenting on it: while I view it as in every respect con-
> firming the justice of the opinion I have formed. As when confidence,
> on one side at least, is forfeited, the continuance of correspondence
> can hardly be productive of a satisfactory result, I desire that you
> will confine your communication with me to official circumstances,
> until sincere acknowledgement of error and greater accuracy of
> statements entitle me to sanction the adoption of a different course.
> I am, Revd. Sir, your obedient servant, J. P. Manchester.[29]

The years 1850 and 1851 saw two further unpleasant collisions
on the subject of ritualism, both of which provoked an angry
pamphlet controversy. The first concerned the priest and
assistant curate of Ringley Chapel, both of whom displayed mild
tractarian leanings. Choral services were introduced; one of the
Tracts (no. 72) was circulated among the parishioners. Lee sent
his Archdeacon to confirm these details. Although the Archdeacon reported that the 'reading, intoning, chanting, and singing, were audibly and distinctly performed, and the congregation
orderly and devout',[30] Lee appears to have ordered the instant

suppression of the novel practices and to have refused to listen to
the objections raised by the incumbent. The account given in
the pamphlet written by the assistant curate—Edward Fellows—
is hardly credible. Lee is reported to have described the parishioners of Ringley as 'an ignorant set', totally incapable of taking
a prominent part in church services;[31] as for reading the *Tracts*
(Fellows goes on to say) he pointed out 'that the Early Fathers
contained the greatest trash that ever men read . . . that he had
the profoundest contempt for the said Apostolical Fathers—their
intellect as well as their writings—but he had not waded through
all the endless rubbish contained in them, although he had, perhaps, one of the best collections of Patristic Theology in the
country'.[32] Lee's comment on the publication of the first edition
of this pamphlet was that it was 'wilfully and deliberately false
. . . too contemptible to deserve other notice than the declining
communication with the weak and foolish person who has
degraded himself and his calling'.[33]

In the following year came the affair of Broughton Parish
Church which gave rise to a vitriolic correspondence in the
Morning Chronicle and a pamphlet worthy almost of Thomas
Gutteridge and James Crossley in the savagery of its attack. The
author, who signed himself 'D.C.L.', was A. J. B. Beresford Hope.
The chief actor of the scene—'the Right Reverend Dr. J. P. Lee,
Lord Bishop (as every one knows) of Manchester'[34]—who had
previously celebrated in Broughton Church, suddenly decided to
launch an attack on the allegedly 'Popish' fittings of the chancel
which had been added by the previous incumbent of the church,
a Mr. Bayne. The attack followed the publication of Lord John
Russell's famous letter to the Bishop of Durham on Papal
Aggression, so that it had the appearance of being a deliberate
attempt to find a victim for the sake of the 'public justice of the
diocese of Manchester'. The various objects complained of were:
three sedilia on the south side of the church, a piscina, an 'almorie
for such as come to pray for the souls of the departed' and a
representation of the Virgin Mary in stained glass, with various em-
blems suggestive of Romish symbolism on the pavement beneath.

The churchwardens published an explanation of the fittings
and decorations of the chancel, whereupon Lee issued a further
rebuke, pointing out the similarities between Bayne's additions

and the decorations recommended in Pugin's *Ecclesiastical
Architecture*.[35] It is only possible to give here one illustration of
Beresford Hope's biting reply to this second rebuke. Lee had
written of 'an almorie for such as come to pray for the souls of
the departed'.

> Can I venture [the author of the pamphlet asks], in the face of the
> Bishop, to give Pugin's *real exact* description? 'Adjoining the
> chancel, a sacristy, or revestry, for keeping the vestments and
> ornaments; or, in any small churches, an almery may be provided
> for this purpose on the gospel side of the chancel, within the
> chancel.' The truth, then, is that the almery (not *almorie*, as the
> Bishop writes it) has nothing to do with the souls of the departed,
> but is simply a cupboard or press for the dresses of the living, and
> for the vessels needed for service. It is in fact, that very same word
> which, in its French form 'armoire', is so innocently used for a
> common, and not, I believe, unorthodox article of furniture in
> everybody's dressing room. The truth must be (incredible as such a
> truth is when fastened upon an eminent scholar, such as one used
> to hear Dr. Lee called) that his Lordship, finding that the first
> three letters of almery were ALM, jumped to the conclusion that
> it must have something to do with ALMS (which any boy in the
> lower form at Birmingham might teach him was derived from
> *eleemosyna*); and seeing an alms-box, with a slit to let money
> through in its lid, in the chancel of Broughton, he decided on the
> nonce that this was an almorie – perhaps, too, he had some misty
> notion of the Almonry at Westminster in his head.[36]

He concluded his pamphlet with a refutation of Lee's interpretation of Sir Herbert Jenner Fust's ruling on stone altars, in
the case of Faulkner *v.* Lichfield. 'Is it not a little surprising that
the Bishop of Manchester labours under a positive inability to be
accurate on any point of ecclesiastical law which he ventures to
handle?'[37]

These three incidents—together with the quarrel with the
Dean and Chapter of the Cathedral—took place in the opening
years of Lee's episcopate. It is not surprising that Lee, who was
acutely sensitive and in bad health, felt that every man's hand
was turned against him and so shut himself away from all but
official contact with the majority of his clergy in his great palace
—Mauldeth Hall. There Mancunians pictured him as 'living in
the style of a great Northern magnate';[38] 'his whole way of

living and ruling was such as would have become a Cardinal of the Renaissance'.[39] The clergy were 'kept at a distance, and treated . . . like schoolboys', received, not at Mauldeth, but at 'a dismal office in St. James's Square'.[40]

It was generally supposed that he had a marked dislike for clergymen. The charge is understandable. Lee seemed to delight in seeing the Church humbled by the State; his loathing of sacerdotalism became so intense that he saw the spectre of Rome behind the most trivial and harmless deviations from the strict instructions of the rubrics; he entertained prominent laymen with lavish hospitality (possibly because they were potential subscribers to the Church Building Fund). But the circumstance which gave most substance to the belief was his treatment of his elder daughter Sophia on her marriage to the Rev. John Booker. The full story is not known. All that Lee gave in the way of explanation may be found in the dreadful passage in his Will:

> I give to my eldest daughter nothing but deprive her of all interest in my property. I do this not in anger but because I hold it to be a duty not to let conduct like hers and the person she has married prove successful.

The marriage took place in 1854; fifteen years later he had not forgiven her. On the publication of the Will, Archdeacon Rushton wrote an explanatory letter to the *Manchester Guardian*. John Booker was his senior curate, a Fellow of the Society of Antiquaries, a graduate of Magdalene College, Cambridge—in every respect he would seem to have been a suitable husband for Lee's daughter.*

> Up to a certain period [Rushton wrote], Mr. Booker was the frequent guest of His Lordship at Sedgley,† and the one unpardonable fault he committed was understood to be, that he did not make the Bishop acquainted with his change of views respecting his daughter, which had once been challenged.[41]

In a letter from Mr. T. C. Greenwood to C. W. Sutton, the author of the article on Prince Lee in the *Dictionary of National Biography*, a more comprehensible account is given:

* He was a member of Chetham's Society and clearly knew James Crossley. But there is only one letter from Booker to Crossley in the Crossley papers in Chetham's Library and this makes no reference to Lee.

† Lee's official residence before he moved to Mauldeth.

I remember only one occasion on which the Bishop referred to this painful subject. I cannot pretend to repeat his words, but their substance was that he had been frequently in the habit of gravely and sternly censuring the alleged tendency of young clerics to use the opportunities which their profession gave them to promote their worldly fortunes by matrimony; and therefore he felt bound to signalise and enforce this judgement in this instance. Moreover, it was always understood that Mr. Booker had in the most deliberate manner repudiated any aim of the kind, or at least consented to abandon it.[42]

Where—in all this—was the 'Mr. Lee' whom Benson, Lightfoot and Westcott loved and reverenced? Both Benson and Westcott were ordained deacon by their old master. Westcott noted a change at once. 'He was greatly disappointed', his son later wrote, 'at the lack of fatherly sympathy for which he had hoped, and grieved at the general undevotional character of the proceedings.' He later told his sons how deeply he felt 'the cold formality', especially regretting 'that he was not allowed even to retain the Bible placed in his hands when he was commissioned. Shabby volume as it was externally, he would have treasured it beyond all other books, had it not been sternly taken from his reluctant hands.'[43] In 1862 he wrote to J. F. Wickenden, rejoicing that his former school friend could still find reasons to approve of Lee's conduct, even if he had reluctantly to admit that 'his whole career seems to me to have been one series of disasters'.[44]

From time to time flashes of the old warmth and liberality would return. When Benson obtained a Trinity Scholarship, he received an affectionate letter from the Bishop asking him to send up some of his Latin verses;[45] the foundation of the Manchester Free Library was achieved largely through his organising powers and oratorical gifts; Owen's College, Manchester, received as a bequest the whole of Lee's magnificent library—one of the finest private collections in the country. When old pupils came up to visit him at Mauldeth, they felt something of the old power. Westcott noted that as he grew older he became more tolerant of opposition and of views to which he could not subscribe.

He had set aside that hasty love of paradox. He loved to speak of the old days and when he grew sad in thinking of recent failures

and disappointments, his eyes would fill with tears and he would
draw comfort from the words of the Gospel of St. Mark—the four
words which expressed for him the fullness of Christian hope—
'Fear not: only believe'.[46]

*   *   *   *   *

He should never have gone to Manchester: that is plain. He was
never happy there. For over twenty years, this incomparable
teacher wore out body and mind in incessant administration. He
was working up to a few days before his death. The organisation
and machinery to which Fraser succeeded was remarkably
efficient—the new Bishop was the first to say so.[47] Yet when it
is recalled that Lee was one of the foremost scholars of his day,
his legacy of published works—two charges, two printed sermons
and a discredited work of scholarship—may make one deplore
the wasted talent, the misdirected effort of years which should
have seen him at the height of his fame. It was once suggested
to him that his powers were being wasted. His reply was: "I do
not think that my thoughts will perish with me, for there are
some who will not, I believe, forget what they have learnt from
me."[48]

He was right, of course. If his pupils were saddened by events
at Manchester, they never forgot his teaching; never ceased to
pay him homage. In Westcott's study, the portrait of Lee took
pride of place: at Addington, a bust of Lee stood always on
Benson's desk.

Others, too, noticed the kinship between master and pupil.
John Wordsworth, when Bishop of Salisbury, commented in his
diary on Benson's masterly judgement in the celebrated trial of
Edward King, Bishop of Lincoln: 'Fit to stand by the strong work
of his two school-fellows, successively Bishops of Durham.
Character of their work: constructive and uncontroversial, seeking
for the great abiding elements in the past yet not shrinking from
minute details and patient study—not always without a certain
idiosyncrasy and quaintness, inherited from Prince Lee.'[49]

Twenty years after Lee's death—over forty years after his
schooldays at King Edward's—Westcott wrote to Benson, following a short stay with the Archbishop at Addington:

The sight of your cares makes me ashamed, but I am sure that there is strength provided for the work given to us. In my better moments I can even feel it. And it is with the greatest as with the least. The old words came back to me at Addington: ΜΗ ΦΟΒΟΥ ΜΟΝΟΝ ΠΙΣΤΕΨΕ (Fear not: only believe). It is enough.[50]

When Westcott succeeded Lightfoot as Bishop of Durham in the following year, Benson summoned a gathering of Prince Lee's pupils for a service in the chapel of Lambeth Palace. 'It was thought fitting', Arthur Westcott wrote, 'that former members of the school . . . should meet together . . . to pray for the well being of the new Bishop.'[51]

One of the strangest instances of the enduring quality of Lee's teaching, however, is this: Writing of Bertram Pollock, Bishop of Norwich, in the introduction to Pollock's autobiographical study *A Twentieth Century Bishop*, Harold Nicolson recalled the singular charm of Pollock's teaching of Classics in the days when he was Master of Wellington.

His method of teaching Latin was wholly personal [he wrote]. When one entered the Upper VI he would present one with a little printed card containing what to his mind were the five or six most beautiful lines in the Latin language. Of these the one he himself most preferred was the startling line of Persius: *Virtutem videant intabescantque relicta*. Often and often would he murmur that line, sighing to himself, sighing sometimes with the words 'and all the dreary round of sin'. . . .[52]

Now Pollock as a young man had studied for the priesthood under Westcott. He often spoke of the deep impression which this close association with Westcott had made upon his mind. Westcott, in 1893, in his address on the opening of the new girls' school at Camp Hill, Birmingham, recalled how Prince Lee would speak

with proud delight of his favourite classical authors, as if they were still his familiar companions. He poured out quotation after quotation as we used to hear them at school, and dwelt on that finest single line, as he said, in Latin literature, *Virtutem videant intabescantque relicta*.[53]*

* "May they see virtue and should they forsake it let them rot away."

146

Nicolson wrote in 1946—a little over a hundred years after Westcott had listened to Lee repeating that line. From Lee it passed to Westcott; from Westcott to Pollock. One wonders whether any of Pollock's pupils are in their turn repeating to their own pupils their favourite line in Latin literature.

James Prince Lee died on Christmas Eve, 1869. 'To die on Xmas Eve,' wrote Benson to J. F. Wickenden, 'to pass into Paradise on Xmas Eve—and perhaps catch whispers of angels or prophets telling what Heaven was like when first *He* was gone from among them to be a child.'[54] The Bishop had expressed a wish that upon his gravestone there should be a single word: "It is a Greek word of course," he had added with a smile. "It is the word ΣΑΛΠΙΣΕΙ—The Trumpet shall sound. Yes," he had repeated after a pause, "The trumpet *shall* sound."[55]

The Exemplar:
Martin White Benson

ON Saturday night 9 February 1878 about 10 p.m. our sweet eldest boy breathed out his soul. It was the hour he was born into both worlds, and he was aged xvii years v months xxi days all sweet and without reproach. His Saviour knew his secret soul not only because He knows all things, but because Martin laid it open to him.[1]

These are the opening words of an account, covering thirty-four pages of an octavo-sized diary, of the life and death of Martin White Benson, eldest son of Archbishop Benson, written by his father only a week after Martin had died. Benson was then in his second year as Bishop of Truro. At the Bishop's Palace, a stately Queen Anne house with large gardens on a hill overlooking Truro and the tidal estuary, he poured out on paper while his memory was still fresh the details of Martin's life: his sayings and doings, his hopes and ideals. His other children one day would read it; perhaps the story would be made known to the world. For the world would be better for the knowledge of what Martin had been: what he might have become. For a brief desperate moment, life seemed to have no longer any meaning to the father who had loved the boy so much and who had seen in him everything he ever prayed for in an eldest son. He would never understand the mystery of God's purpose. But since it was in his nature to work out all his problems on paper, to record the severest trial to which his faith had ever been subjected helped him to adjust himself to a new concept of life. So he wrote.

The loss of a child from disease was a more common occurrence in Victorian family history than it is to-day; and the cause of Martin's death—meningitis, or brain-fever as it was then popularly called—claimed many more victims then than now. If the event which Benson described was by no means unusual, the description of the event, however, can have had few parallels.

Temple Grove School in the 1870's

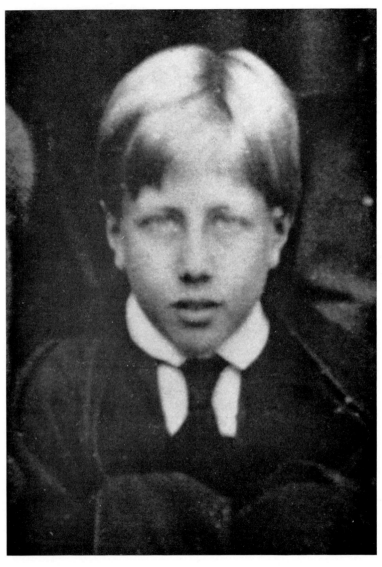

Martin White Benson as Scholar of Winchester, 1875

The most striking parallel is certainly the published record of the tragedies endured by the Tait family, compiled by the Archbishop—Benson's predecessor at Canterbury—and W. M. Benham in 1878, the very same year in which Benson wrote of Martin. Catharine Tait had written the tragic memoir of her five little daughters, who all died from scarlet fever in 1856, only a few days after their death; and when Catharine herself died in 1878, six months after the death of her only son Craufurd (aged twenty-nine), Tait gave the full details of his domestic tragedies to the world.

It may cause us wonder that those who suffered 'as much as it was possible to suffer'[2] could inflict upon themselves the agony of describing in such detail the most tragic moments in their lives, when the writing of every word must have torn open the wound which faith and time were battling to heal. Yet, as historians, we may be thankful that they did. For the value of these memoirs as historical documents is very great. Benson's study of Martin gives us a wonderfully clear picture of Victorian family life, the ideal of boyhood at that time, the enthusiasms and delights of a boy brought up in a godly and scholarly home. Inevitably, too, we learn much about the father and his world: the unashamed emotionalism, the strange fascination for morbid thoughts, the theocentric concept of life—all pronounced characteristics of those of Benson's class and calling—are here magnified under the stress of domestic catastrophe.

In the previous study we examined the aims and actions of James Prince Lee—an educational idealist. His influence over his pupils in bringing them up to be true lovers of godliness and good learning was seen to have been quite as powerful and enduring as anything that Arnold ever taught or inspired. What is needed to complete this picture of high idealism and determined activity is a biographical sketch of a boy who exemplified the ideal which Arnold, Lee and Benson sought to realise. The story of Martin Benson's life fits this requirement well. In the first place, it is possible to reconstruct a large portion of his very short life: not only from what his father wrote in his memoir, but also from the rich collection of Benson family papers, including many of Martin's own letters, preserved in the Bodleian Library,[3] and, again, from the vivid childhood recollections which provided Arthur and E. F. Benson with material enough to write no fewer than ten books about their family affairs.[4] Secondly, Martin possessed to a remarkable extent the qualities which his parents and teachers most hoped to find and to develop in a boy. He was—let it be said at once—by no means perfect. As Arnold well knew, it was not in the nature of boys to be perfect. And there was nothing particularly abnormal about Martin. He could be tiresome. He got into scrapes. The point is that Martin's virtues were exactly what those who taught him deemed to be the essential virtues. His progress towards manhood, therefore, was regarded with deepening satisfaction and confident anticipation of great work ahead and of heavy responsibilities which would be nobly and manfully shouldered.

Finally, Martin belonged to a different generation from those who have so far been the subject of these studies. It is interesting to reflect that had his life been spared, he would have been fifty-three when the First World War broke out, and would have reached his seventieth year in 1931. This was the generation which saw the abandonment of many of the leading assumptions of the Victorian age, among them the belief that godliness and good learning were the main essentials of any educational system. At Winchester in the 1870's Martin must have felt the impact of new influences and ideas which were foreign to his father's way of thinking. Had he proceeded to Cambridge in the early 1880's the differences must have become plainer. How he would have reacted to these new influences is impossible to say. His brother Arthur became a critic of the exclusively classical curriculum, and developed a marked distaste for mounting athleticism and for organised religion. Fred became an Edwardian in heart and soul, and made a name for himself by writing society novels. Hugh remained the impulsive and emotional child he had always been and eventually abandoned Anglican orders for those of the Roman Church. Martin, however, had always been much more like his father than the others. What we can see of his life and thought in the short period in which he was allowed to leave his mark clearly suggests that Martin was more at home in the world of 'godliness and good learning' than in a world which enthused over the Empire, indulged in agnostic speculation and delighted in playing games. He was by nature mid-

Victorian, not late Victorian. And since we have said a good deal
about Martin's father, and more about the man who made his
father what he was, it is perhaps fitting to conclude this study of
an important phase of educational idealism by looking at the way
in which their ideals and principles were transmitted to the most
receptive of Benson's sons.

2

Martin White Benson was born on 19 August 1860 in the
Master's Lodge at Wellington College, a school which had been
opened by the Queen a little over a year before as a memorial to
the great Duke of Wellington, and which was intended to house
and educate a limited number of sons of deceased army officers
on virtually gratuitous terms. The building, a somewhat
audacious rendering of a French château in red brick and Bath
stone by John Shaw, was set in a desolate portion of Bagshot
Heath, amidst scrub and heather and pines, four miles from the
nearest town (Wokingham, in Berkshire) and a little over a mile
from the nearest building of any size (the Criminal Lunatic
Asylum at Broadmoor), then in the course of erection. Sandhurst
was two miles away to the south-east, the villages of Eversley
and Finchampstead about three miles to the south-west; and away
to the west stretched the wild tract of forest known as Bearwood,
a huge estate owned by the proprietor of *The Times*, Mr. John
Walter. In 1860 the buildings of the College still looked gaunt
and unweathered, the countryside around wild and untamed.

When Martin's father had entered into his new kingdom,
appointed on the recommendation of Dr. Temple by a very distinguished Governing Body presided over by the Prince Consort,
his subjects had been equally wild and untamed. But among
Benson's many qualities, the one which the boys instantly
recognised was his natural ability to assert his indisputable
dominance over any society in which he found himself. He was
dignified in bearing, terrifying in his anger (which, in these early
years, was frequently displayed) and perfectly prepared to wield
a cane with devastating effect. Also he knew exactly what he
wanted.

As Martin and the other Benson children passed from infancy
to childhood, so Wellington moved step by step away from the

intention as expressed in the Foundation Charter and so dearly cherished by the Prince Consort, and became more and more like Rugby. The numbers increased; several foundationers were admitted; the curriculum became steadily more classical; Rugby customs and traditions were introduced. Such a transformation was only achieved by phenomenal industry and driving power on the part of the headmaster. Also it involved bitter quarrels with the Governing Body. But of the drama of all this the Benson children were blissfully unaware. Arthur Benson has written:

> As children . . . we were proud of my father, proud of being his children, profoundly convinced that he could do everything better than anyone else; we never regarded the school as his creation, and not at all as the subject of his constant preoccupation and anxiety— it was beyond the power of imagination to regard him as anxious or troubled about anything; we rather thought of it as an institution which he was good enough to preside over, and even punish the boys, when necessary, if they deviated from the rules of rectitude which he laid down for them.[1]

Martin was named after Edward White Benson's dearest friend among the Trinity dons—Francis Martin, subsequently Vice-Master of Trinity. His godfathers were Frederick Temple and J. B. Lightfoot. His mother had married at the age of nineteen and her first son was born a little over a year later. The first years of her married life had not been very happy. Benson was the type of man who desperately needed love and encouragement; he was acutely sensitive and apt to take the smallest trifle amiss. Mary Sidgwick, however, was a vivacious, high-spirited girl who had known from about the age of twelve that Edward had chosen her as his future wife. Her diaries of the months after her engagement—Mary was then seventeen—and of the first year of the marriage make sad reading.[2] She was trying so hard to live up to Edward, to develop his interests, to educate herself sufficiently to be able to talk intelligently with him and in the circle of his intellectual friends. There is something rather pathetic in her industrious notes on ecclesiastical architecture, in the hours she spent in learning German and in ploughing through indigestible books. She began to write curiously stilted letters, and Edward wrote to her aunt asking her to try to take 'Minnie' in hand:

How curious it is that some people are without the power of writing themselves down in their letters. Minnie is a most affectionate creature, but from her letters one could scarcely think so . . . I don't mean that I would wish her for a moment to write love-letters, but one would suppose that she would say something friendly to any affectionate friend.[3]

For a while she seemed to be a little afraid of him, particularly if she had occasion to infringe any of the rules he had laid down for the household economy. She carried out her duties with a sort of hectic eagerness and duly noted in her diary how each day had passed—she had been entertaining Lord Derby for luncheon; Edward had been worried over the behaviour of some mischievous boys. Then occasionally the narrative would break off and she would accuse herself of being a pompous little humbug who deserved—and wished—to die.

In fact Mary Benson was not the failure that she sometimes made herself out to be. She was a typical Sidgwick—quick, shrewd, capable; blessed with a delightful sense of humour. She was naturally kind and loving; instinctively she would take the troubles of others on to her shoulders, rarely speaking of her own secret sorrows. This in part explains the misunderstandings of the first year of her marriage. She could not bear to see Edward unhappy through any fault of her own. Also she had enough sense of humour to appreciate some of the absurdities of their life. As a mother, she was adored by all her children. As Arthur wrote of her: she 'opened, one by one, the doors of life to me. I suppose that she was really so near her own happy childhood that she knew by instinct what we were thinking and caring about.'[4]

The birth of Martin put an end to what had really been an artificial sort of existence for both husband and wife. Henceforth, Mary Benson, if she was still inclined to be ruthlessly critical of herself in her diaries, became more and more the effective—in time, indispensable—support to her husband. She restrained his impetuosity; quietly guided him out of the fearful moods of black depression which frequently assailed him in those early days and which were always liable to recur throughout his life. She gave him everything except, perhaps, her complete confidence. Some of the things she thought or feared or doubted would have given Edward pain: all these were hidden from his sight.

So the household expanded. When Martin was born, 'Beth'—
Elizabeth Cooper—who had been Mary Benson's nurse at Rugby,
came to live at the Lodge. She had entered the service of the
Sidgwick household at the age of fifteen, staying there nearly
thirty years. When she came to join her beloved Minnie at
Wellington, she was not to be parted from the Benson family
until her death at the age of ninety-three.

> She was wholly and entirely devoted to us children [Arthur wrote],
> though she seldom played with us or told us stories; and when she
> did, they were generally pathetic tales of illness and death, which
> we knew by heart, and corrected her if she deviated by a single
> word from the traditional form. But we felt her love instinctively.[5]

And other children came—Arthur Christopher in 1862, Mary
Eleanor (Nellie) in 1863, Margaret (Maggie) in 1865, Edward
Frederick (Fred) in 1867 and Robert Hugh in 1871. It very soon
became necessary for the Bensons to move house. The original
Lodge, on the east side of the main gate, was inadequate for their
needs, and in 1866 Benson saw completed to his satisfaction a
large semi-Gothic building—with the gables, tall chimneys and
solid stone mullions so typical of the period—which he had
designed as the ideal residence for a headmaster. Everything was
perfectly arranged—the study to the left of the porch to which
boys could be admitted without entering the house, a large central
hall with all the main rooms grouped about it and a gallery
running round. Pitch pine wood, lilac distemper and stone
mullioned windows gave the interior a somewhat dark and
melancholy look, but the nursery was a notable exception. The
walls were covered with pictures cut out of illustrated magazines,
the labours of wet afternoons when the children would sit in a
row of little chairs with their father, cutting edges, pasting and
varnishing for hours on end.

It was an exciting setting in which to grow up. There was constant coming and going at the house. Every day some boys would
come to breakfast and the children would speculate on the degree
of embarrassment they would display, unless of course the guests
were A. W. Verrall or Prince Demetrius Ghica whom the
children adored and often invited to their nursery tea. Relatives
and friends were frequently staying at the Lodge: Henry and

Abandon immoral customs.

Abandon immoral customs

Abandon immoral customs b

Abandon immoral customs

Abandon immoral customs

Abandon immoral customs

Abandon immoral customs

Abandandon immoral custo

Abandon immoral customs

Abandon imoral customs

Abandon imoral customs custo

Abandon immoral customs

Extract from Martin Benson's Copybook, *Bodleian Library, Oxford*

Arthur Sidgwick, special favourites with the children, Ada Benson (Mrs. McDowall) whose visits were always short because she tended to compete with her brother in making a forceful impression, Aunt Etty, a regal figure in purple silk and a majestic cap, with a deep masculine voice, Dr. Lightfoot with his extraordinary explosive laugh, Francis Martin with his high collars which rasped and scraped across his chin. Sometimes the children would sense from their father's manner that he was in the presence of an equal—Lord Derby, the Premier, perhaps; the second Duke of Wellington who seemed to have the astonishing power of making their father look uncomfortable; and once—on a day of taut nerves and bewildering temporary regulations—a lady even more dignified than Aunt Etty, of fresh complexion and dressed in black, to whom Martin was introduced and whom Beth addressed as 'My Majesty'.[6]

The countryside around was full of strange excitements. There were wild regions of scrub and bog where gipsies could be seen and vipers were said to lie in wait for the foolhardy; distant smoking brick-kilns from the area of which an odd Irishman called Pat would emerge at night-time to prowl round the College with a lantern and a fierce dog; heather-topped hills like Edge-barrow and Cock-a-Dobby; the mysterious fastness of Broadmoor, whose inmates—out on exercise accompanied by warders—might sometimes be encountered in the course of a walk. Favourite family walks were to Caesar's Camp, not far from Broadmoor, along a path carpeted with pine-needles through a wood which Benson used to call 'The Eternal Calm'; or down into Yateley, a beautiful walk alongside a brook fringed with ferns, wild flowers and high trees; or to Eversley to see Charles Kingsley who would entrance the children with his curious assortment of stuffed birds and exotic ornaments and tell them stories of romantic people in far-off lands.

Much of Martin's early life was spent in the open air—walking, exploring, playing. For his first few years he was taught by his mother. Arthur recalls that her French, history and geography were not strong points, but that she was 'brisk and clear'.[7] Martin was furnished with a copybook and instructed in the art of forming letters. One of his early copybooks (he must have been about six at the time, possibly younger) consisted of twenty-five pages, each of which was headed by an appropriate moral precept, the initial letter of the first word of each precept following the sequence of the alphabet. Under each precept was a space of eleven lines in which the flowing, professional script had to be copied eleven times. Thus on page one the precept was 'Abandon immoral customs'; on page two, 'Bounty commands esteem', and so on until, on page 25, the pupil was reminded that 'Youth should learn wisdom'. The compiler was unable to find a suitable precept beginning with 'Z', but his solutions for 'Q' ('Quit quarrelsome companions') and 'U' ('Undauntedly defend innocence') and 'X' ('Xenophon commended art') showed some ingenuity.[8] Thus—at a very tender age—the child was introduced to the union of godliness and good learning.

The first letter that Martin wrote, preserved among the family papers, was obviously written some time before he reached the copybook stage. Unfortunately it is indecipherable.[9] A letter written to his father in March 1868 (when Martin was aged seven) is perfectly clear and firm. His father was away, apparently at Rugby:

> My dear Papa. I am very glad you are so nearly well. Baby* has been out twice. I have been running three times round the south glen without stopping. I wonder how godpapa is? Tomorrow if all is well we are going to Yatley church. We fetched sand from the glen to the corner. I wonder how the Lakes look at sunset I suppose they look very beautiful? Everything looks rather dull now the boys have gone away. My best love and 300 kisses to you and godpapa. Your affectionate son, M.W.B.[10]

Certainly the boy was very precocious. The following account of these early years, written by his father, gives an abundance of examples:

> From a little one he gave us the promise which he has ever realised. People that were above foolishness were struck with his almost infant face, and said so . . . He was not two years old, when he recognised 'Jesus' in Morghan's engraving of Raffaelle's Transfiguration, and with fixed eyes and open lips he sate in my arms gazing at it for two or three minutes motionless. I never saw, and Mrs. Sidgwick said at the time, she had never seen such fixity of high pleasure in stillness in any child. From five years old he was so clear

* Fred Benson.

and clever with his Definitions—His mother constantly asked him how she should best explain some word to his little brother or sister —and always his answer was as clear and neat as it was ready.

His lessons were very short—quickly over, and never continued for a moment if he looked tired within his little five or ten minutes. He was naturally very fond of them with his mother's engaging way of teaching him and used to listen with the nursery door open for her signal. One day, about six years old, he came down singing to himself, and his mother knew that it was about his lessons, the text which he found made two singable lines 'His ways are ways of pleasantness And all her paths are peace'. Peace and Pleasantness and Love of Wisdom, my laddie's ways were all these and these only.

One day sitting on his mother's knee, at five or six years old, he said to her "I love you till my heart stands still." So early began those strong picturesque expressions which delighted us all his life, and which still we were afraid to notice too much. He must have been about seven or eight years old when on my mentioning 'idle boys' he asked, "But *why* are they idle?"—I said, "They don't want to know what they are being taught"—"Not to *know*?" he said, stopping as he bounded along. "Not to *know*? Not want to *know* things? Oh! no—can't be *that*!" I never forgot the intensity of his look.

At 8 years old he was at a Xmas Tree. Some children told their Aunt that some missing things had been taken by Martin. Their aunt with great reluctance told his mother as a duty to the child. She asked him, and he denied it, saying, "No, I don't think I did. I feel sure I didn't." She then said, "We will go up to the house, and you shall tell Miss —— the story you tell me. I hope it is true. But you must think very carefully before you go, whether you have done anything of the sort." The little fellow went straight to the nursery, and kneeled down, and prayed that God would tell him if he had done anything of the kind. Then he came down to his mother and told her he was sure he hadn't. When they reached the house, the little delinquents at home had already confessed their own doings and their imputation. I never, his mother never, no master ever found any falsehood in his life. Once he wrote to tell me of an untruth of years before which he said had made him *always* unhappy since, and wished that the offended person should be told of it, in terms which assure me it was a solitary lapse and a holy penitence.[11]

Martin always talked more easily and more frankly with his father than did any of his brothers or sisters. 'From the time he was six years old', recalled his father, 'I always said he was "better company" to me in the diversity of interests which he awoke and pursued than any friend I had except two or three.'[12] Benson loved the society of his children: he never chastised them.

> We used to go and talk to him [wrote Arthur], while he shaved before breakfast; in the afternoons he used to walk with us from the time when we had almost to run to keep up with him. In the evenings we often went to him to look at pictures, such as Flaxman's illustrations of Homer, or those in the old *Penny Magazine*, and at dinner we always sat at the table with him and my mother, reading or drawing, and partaking of dessert.[13]

He delighted to sketch with them and would draw with careful detail Gothic castles and cathedrals, occasionally asking for advice and often devising with their aid suitable inscriptions in Latin or archaic English to apply to the subject he was sketching. Sometimes he would play boisterous games and hide in the ferns, emerging from time to time in the guise of some creature which the children were expected to recognise.

Benson was at ease with them: the feeling, however, was not entirely reciprocated. The trouble was that Benson did not know how to relax. Amusements—to his mind—should never be idle. On the family walks the children would be expected to observe things; games to test intellectual ingenuity were devised, such as making up appropriate rhymes on a given subject, which would be earnestly discussed and criticised by all the members of the party. Later, at Lincoln, it became a custom that when certain delicious freshly-made rolls were served at breakfast, these delicacies had to be purchased by a rhyming couplet, such as:

> Roll hither, roll, and let the word be said,
> Which gives my palate something more than bread.[14] *

'He used', recalled Arthur, 'to give us odd little old-fashioned books to read, of an improving kind, like *Philosophy in Sport*, where the poor boy cannot even throw a stone without having the principles of the parabola explained to him, with odious diagrams.'[15]

---

* Temple, on one occasion, was obliged to obey the rule of the house and was unable to make an effective contribution. At last, since nothing was offered him, he burst out 'in loud harsh tones: "An egg I beg—."'

Benson expected so much from his children. He was an idealist, both as a parent and headmaster. He saw clearly the goal to be reached, the pitfalls which might impede or prevent its attainment. His pupils, and especially his children, were expected to see things as clearly as he could. Misconduct, a slackening of effort, childish flippancy all pained him deeply. It was as if the offender were consciously letting him down, deliberately flouting the most sacred principles of life. His children very soon realised this and therefore went to very great lengths to avoid incurring his displeasure. His disappointment in them would be so intense that a shadow of gloom would descend over the whole household until the incident had been forgotten or the offender showed by word or deed that he was truly contrite. And since one could never be quite sure what innocent remark or act of childish impetuosity might be taken seriously amiss, there was often an unnatural sense of strain when the father and the children were together. Arthur, strumming on the piano before breakfast one morning, was tenderly reproved with the words, "Hadn't you better read a useful book?";[16] a 'harmless, chattering hairdresser' who had come to the house to cut the children's hair indulged in a political harangue about Liberals and Conservatives in response to Martin's and Arthur's insistent entreaties. The boys discussed it delightedly at lunch. Their father saw to it that the hairdresser never came again.[17] Once Nellie retailed an imaginary conversation between Jonah and the Whale which her Granny had told her. A cloud passed over her father's face. 'I knew dimly', wrote Arthur, 'that not only were we rebuked, but that we had got the dear Granny into trouble as well.'[18]

Martin, being the eldest child and showing from an early age such a close identity of interests and ability with his father, was expected to set an example to the others. His misdemeanours were most deeply felt. Once while the children were waiting in the study for their father to show them pictures, Martin knocked down and broke a large ivory-handled seal. All that Benson said was: 'Martin, you naughty boy, you must forfeit your allowance to pay for mending that.' Arthur, who was present, subsequently wrote:

Apart from the consequences of the deed—for the seal appeared to us of priceless value, and my own idea was that my brother would sink into an indigent old age with his allowance still going to pay for the damage—the terror of the incident is even now indelibly stamped on my memory.[19]

It is certain that Benson had no idea at the time what awe and fear his displeasure cast over his children. Perhaps when he ceased to be a schoolmaster, he came to realise the necessity of tolerance and the danger of guiding too much the conduct of other people's lives. While he was a headmaster, however, he was always tempted to compare the behaviour of his children with that of his pupils, feeling—as it were—professionally bound to ensure that his family presented a model for his pupils to emulate.

Thus when the time came for his eldest son to go away to school, Benson expected Martin to become a model pupil. And the pressure which he exerted on Martin shows plainly in the letters which passed between them.

3

Martin went to Temple Grove in September 1870, at the age of ten. A letter which he wrote to his mother, while staying with old Mrs. Sidgwick at Rugby earlier in the year, tells us something of his mental development and interests at this time:

> Can you bring some jaspar for us from Budleigh Salterton? I have been reading Capgraves *Chronicle of England* which is in most delightfully old English like Seint Jameses, deped, on for one. This reminds me of an inscription in Arundel Castle in which Paris is spelt parysse and Arundel Arundelle. . . .My soldiers are in prime condition. . . . What's a Bachelor of Arts and what does he do. But there is Granny ringing for us.[1]

He was taken to school by his parents, received by Mr. O. C. Waterfield, the headmaster, and his wife, and then shown round the premises and grounds, all of which delighted him. Temple Grove was an old-established private school (founded about 1810) and situated at East Sheen in a villa formerly belonging to Sir William Temple which had been built in the early seventeenth century. Its change of function had led to some considerable adaptations and additions. Adjoining the dignified

161

old house were wings of bare brick, housing a low dining-room, smelling faintly of years of institutional cooking; and a large gaunt schoolroom in which five classes were taken simultaneously. The boys slept in cubicled dormitories above this. The show-place of the school was the beautiful panelled library in the body of the main building, communicating with Waterfield's study. Benson no doubt was as impressed as any other parent, parti-cularly approving of an arrangement which he had himself introduced into Wellington—a special compartment of books for 'Sunday reading', among which could be found *Basil the School-boy*, *Sunday Echoes*, *Sacred Allegories*, *Sundays at Home*, *Good Words for the Young*, *Hebrew Heroes* and Neale's *Tales from Church History*. The library register shows that the most popular books for week-day reading during the 1870's were Cooper's *The Last of the Mohicans* and Captain Marryat's *Masterman Ready*.[2]

The grounds, too, were impressive and spacious—some twenty acres of garden and shrubberies with towering elms and cedars.

I remember [wrote Arthur Benson], a curious stone summer-house, of rough rustic work, with a pediment like a Greek temple, of which the front had been boarded up, which ruefully surveyed the arid gravelled playground, . . . a dense shrubbery . . . and some little mounds inside, with headstones, much overgrown with peri-winkles, the graves no doubt of dogs, but which in my own mind I believed to be the graves of children—perhaps of boys who had died at the school, and which I regarded with a mournful pleasure.[3]

Temple Grove was larger than most private schools. There were over a hundred boys in the school when Martin went there and about a dozen masters. Socially and academically it had an excellent reputation, and every year some eight or so of its pupils won high-ranking scholarships to the major public schools. Among Martin's contemporaries were Lord Grey of Falloden, M. R. James, later Provost of Eton, Sir Arthur Hort (F. J. A. Hort's eldest son), E. C. Cumberbatch (son of the eminent doctor), C. L. Cust and William Goodenough, who later became admirals, and John Capper and C. C. de Crespigny, both future generals.

From the number of published memoirs of Temple Grove in the 1870's,[4] one feature stands out—the dominating personality of O. C. Waterfield. He was a tall, commanding figure, with a fearsome beard and grave, but kindly, eyes. He was always immaculately dressed and lived in a style befitting a gentleman of considerable means. An Old Etonian and Fellow of King's, he had been an Eton master in the early fifties and was still a very able classical scholar. In some ways he was a typical schoolmaster of the period, stern in demeanour and severe in chastisement. For mistakes in lessons he would commonly apply a thick ruler several times across the hand. (Once he broke a boy's finger in the course of this exercise and collapsed in tears on the spot.) For misconduct he would wield a birch, standing stiffly—a perfect figure of dignity—drawing the lapel of his frock coat across his breast as he delivered the stroke.[5] A characteristic schoolboy reminiscence of him is that he had 'a pimple on the side of his nose which used to swell up enormous when he was really angry'.[6]

He was by no means a heartless brute. He cried copiously when he had to send boys away;[7] after a terrible harangue, he would commonly kiss his victim to show that all was forgiven.[8] And much of what he ordered for the school was wise and enlightened. The boys were permitted a great deal of freedom in their leisure hours and were at liberty to ramble at large within the grounds. Those who were top of their class were given the very desirable privilege of unconducted visits to Richmond on half-holidays. The curriculum was largely governed by the requirements of the public schools: Greek, Latin, Divinity and Mathematics occupied most of the time; but a little French and German (taught—as was the custom then—by foreigners) and History and Geography were also included. There were facilities for most games but very little organisation. A school sergeant conducted regular morning drill on the school playground in the interval between school periods; there was a professional to coach the cricket XI. Otherwise the boys chose their own recreation and if they wished to play team games, they often played to rules of their own making.[9]

The staff was efficient, displaying that blend of capability and eccentricity which boys expect to find in those that teach them: Mr. Edgar, the second master, who took over the school from Waterfield in 1880 when the latter's affluence and acumen earned him a directorship of the Ottoman Bank; Rawlings, a fine scholar who went down in the world and ended life as a bookmaker; the one-armed Geoghegan, bearded and fierce; and the persecuted writing-master, Mr. Prior ('Mr. Abbott' in A. C. Benson's reminiscences), who had never lived down the occasion when, in one of those sudden silences that sometimes fall upon a large gathering, his rich voice was heard throughout the dining-hall saying, "My uncle is a man of large property in the North."[10]

Into this world came Martin for his first experience of living away from home. 'Remember,' his mother wrote to him, 'you are my first pupil, and you must do me credit.'[11] When he had been there a week, he wrote home to describe his impressions:

> I like this school very much. I am in the 4th form and Mr. Gehogehan's class. Mr. Gehogehan's name is pronounced Gairgan. There is a fellow in my dormitory who has got an alarum which he always sets to 5.30 (an hour too soon) which *punctually* makes an alarming noise which wakes every fellow in the dormitory except himself who snores on until 7 when somehow he manages to get dressed and put his boots on before 7.15. I have been reading *The Antiquary* and I like it very much particularly the song-dialogue between 'Patrick the Psalm singer' and Ossian 'the son of Fingal' . . .
>
> At 10.30 we have to get ready to go to church. When you write mind you tell me if the canaries are safe and well and if Fred's canary sings. I really don't know what to write now except that every Saturday afternoon any boy with one or two others is allowed to go out into Richmond and buy whatever he likes. There is also lots of horse chestnuts here and we take advantage of it by putting *one* on the end of a string and then swinging them together or 'fighting' with them till one snaps in half and then of course there's an end to it. I believe that 9/10 of all the boys are writing home now. Please send me if you can a photograph of the Chapel or College. Tell Beth I will write to her very soon and also give my best love to Arthur, Nelly, Maggie and Freddy and Papa and I will write to Papa tomorrow. Goodbye. Your affectionate son, Martin White Benson.[12]

He wrote to his father as promised.

> I have been playing croquet with Mrs. Green this afternoon. Whenever any of Mr. Gairgan's class are stupid he calls them 'little pigs'. Only two masters can cane here—Mr. Waterfield and Mr. Edgar. . . . Our work is as follows:

6.30. Get up	12.30. Play
7.00. Go to get boots	1.00. Dinner
7.15. Work till 8.30	4.00. Work
8.30. Breakfast	6.00. Tea
9.30. Work	7.00. Work
15 to 11 [10.45]. Drill	8.00. Prayers
11.15. Work	8.30. Bed

To-day and Saturday are half-holidays and sometimes Mr. Waterfield lets off an hour or gives an evening which means no work from 6 to 8. And he always gives a whole holiday (so Boyle says) when any scholarship is obtained. . . . Our class is doing the Greek declensions.[13]

He also told his father that the Waterfields had taken him to the zoo.

Mr. and Mrs. Waterfield were indeed kind [replied his father]. You must show by good work that you feel how kind. . . . I want you to tell me how your Greek Grammar and Verses get on. . . . Dr. Jarvis has given up his Professorship and I hope Canon Westcott will be made Professor of Divinity at Cambridge. . . . God bless you, my dear son, steer by the Pole-star, you know what that means.[14]

More information reached home during the next month. 'Before every Sunday we have to learn part of the Catechism, part of the Vth chapter of St. John and the Collect and say it on Sunday morning.'[15] He was still reading Scott. In October he had embarked upon *Redgauntlet*. In a letter dated 13 October 1870, he discussed the Franco-Prussian War and the fall of Strasbourg. He continued: 'In Greek we are doing sentences almost as long as this, "You will not then write with water." We have to do maps here on tracing paper. . . . P.S. We had "Holy, Holy, Holy, Lord God Almighty" this morning.'[16]

His account of the 'crazes' or 'manias' which from time to time seized hold of the school is very evocative of private-school life:

There has been a great Panorama here which consisted in a kind of small windowpane set in wood with two rollers at each side on which several pictures were wound and then one roller was turned and the pictures went on and on.[17]

Three days later he wrote to his father:

There has been another attempt to get up a Panorama. . . . Thank you very much for the sermon you sent me. I think there is only one *decided* bully in the school. . . . There have been 5 decided changes in mania during the last month. They were as follows—chestnuts, elastics, ticks, transferable pictures, panoramas.[18]

Arthur—at home—attempted to keep pace with his brother's enthusiasms, soon discovering that 'manias' end as quickly as they catch on. 'Tell Arthur', Martin wrote to his mother, 'I am afraid I really cannot send him a tick as they are sadly out of fashion now.'[19] Then, 'The Panorama mania has broken out again and is very fierce now. A fellow called Hobday who is the best drawer in the school does nothing all his play hours hardly except draw, draw, draw for them.'[20] A week later he wrote:

There is *no* mania going on now which is a very extraordinary thing but I expect from preparations which are going on that Fantoccini will be next. . . . We are doing Rule of Three in our Arithmetic classes. The drawing master Mr. Allen says I have a very good idea of drawing which I am very glad of.[21]

Then Martin's school report on his first month's work was sent to his father. Benson's letter deserves to be quoted in full:

My dear Martin, I received yesterday from Mr. Waterfield your first monthly report, and I am sorry to say that neither Mama nor I are at all satisfied. There is only one point which comes up to our hopes, and that is 'conduct out of school' which is what we desire. But the report for your class is 'his work is much hindered by inattention in class'.

Now, my boy, we did *not* expect this. You *can* concentrate your attention and give your whole mind to your work, and this is a report I hope never to receive again. Mr. Edgar goes on to observe that it is a 'new boy' kind of fault, and so it is. But I hoped it was one from which you would be exempt because you have heard it spoken of. I did not think you would play 'The New Boy'. Mr. Waterfield also remarks on your *carelessness* in *writing*. Think of Mama's pains thrown away!

—Well, now what does it all come to? What sort of report for form work? What place in form? How does 'inattention' answer? Why, there is not one single 'good' report for any one subject— still less 'very good'. It reads thus.

Latin—fair.
Greek—tolerable (*worse* than fair).
Divinity—tolerable.

Mathematics—*poor*.
History—fair.
Geography—tolerable.
French—fair.
Writing—fair.

Now, my dear boy, you must *never* let me see such a poor report again. Place only 6th out of 11. Your affectionate father,

E. W. Benson.[22]

Martin's reply was cheerful, though penitent: 'I am very sorry indeed about my report and I will endeavour to make it a much better one next month. . . . Will you always send me my report? Because I would like to know how I am getting on.'[23] His father's next letter was even more peremptory. He had received a complaint from Mr. Edgar of Martin's inattention in class.

It seems that you have not yet begun in earnest to amend. . . . What is the use of our sending our boy to be *taught* if he is so silly as not to give attention to the Teaching. . . . Those who wish well of a boy are obliged to procure his attention by *some* means— severity, if he is wanting in will. . . . I could tell you of many and many a boy who might have attained great powers of mind and a full store of knowledge, who has been obliged to leave school and go into some poor occupation because he was inattentive to his lessons. Now let me have a different account in a week's time.[24]

The account of Martin in Benson's memoir gives the impression that he was always an exceptional boy both in ability and in his serious attitude to life. The Temple Grove correspondence somewhat corrects this picture. At home, the atmosphere of classical learning and deep religious conviction, the relationship between the father and his eldest son, all served to quicken the boy's intellect and to acquaint him with problems and literature of a more adult nature than one would expect a boy of ten to encounter and to assimilate. Benson treated Martin as a boy but often talked to him as if he were a man with an adult's interests. It is for instance significant that Benson should speculate with

167

Martin on Westcott's chances of securing the Cambridge chair of Divinity, expecting Martin to share his enthusiasm over such an event.

At school, however, Martin was a boy amongst boys. He was neither abnormally over-diligent nor conspicuously pious. As is normal, his enthusiasm for school soon waned. ("Twelve weeks at this beastly place!" were the comforting words he spoke to Arthur, who joined his brother in 1872, when they had said good-bye to their parents at the start of a new term.[25]) And he frequently got into mischief. 'To wilfully cutting a table-cloth —ten shillings' was an item on one of his school accounts.[26]

> Martin was not by any means a retiring little secluded scholar [Arthur wrote of him many years later]. He was quick-tempered, entirely fearless, combative, distinctly law-breaking. . . . He was full of liveliness and wit, and was rather a good-humoured auto- crat in the nursery circle, impulsively affectionate, but severe.[27]

His letters show him passing through the various enthusiasms, whims and affections common to boys of his own age; yet—at the same time—they are always distinctive compositions, alert, perceptive, inquiring. The following extracts all come from letters written before his eleventh birthday. Writing to his mother, he inquires after Arthur's ticks:

> How many ticks have you had to confiscate yet? About 6,000,000,- 000,000,000,000,000 and 2. Has the ice grown strong enough to bear yet? I hope when I come home at Christmas I shall have many and many a skate on it. . . . Next week will be the last week but one. By the by there are some customs here which are in the last week but one—thumping violently on your hands and saying

> > 'Last week but one
> > Take it all in fun'

> And in last week pinching your arms and saying

> > 'Last week
> > Don't squeak!'[28]

A little later he wrote to his mother from Wellington:

Arthur construes 'Omnia vincit amor' as 'All things conquer love'.
. . . I can play 4 tunes on the music which are 'God save the
Queen', 'Magnificat', 'To thee O dear dear Country' and 'Ten little
Niggers'. Arthur will persist I oughn't to strike E in the last but
I don't believe him. . . . In Punch somebody translates rather
oddly 'Les Chevaliers du Bouillard' The Cavaliers of the waste-
paper basket ! ! ! ! ! [29]

A month later he was back at school again, with a new nickname ('the whitewashed Marmot') and new manias to record
('silkworms—nearly all the school have got either cocoons or
moths or worms . . .')[30] and fresh troubles with his work
('Mr. Edgar said that my being down at the bottom was no
criterion (what does that mean?) of my work').[31] The two years
that followed were not especially eventful. Martin's work took
a turn for the better. In March 1872 he was top of his form by
23 marks and was rated 'very good' for divinity. He succumbed
to the various infectious diseases which struck the school from
time to time. When Arthur joined him there, they both fell
victims to whooping-cough and during their convalescence they
were ordered by an eccentric medical officer 'to go to a neighbouring gas-works, and to spend an hour in being fumigated, by
the simple process of pacing about in a high-walled yard into
which some refuse from the retorts had been cast'. Mrs. Waterfield took pity on them and accompanied them in coughing and
spluttering over the 'filthy, burning offal'.[32]

The tone of the school seems to have been good and wholesome. Occasionally a reference to bullying occurs in Martin's
letters;[33] a sentence in one of Benson's letters—'Be sure you let
me know if there is the *least* budding out again of the Abomin-
able'[34]—suggests that sometimes something worse took place.
But neither Martin nor Arthur appears to have encountered any
impurity at the school and they were spared the experience of their
brother Fred who came to the school after both the elder boys
had left.[35]

The pressure on Martin from his father was still keen. 'Let
me know your marks', he wrote in March 1871. '. . . I want to
see you in the Honours. . . . N.B. Write well.'[36] Occasionally
there came hints of what the future should hold in store, which,
if jocular, were none the less purposeful:

You and Arthur [Benson wrote to Martin early in 1874] had better found an order of Preachers—Preaching Friars, you know! They are very much wanted nowadays. Well, *in the meantime*, you had better stick to your Greek plays and Latin verses. You'll be all the better Friars, for the old ones failed thro' ignorance.[37]

4

It was when Martin reached the age of twelve that the most striking advance in his intellectual development took place. This coincided roughly with Arthur's joining him at Temple Grove. His letters became more mature; his scholarship more accurate; his reading power—which had always been remarkable—increased in its intensity. His father recalled that at this age he read during one vacation 'with intense enthusiasm Carlyle's *French Revolution*. Then, finding he did not know enough minute facts he read other accounts, and reread it. Since then he has been ever freshly informing himself about it, and a new life of Camille Desmoulins was his last.'[1]

Shortly before his twelfth birthday he and Arthur visited Chichester Cathedral, and the description of the visit which he appended as a postscript to one of Arthur's letters home shows that he already possessed a keen eye for architectural detail and his father's love of ecclesiastical antiquities:

Chichester Cathedral is very venerable and there are in it several curious pieces of ancient art, particularly two sculptures, about A.D. 800, both referring to the raising of Lazarus. The steeple is new, but it is copied from the old one which fell in in 1861. On the wall there are painted portraits of the Bishops of Chichester, and two pictures of Ceadwell—King of the S. Saxons granting the monks of Selsey (where the old Cathedral *was*) a Charter and another of King H. VIII confirming it. In the Church at Arundel there are 3 frescoes, the two most important were the 7 Acts of Mercy and the 7 deadly sins. There was another less important of an angel holding a garment in its hands. 5 of the Earls of Arundel and Dukes of Norfolk are buried in the Church there and one at Chichester. There is an ancient British coffin at Arundel, The park is very beautiful and there is a fine view, from the top of a hill which Arthur and I *attempted* (I say *attempted* advisedly) to draw. . . .[2]

170

Reports from Temple Grove showed that the work was going well. In March 1873 Martin wrote to tell his father that the mania was now for writing books. 'Hobday is writing a book called Stories of the Sikh Wars and Morris ma. . . . is writing one called Bannockburn and I am writing one called Virginians. . . . I have had the highest marks with Mr. Waterfield for Euclid.'[3] The next letter reported that he was top of the school by 23 marks.

In the same year, the Benson family said good-bye to Wellington and moved to the stately but rambling old house in the Lincoln Cathedral close which traditionally belonged to the Chancellor of the Cathedral. Benson had accepted Christopher Wordsworth's offer of the Chancellorship and a Canonry in December 1872. In his diary, he recalled Martin's reactions to this upheaval:

He was exceedingly devoted to country life and country sights and sounds. The old home at Wellington was more loved than any; the fir woods, the heather, the 'Ridges', and the great beech trees. He often hoped it would never be his lot to live in a town, and when we went to Lincoln it was a trial to him. . . . One of the first evenings that we were there, having tea in the Schoolroom, the ancient private chapel, as it had been, of the Chancery, when we were all rather low at the change from Wellington (in spite of our long before forward love of the Minster) I said to the children, "I hope you will all be happy here. You won't be so well off as at Wellington, for our income will be less than half of what it was there—and we must do without many, many, enjoyments. But you know I've come here because I thought it was right to come and try to revive the ancient life and energy of cathedral institutions—which will be destroyed if they can't be made more serviceable to the Church." There was a little pause; we had often in walks and talks (Martin and Arthur especially, and even Nellie and Maggie) chatted of St. Hugh and Grosseteste, and they had all read short lives of them, and we had often imagined the Cathedral stalls full of prebendaries and busy sacrednesses going on once more and frequent services, for the visits of the whole troop to Riseholme * had been frequent —But my heart rather sank, thinking that the City life among strangers, subsisting on the canonry alone, might curtail some good and many pleasures for the children—and all this came back in

* The Bishop's palace.

171

the pause, when out spoke Martin: "*I* think it's quite right to have come here; and I am very glad, Papa, that you *have* come."[4]

Joys there were in plenty at Lincoln: a house 'expressly devised for the most gruesome forms of hide-and-seek—for it was full of dark corners and empty cupboards and dreadful angles of ambush';[5] a garden containing ruins of the old city wall, in exploring which Martin nearly came to grief during his first holidays there;[6] a maze of little paths through shrubberies and fruit trees along which Benson used to walk in his cassock, note-book in hand, practising the art of extempore preaching; a lawn on which a primitive tennis court was devised, marked out by tape which was fastened down by hairpins. ('A singular game', Arthur observed, 'one interesting feature being that if a player caught his foot in a tape, the whole marking of the court was transformed into a sort of rhomboid, instantly obliterated, and the ground strewn with hairpins.')[7] Martin and Arthur were allowed to borrow their father's pass-key to the Cathedral at any time, and explored every nook and cranny of the enormous building. Once the two boys scrambled on to the nave clerestory from the north-west tower—a narrow stone ledge without railing, some 60 feet above the ground. Then Martin discovered that he had little head for heights.

> Every few yards [wrote Arthur], between each window, the gallery entered a narrow passage, behind the shafts which supported the vaulted roof. We had crossed about four of these spaces, my brother in front, when, as I was advancing along one of the open ledges, I heard ahead a stifled gasp. He was ensconced in one of the narrow passages; I found him white and shaking. "I can't go on", he said, "and I can't go back." . . . I said, "Will you sit down here and wait, while I go and fetch someone?" "Oh, no," he said, "I couldn't wait here alone—I don't know what I might do." At last I persuaded him to come back, holding my hand. It was, though I did not think it so at the time, really rather a ghastly situation. If he had reeled or staggered or grown faint, I could not possibly have saved him. We said nothing about it to our parents, but my brother would never venture out on an open gallery again.[8]

In 1874, as Martin was nearing his fourteenth birthday, the time approached for a serious attempt at a scholarship. In the previous year he had been awarded one of the Eton scholarships, but it was generally agreed that a top scholarship was clearly within his reach. His father favoured Winchester.

> Winchester would perhaps suit *you* best as a school—but they say the examination is harder. Can you put *powder* into your work . . . Your fault intellectually is to be rather *dreamy*, and let the grass grow while you are turning round. It is a weakness which you should try to cure. But I am afraid that you rather foster it than otherwise by reading novels. Novel-reading is a great cause of dreaminess. The characters and situations rise up between you and your work—and then also they awaken ideas which have no reality and you feel as if the real world was duller. But then you know 'A living dog is better than a dead lion'. Also the reading of novels is as tiring to the head as any other reading—(perhaps more, because of the excitement)—and so you come with tired powers to your work. I hear from Mr. W. that you are in this weakness of novel-reading, and considering how inescapably important this term's work is to you and to us all, and looking on yourself as a boy of sense, I wish you would make a resolution to open no more novels and dream no more till the holidays. I am glad you like the *Antigone*—It is a Tragedy indeed. You will wonder at it more and more as you grow older. It took possession of me entirely when I read it first, a little older than you. The lines and thoughts were never out of my ears and head. And I read it last term with more appreciation than ever. . . . Was the Euclid you sent me in miniature written without Book? or copied? . . .⁹*

In a letter written a week later, Benson was still considering the rival merits of Eton, Winchester, Marlborough and Charterhouse. Martin must make up his own mind.

> Don't think of it in lesson time tho' except as a stimulus! Don't be planning and DREAMING *then*. Your letter is all I could wish and I hope you'll carry out your good resolution about '*powder*'. What you seem to want intellectually is concentration of mind and body. For Listlessness of Attitude (want of smartness) springs from and then tends to reproduce Listlessness in Attention.

* Benson's remarks on novel-reading are a fair reflection of the views of many of the advocates of godliness and good learning. See his letter to Sir Charles Phipps in W.C. MSS. I.57. Benson complains of the 'flood of fatal "yellow novels", translations from Dumas, etc., which pour in upon us from the railway stations', 1 February 1861. See also Arnold's remarks on the dangers of novel-reading in *Sermons*, IV, no. 4.

You should determine to commence work *sharp,* and to put your whole Force into it *while at it.* You don't want interest in work, nor ability, nor good attention. But you do want concentratedness. I hear the echo of your mistakes. Appar*eu*nt! Don't you remember making that identical mistake in the holidays in a verse? I do—and here you have done it again! Appar*eu*ntly you think it has something to do with *eo* 'to go'!!! There are others—but I spare you, only do be careful—Remember Accuracy is the very soul of a scholar.[10]

In July, shortly before his attempt at Winchester, Martin was examined with the rest of Waterfield's VIth form by Dr. A. W. Verrall, Benson's old pupil. His report was:

All four boys did well. Benson, ma., is, I should say, the best and on this occasion *knew his work* better than the others. In the unseen work and composition there was very little difference between Benson and Boyle. . . .[11]

Not unnaturally, Verrall wrote to the boy's father who passed on all his remarks to Martin.

You did very well. . . . You keep your place in the order he brings out. . . . Your prose was good, but . . . there were one or two instances of a fault which seriously impairs the style of your composition—viz. the *repeating* of the same word or construction within a few lines.[12]

Mary Benson's letters to her son over this period must have given him more comfort. 'I do so want you at home, dear Boy: the time is very long till you two come back. Please God we will have a happy time in August. Shall we have to welcome a Wintonian or a Carthusian, I wonder?'[13] Then, when the examination was over:

Papa told me about the examination, and how you had certainly done your best, and done creditably. And it made me very happy, for much as we desire the scholarship, we desire the other more—so whether you get it or not, I am glad and proud and *won't* we welcome you home.[14]

Martin, then head of the school at Temple Grove, was awarded the top scholarship at Winchester. His new career began in September 1874.

Dr. Ridding had been headmaster of Winchester for eight years when Martin joined the school. He had taken full advantage of the recommendations of the Public School Commissioners to escape from the old oppressive control of the Warden and Fellows and to initiate a sweeping programme of reform—new buildings, the abolition of 'Commoners' in 1869, a widening of the curriculum (including the establishment of a Modern School), and an increase in the size of the staff.[1] He sought, with striking success, to do for Winchester what Temple had accomplished at Rugby. At the same time, Ridding was a Wykehamist through and through. He had been born at Winchester (his father being Second Master), educated as a boy there under George Moberly, his future father-in-law, and had himself been Second Master at the College for the three years prior to his appointment as Moberly's successor. He was not likely to sacrifice cherished Wykehamist traditions on the altar of reform. Indeed, this blending of the old and the new was his most remarkable achievement, making of Winchester—in the words of Dr. Abbott at the second Head Masters' Conference in 1888—'a place where everything was antique and nothing was antiquated'.[2]

These traditions Martin grew very quickly to love and to respect. His first letters home show that despite the exigencies of fagging, he was delighted at his new life and very proud of 'the honour of being William of Wykeham's son'.[3] In October 1874 he wrote to his mother:

> The lengthened description of my fagging is—
>
> Get up 6.15 and put up cold baths every 5 minutes, dressing in the meanwhile.
>
> 8.30, take my proefect's books through to Moberly Library.
> 12.00. Play football.
> 6.30. Wash up 3 cups and 3 saucers, etc.
> 6.45. Swill mop.
> 6.50. Sweep up. (6.00 get Proef. books *from* Moberly)
> 8.30. Wash tooth mugs and clean tablecloths.
> 8.45. Take letters to post . . .
>
> Only fancy I got 55 marks out of 60 for my Verse Task. Senior marks in the Div! I have been learning no end of slang. Guess

what this means—'You brockster, to splice hollises at a man's duck by Salve diva potens.'
Alias 'You bully, to throw stones at a man's face by Salve diva potens corner.'
When I come back for the holidays I think I shall draw pictures of the life of a Winchester Junior. . . . I am going to the Deanery after Cathedral . . .
Been, and oh horror a man has sat down on my cathedral, alias topper. Result—*collapse* [*there follows a drawing*]. . . . The notion is to have small rich cakes. 'Notion' by the bye is a remarkable word. To 'sport notions' is to say anything. To 'have a notion' is to pride oneself on anything especially.
Vale. Your most loving and affectionate son,
Martin White Benson.[4]

He was singing alto in the choir ('You should hear my lovely execution')[5]; the work was presenting no difficulties:

I came out Senior in monthly exam.: scoring 290 out of 300, getting full marks for everything except French and 40 out of 50 for that. I hope Papa will get the Facciolati and dictionary of antiquities soon.[6]

His father and mother were very relieved. 'Your happy letters are a continual joy',[7] Mary Benson wrote to him. 'My dear lad,' wrote his father, 'Mind you work and walk worthily. . . . You begin where I end. Take care that you may not have your good things and pleasures at the beginning of life—but let them, through your goodness and gratitude for them, ripen on to still greater friendships and more confidence on the part of those who love you.'[8] A month later Martin was a little less content. Beatings—or 'tundings'—were very frequent; also there was a good deal of cheating, especially amongst the Commoners.[9] 'Don't taste that ground-ash for my sake,' his father replied. 'I shouldn't like it. You have done well to escape it if it is as active as you imply, but don't get it pray—at least not for any carelessness or anything in that line.'[10]
As for the other matter, 'I am very sorry to hear about the commoners cheating. Oddly enough, Arthur in a letter I got the day after yours, says just the same of the Oppidans.'[11]

Martin soon found that a weakness in mathematics, especially in Euclid, was beginning to pull him down in his place in form.

Benson maintained his custom of sending Martin his monthly reports, and his letters were full of a nervous anxiety lest Martin should fail to realise the high promise he had shown. 'Pray pick up directly', he wrote in January 1875. 'Do not flag with the goal just in sight.'[12]

At Easter 1875 Martin moved up to a higher division, in which there were a number of boys older than himself who had failed to gain promotion. His letters suggest that his diligence was scoffed at by these older boys. Feeling very wretched, he wrote to his mother telling her that on top of everything else he had mislaid a railway ticket which his father had sent him.

Dearest of dear old boys, [his mother wrote back] So glad to get a note and so sorry to hear of your misfortunes. [Then—in tiny writing—she added:] (Don't tell anyone, but *I* lost a ticket myself once.) [She continued:] I have missed, missed, missed you so! Our morning walks and talks were so delightful. In the summer we must have many more.

'Sweet are the ways which we went together
Gladly thou wentest, and one glad with thee.'

. . . I am so sorry about your new form—but you will do the 'beasts' good.[13]

Later in the year he had a poor report on his Euclid again, and Ridding complained that he was 'a little fond of scribbling at times'. His father wrote in dismay:

The low place, the Euclid, and the want of attentiveness in Dr. Ridding's report are all blows. As to 13th, you must indeed recover yourself. I shall be displeased more than I remember being with you, if you do not. . . . I am intending for you a really handsome Christmas box—But, my boy, you must *deserve* it. . . . I send you a prayer of Dr. Arnold, which I began to use just about your age. It was very useful to me and made my work more true and real. I hope you will like it and use it.[14]

At the same time Martin received his first 'tunding' for an offence which is not specified.[15]

All the adverse criticisms of Martin's work amount to the charge of 'dreaminess' or 'inattentiveness'. This appears to have been a characteristic which he occasionally displayed at a very early age. In a letter written by Temple to Benson in 1868—when Martin was only eight—he commented: 'I am glad my

godson is dreamy. I was and am very dreamy.'[16] Certainly it was
not a dreaminess that sprang from apathy or intellectual dullness.
It was rather the introspective, philosophical trait of the Sidgwick
character which all the Benson children inherited to a certain
extent and which came out in Martin very markedly. In many
ways Martin resembled Henry Sidgwick as a boy. Henry at
Rugby had been noted for his 'unusually wide reading, his
exceptional taste for poetry . . . showing during his schooldays a
certain want of physical vigour, and no special aptitude for
games'.[17] In January 1866 Henry Sidgwick wrote to Mary
Benson about Martin, then aged five:

> I am glad that you think Martin is like me. I hope he will turn
> out better; I think there was once a tide in my affairs—a few years
> ago—which if I had taken might have led me to greatness. May
> Martin have as good opportunities and make more use of them.
> He certainly startled me by the extent to which he appreciated
> things; my idea was, however, that he had less character than
> Arthur, which perhaps is also my case as compared with either of
> my brothers.[18]

Arthur Benson also noticed the similarity between his elder
brother and his uncle. In *The Trefoil*, he wrote:

> I believe he had a mind somewhat resembling Henry Sidgwick's.
> His memory was very accurate, he mastered subject after subject
> with perfect ease, and abstruse and complex ideas seemed never to
> baffle him. He had too a firm and devout Christian faith, very
> mature for a boy. I know that Mason once said to me not long after-
> wards that he thought that my brother might have been destined
> to treat the subject of Christianity on profound philosophical lines.[19]

There is no puzzle, either, about Martin's 'scribbling' in class.
Amongst his papers in the Bodleian are a number of sketch-
books and notebooks of drawings—fantastic demons, weird little
Chinamen, fearsome savages in panoply of war, priests and
acolytes, beautifully executed heraldic devices.[20] Sir Charles
Oman, who was at Winchester with Martin, recollects that he

> had a nice taste in manuscripts, could imitate something very like
> fourteenth or fifteenth-century script or illustration—his speciality
> was the painting or small miniatures such as deck the initials of
> choir-books or of charters. I remember that he once produced a

properly crumpled parchment, with a glorious initial, which gave some absurd privileges to members of Wykeham's foundation, and succeeded in persuading certain simple souls that it was an original, newly discovered. He was a delightful companion. . . .[21]

He was a passionate and informed collector even while at Temple Grove. At Winchester he built up for himself a library which—according to his brother Fred—'must have been unique for a boy of his age. Already at Lincoln he had spotted an Albert Dürer woodcut pasted on the fly-leaf of some trumpery book at a penny bookstall, and had breathlessly conveyed the treasure home.' Fred also writes of his 'exquisite ridiculous drawings' and 'poems as ridiculous' and a 'boyishness, which verged on the fantastic, for once he appeared in school with four little Japanese dolls attached to the four strings of his shoe-laces, and gravely proceeded with his construing'.[22]

His father saw most of these things. He became painfully anxious to impress upon Martin that while at school he must learn to give his full attention to the tasks which were set him and that he must conform to the rules and routine which the authorities had devised for his good:

> You don't tell me anything about your games [he wrote in May 1876]. I hope you are playing hard as well as reading hard—or you'll turn out a dull boy after all. There is a great power to hold up your head 'in the pride and delight of fresh work' as you say to your mother, but there's also great power for the same in the energetic play of a couple of hours in which your work doesn't come into your head for an instant.[23]

Martin's career at Winchester followed very much the same pattern as his career at Temple Grove. For the first two years his intellectual attainments were not especially distinguished. Then came a new confidence, and with it rapid development. If a marked change can be discerned in his work and writing at the age of twelve, so too in 1876, when Martin was sixteen, the year in which he was confirmed, his reaching of maturity shows itself clearly in his letters and in his relations with his family.

> Dearest mother, [he wrote at the beginning of the Easter term]
> . . . Tell the girls that I will give a prize at Midsummer to which-ever of them has in the interval between then and now written the best prize poem on Lincoln Cathedral in any rhyming metre

they like except totally irregular ones like some of Southey's. Minimum 30 lines. (In confidence I will tell you but you must keep it STRICTLY PRIVATE that the prize is a collection of Shakespeare's sonnets, v. well illustrated by a man named Gilbert.) [24]

Benson remarked upon the exceptional progress of his work at this time:

Natural Science he did with great care and great delight. Italian was an extra which he did voluntarily, without consulting us, and here his progress seemed to me half magical. One evening in the holidays he asked me to read some Manzoni with him, and I thought I had never before been so struck with his immense ability. Sentences seemed to become luminous to him in a moment, and he darted down like a king-fisher on origins and meanings and shades of meanings in words.* But just as in reading for his essay on Mahometanism, for which he gained his Sixth Form Prize at 16, and in his present reading of Milton and Taylor for a Literature Prize, so always there was the same easy unexcited enthusiasm for all he read—whether it was Ruskin or Burke to please himself or books fixed by others. As Beth says, "He always worked as if he were not working at all."

Dr. Ridding said that, "His great charm was the enthusiasm which made him always the centre of a group of boys whether in their own rooms or in his drawing room; and, together with a religious feeling, so evidenced as ever present, the childish absence of self-conscious, morbid broodings—so much life and so much merriment."

He was greatly delighted when he became a member of the Debating Society and spoke two or three times, as he described it to me, with horrid sense of failure; as others described it, with a torrent of words directed throughout to what was high principled and free from paradox, and sympathetic with the ignorant at home and the oppressed abroad. . . . All seemed to come simply and naturally because it was Martin and we were not vain of him, only loved him because he was Martin. History was his favourite school work, but he was doing exceedingly well in classics, having set his heart on 'making his scholarship good at least' and some of his English translations into verse are certainly *very* good.[25]

The letters that passed between the father and his eldest son in the last eighteen months of Martin's life are remarkable docu-

* On Benson's and Prince Lee's love of 'shades of meaning' see *supra*, p. 107.

ments. They wrote now almost as equals; they discussed texts as one scholar addressing another; their letters were full of the excitements of the new responsibilities which faced them both. Indeed this was the happiest time in both their lives. Benson left Lincoln, early in 1877, to become first Bishop of Truro. He had to build up a new diocese; to organise an effective counter-attack on the firmly entrenched ranks of nonconformity; to fulfil a long-expressed ambition to make a cathedral (which had yet to be subscribed for and to be built) the effective, active centre of spiritual life within the diocese. It was a challenge which drew forth the finest of Benson's qualities and made supreme demands upon the energy and industry of this phenomenally industrious man. Also, he saw in his eldest son a partner in his work. The anxiety was over. Martin was fulfilling daily the hopes he had hardly dared to formulate. At the beginning of 1877 Martin won the Sixth Form Prize; in October 1877 he became a prefect; and at the end of the year, after only a very short time in the Head-master's division, he was runner-up for the Goddard Scholarship —'first with one examiner actually, and only after revision placed a little second' [26]—a certain winner in 1878.

Benson's letters bear witness to his mounting delight: 'I do not know when I have been so delighted', he wrote on hearing that Martin had won the Duncan History Prize. 'It is really a grand prize to have won—I can't add more but that you are a dear lad —Be more and more!' [27]

In October he wrote: 'Your long and delightful letter contains so much matter that we have enjoyed, but I am afraid we shall never satisfy you with our replies. Only don't mind *that*.' [28]

In May 1877 Benson discussed with Martin how he might do something to raise the moral tone of the school, which Martin had described as 'low'. He suggested that the boy should make the acquaintance of Brooke Westcott (one of Dr. Westcott's sons) who with like-minded friends had done wonders in elevating the tone of Cheltenham. [29]

In July he wrote to thank Martin for a birthday present:

I came here last night and found your delightful present awaiting me. I am very glad to possess it indeed, and I believe it is a rare book now, and I particularly like it with *your* inscription in it.

I have never had time to go into the question of the metres or rhythms of these Sequences, which are very musical, and yet elude me. I shall study Neale's theory of them. Do you know whether it is the accepted one? It is not I believe the same as Daniel's. . . .

I think the subject of the Three Revolutions would be, as you say, a splendid one for a brilliant book. But then, you must be first soaked with the spirit and handling of Thucydides. The determination to take into account *all* the phenomena which were real, and the insight into the first principles of action, and the modification of high aims by inferior and selfish ones, and the perception that there are laws under which societies may be traced as acting. I am not at all surprised that you have not got yet into the sense of devotion to that mighty man which will, I think, soon seize your historical sense. Some people have queer superstitious views about the 'moment' of their 'conversion' (though it is really the work of many moments), but I do distinctly recollect the day and hour when I exclaimed sitting over my Thucydides, "Why I am beginning to comprehend exactly what he means! I can understand all this as he goes on, slowly but really!" [30]

Martin's assistance to his sister Nellie (aged fourteen) on the subject of confirmation impressed his father deeply. We may let Nellie speak for herself. On 16 September 1877, she wrote to him,

Dearest Martin, Oh how I miss you, you nice boy. Arthur is going very soon too. Oh! Oh! Oh! Is it worse for you I wonder. I suppose so. Martin I am such a horrid girl, so cross and lazy, and you are *so* good. Was it very hard to you to try to get good for it is to me. You are so much nicer than you used to be. Was it your confirmation communion that did it—I wish you would tell me. . . . I hope your ash has been well boiled. I shouldn't much mind being your fag boy. I don't imagine you are very severe Mr. Prefect. . . . Good-bye, you dear old Prefect. [31]

A fortnight later she wrote in reply to a letter from Martin:

Dearest Martin. You are the nicest best boy in the whole world. No—it's no good saying you aren't. Thank you again and again for your letter. My confirmation will come sometime next year I suppose when Papa goes on his confirmation tour. [32]

Amongst the bundle of her letters to Martin, this little gem may be found:

I Mary Eleanor Benson do promise that when my unfortunate brother Martin comes down in the world so as to be a small trades-

man I will restore him his half-crown . . . to be nailed on his
counter. Signed, M. E. Benson.[33]

This was an unforgettable year for them all. To Martin,
Winchester never seemed lovelier.

The very stones of Winchester were dear to him [his father re-
called]. The gateways and the old flint walls, Chambers and the
Hall, and the 'peals', and the Chapel, and the gowns, and the saints
in the windows were all to him parts of his venerated William of
Wykeham himself. . . . Any offence against the spirit of the place
in prefects or boys quite wounded him. But he never could endure,
and never excused the 'unkind cut' which it was to him, when the
collegiate chapel arrangements were altered for a commonplace
plan in which all looked East, and the surplices were ordered not to
be worn any more by college boys. Such a change after 4 centuries
appeared to him utterly unlovely and unkind.[34]

Truro and Lis Escop (the Bishop's Palace—formerly Kenwyn
Vicarage) were sheer delight to him. He had only two holidays
in which to enjoy them, and Benson recalled how he and the boy
would spend them in rides together two or three times a week:

We had looked forward to the rides of many beautiful years in
this to us consecrated land. And these first rides were our last. . . .
In one ride, he remarked how incorrectly the story of the Tree in
S. Martin's life was generally told, and gave it accurately from
Sulpicius, remarking on the *humour* with which the gentiles
exclaim '*nosmetipsi succidemus hanc arborem*', and he contrasted
it with the miracle of the Oak of Geismar. I asked when he had read
this and he told me sometime he looked it out in Pertz.
We rode one day to Probus where the screen and reliquary and
stateliness of the interior charmed him almost more than the
tower, I think, tho' the date of this interested him exceedingly—
And once we rode to Gwennup pit where we prayed on horseback,
and once a ride which filled him with an exulting delight to Piran,
fast and free against a strong wind which made a glorious sea. He
broke out with joyous exclamations just at the spot on the road to
Piran where first we caught the glimpse of the white waves spring-
ing up the black rocks out at sea and that day almost over them.
We attempted the sands, and rode up the Western hill for a still
grander view. As we came back part of our talk was whether
an advance of scientific knowledge helped poetry: 'Whether our

knowledge of its contents for instance made us less admire that portentous ragged and rugged cloud.'

Our talk was of course frequently happy school talk about all things going on here and Winchester, and about my cathedral plans in which he was immensely interested. . . . How indignant he was at Browning's version of the *Agamemnon* of which he quoted many harsh absurd lines contrasting them with Morshed's translation; he read Philip Van Artevelde with great pleasure, and could not think why Sherief's *Interpretation of Nature* had been written. "I read page after page", he said, "and can get hold of nothing." I delighted to see the boy's growing catholicity of spirit. . . .[35]

Benson's memoir of Martin records many moving episodes of Martin's last year in Cornwall: a visit to a family of Quakers at Falmouth, returning in a steam yacht up the Fal to Malpas, when Martin turned to his mother and said, "Mama—these are *real* people";[36] expeditions with Arthur Mason—and

among the endless poetical quotations which Martin was constantly making on these expeditions, he remembers more distinctly than any, once in a boat on the Tressilian Creek, how he dwelt on the exquisiteness of the words 'Quiet consummation have'—murmuring them over again and again—

'Quiet consummation have
And unharmed be thy grave'.

—and again 'Quiet consummation have'.[37]

Benson thus described the last walk they had together:

Our last walk was on the Piran sands with John Wordsworth. We had driven there—and then walked to the buried church— He was very silent—and as we came back, while we kept near the rocks (Arthur, J. W. and I) there was 'something prophetic' as J. W. has since written 'in the way in which he walked alone in the fading light along the margin of the waves'.

Yes, you were already, dearest boy, on the edge of an ocean greater than the Atlantic—You have crossed it alone—and our light fades while we strain after you.[38]

6

Only a few days after the dawning of the new year, 1878, came the first signs that all was not well. The story of what followed is best told in his father's words.

After the first fortnight of his holiday had passed, he went about we thought rather quietly and except on one or two bright days (when Arthur Mason was with him here and at St. Michael's Mount . . .) there was a languor about him which we attributed to the effect of our soft climate on him, so that for his sake we were glad when he went back to school, and he promised to take more and more active exercise. . . .

I believe he did not read much these holidays. His mother says he was not up to it; that he used to wish to begin, but got rid of his time in a way unusual to him by little drawings and by arranging his room, . . . all his school rolls, his letters from home, of which I believe he never destroyed one, and some poems and translations which we did not know he had been making, all most carefully and orderly . . .; tidiness which he cared little about before, but which we now fear was the utmost his tired brain cared for, for very long together. It is rather strange that the day he went back, about midnight I took my candle, and looked carefully round his room at everything as it was—and I know it was with a heavy heart. I had never done so before. I observed he had taken his mezzotint of William of Wykeham (whom he venerated in a kind of personal way as if he had known him) back to school—and so we afterwards found it over his bed.[1]

For the first week all went well at school. Then—

the Sunday after he went back . . ., his friends were surprised that he asked Hardy to walk with him after Dinner in Hall. He seldom asked anyone, but was asked by others. He was at the Communion, and was at chapel twice besides. This was the 2nd Feb. At tea at the Second Master's, Mrs. Richardson noticed something in him and found he could not speak. They took him out of the room, and he could not write. He printed some letters by which they gathered that he thought it was paralysis. . . .

I was telegraphed for, and arriving on Monday evening had a better account. On Tuesday he seemed perfectly himself and only wanted to get up and have 'fresh air' which he said would 'cure him quite'. It appears that there had been an entire derangement of digestive and internal action which he had not mentioned. He was eager for books. He entered into two or three prayers which I used very earnestly. He was allowed to look at pictures, but found no pleasure in J. Leech, saying that 'after all they were rather coarse in idea'—and looked at some Art Union outlines of *Pilgrim's Progress*, much displeased with the 'meaningless, unreal, uncharacteristic large stones' in the Combat and with the want of spiritual power in the demons. . . .

The doctor said he was so well that there was no fear, he should keep him quiet till he had got his digestion into order, and that he should not have sent for me if he had anticipated so good a change. I remained however until the Wednesday evening . . . I had a meeting of Sunday School Secretaries in Truro, and in spite of Dr. Wickham's assurances I felt a little less happy as I watched him on Wednesday. He was exceedingly bright when I asked whether I should read the evening psalms aloud to him. "O I *should* like it," he said. Dr. Wickham thought he must not come so far as Truro at first, but Mrs. Ridding and the Dean were both kindly anxious to take him in. He said, "Oh if I go to Dr. Ridding's it would be dreadful afterwards to break down in scholarship. A false quantity would seem like a breach of hospitality!"

On Wednesday morning he said to me, "One's views of life change strangely fast. On Monday I wanted so to go back to college and to the work. And on Tuesday I only wanted to see the men and talk about it. Then on Tuesday I wanted to be allowed to get up and walk in the air, now to-day I only just want to get up and sit in the room." Did thy dear views of life, dearest lad, go on changing day by day until thy wants became those of immortal lives?[2]

Then on the Sunday evening there came a relapse.

He became delirious, . . . on the Monday yet more and his mother was telegraphed for. She arrived on Tuesday evening and he knew her with peace and pleasure. . . . Miss Bramston had been a great deal with him in the week before, and on this Tuesday saw him the last time before his mother came. He had been talking with her on some usual thing, and she noticed that he very slightly wandered. Then he closed his eyes as for sleep, and then turned his head a little towards the room, awoke fresh, and gazed with a beautiful expression at a part of the room where nothing visible stood: plainly saw something and exclaimed, "How lovely." These words were the last he uttered.

The aphasia returned . . . but of the next days much was passed in profound sleep. On the Friday Sir Wm. Jenner saw him, and told us he grieved to say there was cause for the very gravest anxiety. Even then I was praying so for his recovery that I could not realise it. . . .

Next morning his breathing was troublesome and he could not take nourishment. We were allowed to be with him as much as we would from 10 o'clock. We were told we might pray to him and talk to him as we would. His mother almost immediately said to him, "Do not be afraid, darling; you are in the Valley of the Shadow of Death; but do not be afraid; don't fear, darling. God is with you." He looked for a little while afraid. But the fear passed from his face again. . . . His breathing was very sad and laboured, yet he scarcely seemed to heed it, and I never saw his face more full of intelligence and his eyes clearer and quieter. He was quite free from fever. . . . He looked constantly at us both with the most tender and affectionate expression, at other times looked quietly before him. And frequently took our hands for a moment—dropt them and then folded his own together—or placed one of mine against the other that I might pray. Thus he kept us almost continually praying aloud and moved us to continue if we paused.

Soon after we first began thus to pray I worked into my prayer the clauses from the communion service that the 'Body and Blood of Jesus Christ given and shed for us might preserve his soul unto life everlasting' and placed my finger upon his lips, saying "you receive them in your spirit".

But he would not let me then proceed, looked very anxious and imploring, and rather tearful. His mother wiped the tears, and said, "He will wipe away all tears from our eyes"—still he was restless and moved his hands and fingers, until at last I saw and said, "He wants to speak on his fingers"—Then he quickly formed the letter B. I said, "Bread and wine?" and he was happy again instantly. A little Bread was brought, and we all received, when I had consecrated it, and wine in a glass. The Matron put a little wine in a spoon for me to give him, but he would not take it so—and most reverently grasped the glass in both hands, we left but a little drop in it, and he received the Lord's Blood with the happiest look. Again he took my cross, as I held it up to him, fearing that he might be unable to hear from the distressed sound of his breathing, tho' well able to understand he took it and kissed it, and took his mother's.

She began to say close to his ear gently, "When I survey the wondrous Cross" and his very soul was with it. But when she came to the second verse—

> "See from his head, his hands, his feet
> Sorrow and love flow mingling down"—

he with a sudden momentary look of inquiry which instantly changed into an expression of both awe and pleasure—the most perfect look I ever beheld of satisfied adoration—gazed at *something*

—some*one*—tried with his eyes to make us look at the same, and then pointed to it with his finger twice or three times, most reverently directing us to look, which we did, but our eyes seeing saw not. . . . I knew it—but I was so fearful of deceiving myself that I said to the nurse—"Does he want something? He is pointing to something he wants, is he not?" She said, "No—no—He sees more than we see."

. . . After five o'clock they told me his pupils did not contract at light. The nurse said, "He would last until three in the morning. He was very strong." A few minutes before ten the heavy breathing quite passed away. It became quite soft. His lips gathered themselves nearly together, and it looked like a baby's mouth—so soft and sweet and small. The nurse placed his hand gently across his eyes. He breathed in soft little gentle sobs—and these ceased to come—and our Martin was quite gone to God.

My dearest wife understood it all more quickly—better—more sweetly than I. At once she knew she had never cared for anything but his happiness. And that it was come. The dear ones at home were told by John Reeve * and Mary Bramston, who were staying at Kenwyn to take care of them, in the holiest ways. They too felt nothing but the Love of God. Arthur came to us from Eton . . . and he received this letter from Hugh who is just six:—written with a blue pencil between big lines:—His Sunday letter

'My dear Arthur, Martain is dead. Nellie sends you her love. Martin is gone to hefen. Maggie sends you her love. I am so happy that Martin is gone to Jesus Christ. I hope we shall all go to HIM very soon. He is Saint Martin now. Your loving brother, Hugh.' [3]

Of all the letters which Mary Benson wrote on Martin's death, none is more touching and more eloquent of her character, her courage and her faith than the letter which she wrote to Beth on the morning of the next day:

Dearest Friend and Mother Beth,

Be comforted for Martin. He is in perfect peace, in wonderful joy, far happier than we could ever have made him. And what did we desire in our hearts but to make him happy? And now he will help us out of his perfect happiness. He died without a struggle—his pure and gentle spirit passed straight to God his Father, and now he is ours and with us more than ever. Ours now, in a way that nothing can take away.

* The Rev. J. A. Reeve, Curate-in-Charge of Kenwyn Church, later Rector of Lambeth.

Dearest Beth, we are all going to be more loving than ever, living in love we shall live in God, and we shall live close to our dear one.

One is so sure now, that sin is the only separation, and that sting is taken out of death by Jesus Christ. My heart aches for the dear ones at home, but I know you are a mother to them, and will support and comfort their hearts, and keep before them that God is love, and that He is loving us in this thing also. And I want them to think of Martin, our darling, in perfect peace for ever, free from fear, free from pain, from anxiety for evermore, and to think how he will rejoice to see us walking more and more in Love for his dear sake.

We cannot grudge him his happiness.

Dearest Beth, our boy is with God: he knows everything now, and will help us. The peace of God Almighty be with you.

Your own child, your fellow-mother, M.B.[4]

On the Sunday, Benson went to Martin's college chamber to collect his things. There—on the table—were his books and prayer-books annotated and inscribed in his small, immaculate Old English script; fragments of parchment with verses and Latin texts as beautifully executed. He looked more closely at what Martin had written. On the first fly leaf of his prayer book he found: '*Juravi et statui custodire judicia justitiae tuae.*'[5] On a slip of parchment under this *Salvator Mundi*, etc., and Fulgentius' *Rogo te, Veritas, Deus Meus*, etc., and then—as Benson recalled in his diary—'in capitals this from I know not where

> WHO HE WAS AND WHENCE HE CAME
> AND AT WHAT PRICE HE REDEEMED THEE
> AND WHY HE MADE THEE AND GAVE THEE
> ALL THINGS DO THOU CONSIDER.

Opposite was—not written in Old English or capitals like the rest, but in his ordinary recent hand, what gave me some trouble to think of

Deus, Deus meus, respice in me; quare me dereliquisti? . . . *Tu autem in sancto habitas, Laus Israel'.*[6]

But under this, as comforting himself in God's word, again in bold neat capitals

> MISERICORDIA TUA SUBSEQUETUR ME
> OMNIBUS DIEBUS VITAE MEAE
> ET UT INHABITEM IN DOMO DOMINI
> IN LONGITUDINEM DIERUM.[7]

189

[80-285] New Moon.

when gave me some trouble to think of 'Deus, Deus meus, respexisti me. Quare me dereliquisti?' .. In autem in sancto habitas, laus Israel."— But under this, as imperishably burning in Gold and, again in Gold next chapter

    MISERICORDIA TVA SUBSEQUETUR ME
      OMNIBVS DIEBVS VITAE MEAE
    ET VT INHABITEM IN DOMO DOMINI
       IN LONGITVDINEM DIERVM

Verily, my sweet lad, this "Lord's House" which thou lovedst is given thee to dwell in "for length of days—" Did the thought of ___ for at length of days it should be thine really come over thee? so it seems some more ___ than me— And if not, why in this same book didst thou write thy name thus Christianity, but deathfully in its place on the fly leaf

    MARTIN WHITE BENSON
     IN ☧ PACE ..

Then ___ full meaning and ___ a use of that form. But we may say, that, if thoughts and touches of what was preparing for thee did lay hold on thy soul thus from time to time, then not an ensample indeed of "working while it was yet Day", as brightly and as vigorously as if there were nothing but a long life of love & usefulness before thee— The last page has words again in ___ some beautiful old ___ which now seem ___ for us than for him "Secundum te Deus in die tribulationis .... et ne die ___ te."

Extract from E. W. Benson's Diary, recounting the
death of his eldest son, *Trinity College, Cambridge*

Verily, my sweet lad, this 'Lord's House' which thou lovedst is given thee to dwell in for 'length of days'. Did the thought of *how* for all length of days it should be thine really come over thee? So it seems from more signs than one—And if not, why in this same book didst thou write thy name thus Christianly, but deathfully, in its place on the fly leaf

MARTIN White Benson

IN ☧ PACE [8]

*   *   *   *   *

Martin was buried as a Scholar of Winchester in the cloisters of the college. His coffin was borne by eight prefects, his special friends. Under the chantry gable, in the shade of a bay tree, the grave may be seen. And above it is a brass, which his father later caused to be put up, depicting Martin in his Scholar's gown and with—as Arthur Benson has written—'one of the most beautiful and moving epitaphs ever framed by love and sorrow':

> O Amor, O Pastor, qui quem tibi legeris agnum
> Vitali tingis morte, sinuque foves,
> Nos, qui tam dulces per te reminiscimur annos,
> Duc ubi non caeco detur amore frui.[9]*

Benson was dazed—shattered—by the blow to all his hopes. Both Arthur and Fred have written of their first sight of him as he met them at Winchester station—'the pale and agonised face . . . under the flaring gas-jets'.[10] Every year, thereafter, he went to Winchester on the anniversary of Martin's death. In the account, written in his diary, he sought for the consolation and the understanding which his wife had found.

I shared to the full the feeling that several sensible letters, sent us while watching him, expressed—that it was 'inconceivable' that he should not be restored to us. 'Inconceivable'—so much past interest, skill, beauty, power, love were wrapped up in his growth

---

* O Love, O Shepherd, who dippest in life-giving death and who doth cherish in thy bosom the lamb whom thou hast chosen for thyself, lead us, who thro' thee recall such sweet years, to the place where we shall be enabled to enjoy a love that is not blind.'

191

and constant progress—so much hope for the future; such admirable preparation for good work, with such persuasive gentleness; such thoughtfulness and such reverence together. He seemed so sure to be 'a wise scribe furnished unto the Kingdom of Heaven on earth with things alike new and old'. There were such memories about him and he wove them so: such hopes and he knew it not.

It has come as such an interruption not to ambitions, not to pride, I trust, not to hopes of comfort only—But his path seemed ever to run on so completely in God's own way: we thought all *God's* plan for him was running on so sweetly towards some noble God's work.

It has changed all my views of God's work as it is to be done both in this world and the next, to be compelled to believe that God's plan for him really *has* run on sweetly, and rightly for him and for all—and yet—he is dead. "One's views of life change very quickly", he said to me the last hour in which he spoke to me. My sweet boy, thou hast changed mine.[11]

What had caused Martin's death? The diagnosis was tubercular meningitis. His father—and the family—feared that Martin's brain had been over-taxed, over-stimulated at too young an age. Accordingly, Martin's fate caused his father to change his whole manner of training his children. Arthur Benson has written:

It was unhappily clear that my brother's death was in part due to precocious mental development: and it gave my father a horror of any sort of pressure, and a tender desire to subordinate everything to our free happiness, which I think bore much fruit in our lives.[12]

In particular, Hugh was brought up on the very opposite principle to that which had governed Martin's early training.[13] Whereas Martin developed adult tendencies at a very early age, Hugh—it was both his charm and his bane—remained curiously childlike to the end of his life.

On the other hand, there may have been some inherited weakness. Benson himself had some of the characteristics of a depressive. At one moment he was a figure of tempestuous energy and wild optimism; at another he was almost paralysed by a sense of failure and a consciousness of the power of evil to thwart his work. The introspective nature of the Sidgwick family—so marked in Henry whom Martin resembled—has already been noted. All these traits can be seen in the Benson children. At least four of them (five, if we include Martin) possessed talents bordering on genius; also most remarkable energy in intellectual activity, coupled with a tendency to lapse into acute mental depression and sometimes morbid introspection. Nellie, who died at the age of twenty-seven from diphtheria, was in many ways very like her mother, with a bubbling sense of humour and a profoundly sympathetic nature. But Arthur's description of her —'she had a good deal of ill health in her short life and much depression—the result perhaps of her activities'[14]—suggests an affinity with her father and her eldest brother. Hugh—more than any of the Benson family—hopelessly overtaxed his resources. He died in 1914 from pneumonia, contracted when his doctor had already diagnosed a neuralgic complaint ('false angina') and had advised complete rest. With Hugh, periods of breathless enthusiasm were followed by black days of *malaise*. "I'm tired, I'm tired—not at the top, but deep down inside, don't you know",[15] he once said in 1912. And shortly before his death he experienced an attack of persecution mania.

Maggie Benson's end was the most tragic. She died in 1915 after a mental illness which had lasted nearly nine years, the prelude to which was increasing tiredness ('There's nothing the matter except tiredness',[16] she wrote in June 1906), followed by black depression and 'tyrannous fancies'.[17] Arthur himself, for two periods in his very active life suffered from acute mental depression or neurasthenia—in the two years 1907–8 and finally from 1917 to 1923.[18] After each attack he returned to his work with an almost furious determination.

Recalling the intermittent bursts of intense activity which marked Martin's progress through school, his introspective habit of mind, the increasing languor and listlessness of the last weeks of his life, we cannot doubt that he was truly a member of this family.

This, however, is certain: Benson never fully comprehended why Martin had been taken from him. On his sixtieth birthday, when Archbishop of Canterbury, he confided to his diary that this was the 'inexplicable grief' of his life. 'To see into that will be worth dying.'[19] Two months later he wrote—unknown to his family—this poem, found seven years later among his papers:

193

THE MARTIN

The Martins are back to cornice and eaves,
Fresh from the glassy sea;
The Martin of Martins my soul bereaves,
Flying no more to me!

One of them clung to the window-side,
And twittered a note to me:
'There's a Martin beyond or wind and tide
Whom you know better than we.

His nest is hid in a clustered rose,
On the Prince's own roof-tree;
When the Prince incomes, when the Prince outgoes,
The Prince looks up to see.

Calls him hither or sends him there
To the friends of the Holy Three,
With a word of love, or a touch of care;—
Why was he sent to thee?'

Martin I know; and when he went home
He carried my heart from me.
Half I remain. Ere Martinmas come,
Go with this message from me.

Say, 'Thou Prince, he is wholly Thine!
Sent once on a message to me;
Yet suffer me soon, at morning shine,
To see him on Thy roof-tree!'[20]

Finale: Godliness and Manliness

The noun 'manliness' and its adjective 'manly' are words rarely encountered to-day. In the nineteenth century, however, and during the Edwardian age, they were part of the common descriptive vocabulary of the period; so common, indeed, that one might reasonably conclude that manliness was one of the cardinal Victorian virtues.

> His manliness appealed to the manlier side in us [wrote an Old Rugbeian of his headmaster, Frederick Temple, whom he had witnessed clambering over the roof of one of the houses to fight a fire], and we were at our best in his presence.[1]

> The whole efforts of a school [wrote Edward Thring in 1864], ought to be directed to making boys manly, earnest and true.[2]

A passage from a letter written by the Rev. R. Shilleto to Montagu Butler, Headmaster of Harrow, runs as follows:

> Do, my dear Montagu, throw into your Sixth Form your own love of work. Make them feel the manliness, the health, the duty . . . of work.[3]

Horace Annesley Vachell's school story *The Hill*, published in 1905, was described on the wrapper as 'A Romance of Friendship. A fine, wholesome and thoroughly manly novel.' In 1876 Thomas Hughes gave a series of addresses, published three years later under the title *The Manliness of Christ*.

Manliness, as the Victorians understood it, is not easy to define. Sometimes—as when W. C. Lake wrote of Tait at Oxford, 'We quickly began to feel the straightforwardness and manly simplicity of his character'[4]—it meant the qualities of openness and transparent honesty as opposed to the baser elements suggested by such words as subtlety, refinement, luxury or ostentation. Dean Church, for instance, frequently used the word in this sense. Writing of the High Church school of the eighteenth century, he pointed out that there was nothing effeminate about it:

> it was a manly school, distrustful of high-wrought feelings and professions, cultivating self-command and shy of display, and setting up as its mark, in contrast to what seemed to it sentimental weakness, a reasonable and serious idea of duty.[5]

He admired Arnold for his 'manly and open ways';[6] praised Charles Marriott's personal devotion to the Tractarians as being an example of the best form of discipleship, partaking of its 'manly and reasonable humility, its generous trustfulness, its self-forgetfulness'.[7] He upbraided the Heads of Houses for their underhand and shallow methods of dealing with their adversaries, the leading spirits of the Oxford Movement: 'None of the University leaders had the temper and the manliness to endeavour with justice and knowledge to get to the bottom of it.'[8] And in a passage which would have amazed Charles Kingsley had he lived to read it, he defended the Tractarians' pursuit of celibacy as essentially manly:

> To shrink from it was a mark of want of strength or intelligence, of an unmanly preference for English home life, of insensibility to the generous devotion and purity of the saints.[9]

The Victorian enthusiasm for manliness may be best explained and understood by a study of the writings of S. T. Coleridge, especially the *Aids to Reflection*, which we have already described as the most influential of the literary works that shaped the minds of early Victorian churchmen. The full title of the work in the original edition was *Aids to Reflection in the Formation of a Manly Character*. In his preface, the author pointed out that the book was intended

> for as many in all classes as wish for aid in disciplining their minds to habits of reflection—for all who, desirous of building up a manly character in the light of distinct consciousness, are content to study the principles of moral architecture on the several grounds of prudence, morality and religion.[10]

In the *Aids to Reflection*, manliness is portrayed as the opposite of childishness: to be manly was to be mature, to be conscious of the duties of manhood, and so to cultivate the powers of intelligence and energy that one's moral character should be elevated

to a higher plane and one's understanding should aspire to that
perfection of human intelligence which is the Christian faith.
Thus he stressed that his writing was 'especially designed for the
studious Young at the close of their education or on their first
entrance into the duties of manhood and the rights of self-
government'.[11] Thus he echoed—in Aphorism X of the Introductory Aphorisms—the words of the poet:

> Unless *above* himself he can
> Erect himself, how mean a thing is man.[12]

And thus, in commenting on the XIIth Aphorism, he wrote:

What says the apostle? Add to your faith *knowledge*, and to knowledge *manly energy*: for this is the proper rendering of ἀρέτην
and not virtue, at least in the present and ordinary acceptation of
the word.[13]

The influence of this teaching on Arnold is plain. Here is the
source of Arnold's educational ideals, the explanation of his dis-
trust of childishness and of his passion for converting unruly boys
into Christian *men*. Here, too, is the inspiration that converted
such scholars as Benson, Westcott and Lightfoot into men of
action. We may recall that Westcott said of this band of friends
that their motto was 'I act therefore I am'—as good a slogan for
the early Victorian conception of manliness as we can hope to
find.

Yet to Kingsley and to Hughes manliness meant something
very different from this. Whereas Coleridge had equated manliness and ἀρετή—the fulfilment of one's potentialities in the
living of a higher, better and more useful life—Kingsley equated
manliness and θυμός—robust energy, spirited courage and
physical vitality. Whereas Coleridge had regarded manliness as
something essentially adult, Kingsley and Hughes stressed the
masculine and muscular connotations of the word and found its
converse in effeminacy. In this difference of meaning, we see the
distinctive features of two opposing schools of Victorian idealists,
represented by the followers of Coleridge and Arnold, on the one
hand, and by the 'muscular Christian' school of Charles Kingsley
and Thomas Hughes, on the other.

When Arnold exhorted his boys to be manly, he meant that
they were to put away childish things; but when Hughes portrayed

14—G.G.L. 197

Tom Brown as the paragon of manliness, he was expressing his admiration for the sort of boy 'who's got nothing odd about him, and answers straightforward, and holds his head up . . . frank, hearty, and good-natured . . . chock-full of life and spirits'.[14] * When Charles Kingsley encouraged Wellington boys to play at hare-and-hounds, he was seeking to train them to be manly and, incidentally, to become 'handy rifle skirmishers'.[15] On the other hand, when Benson preached his farewell sermon at Wellington in 1873, he voiced his hopes that his congregation would advance in manliness thus:

> For you will be men. You will seek Purity, that the souls and bodies you offer to those you love and to all-seeing God may be white and unspotted; Truth, that your speech may be simple and clear; Love, that your friendships may be sound and that the brotherhood of men may be to you no shadow.[16]

This could have been Arnold speaking. The same could not be said of Hughes's lecture on 'The Tests of Manliness', given only one year later, in which endurance in the face of death and torment was the theme, amply illustrated by gruesome extracts from Napier's *The Peninsular War*.[17] In the 1870's the winds of change were blowing with a vengeance. The ideals of godliness and good learning were passing, along with other distinctive features of the early and mid-Victorian age. Muscular Christianity was firmly establishing itself in their place.

F. W. Maitland, in his *Life of Leslie Stephen*, ascribed the origin of the term 'muscular Christianity' to T. S. Sandars, the *Saturday* reviewer.[18] The *Oxford Dictionary*, in defining it as 'a term applied (from about 1857) to the ideal of religious character exhibited in the writings of Charles Kingsley', fails to establish its origin, but cites an extract from an article in the *Edinburgh Review* of January 1858. The writer, referring to 'the school of which Mr. Kingsley is the ablest doctor', states that

> the principal character of the writer whose works earned this burlesque though expressive description, are his deep sense of the sacredness of all the ordinary relations and the common duties of

* This is East describing to Tom how he has to conduct himself if he is to make a good impression as a new boy; the last part of the quotation is Hughes's description of East himself.

life, and the vigour with which he contends . . . for the great importance and value of animal spirits, physical strength, and hearty enjoyment of all the pursuits and accomplishments which are connected with them.[19]

This is a brilliant description of Kingsley's attitude to religion and life. Here was a creed for the healthy extrovert; here were ideals which the average man could easily attain. Asceticism was unnatural; the preoccupation with sacerdotal conceits and with ritualistic extravagances was both exotic and unhealthy. For ordinary individuals, the quest for doctrinal truths was profitless; obtrusive piety was both unnecessary and harmful. Inevitably there was vulgarization. As E. C. Mack has written: 'In Kingsley, Christian practice seems not seldom to mean little more than being clean and physically well-developed'.[20] Certainly by the 1870's the pursuit of manliness had become something of a cult. We may take a brief look at the phenomenon before we examine the reasons for its appearance.

For schoolboys, Tom Brown had become the model of boyish excellence. Farrar's saintly heroes could not compete with him for popularity. He was an ordinary boy with an ordinary name, of good English stock and with good English ideals. He created a new vogue in schoolboy fiction. In the 1870's the *Boys' Own Paper* was started. Already—twenty years before—*Beeton's Boys' Annual* had been launched, producing in its early numbers *Tom Brown's Schooldays* in serial form. The description of the serial is significant: 'vigorous, manly, and thoroughly English, and . . . as far before the common run of books for boys as are reality and truth before pretence and imposition'.[21] New 'types' who captured the public imagination were confined neither to the schools nor to the realm of fiction. There was James Fraser, for instance, Prince Lee's successor as Bishop of Manchester in 1870; and Manchester's first two bishops exemplify strikingly the transition from the ideals of godliness and good learning to those of godliness and manliness. Lee's character and ideals have already been studied: he personified the principles that were dying. He was succeeded by a man who has been aptly described as 'Tom Brown in lawn sleeves'.[22] It is not surprising that Tom Hughes chose to write Fraser's biography. For Fraser was everything that Lee was not: tall, muscular, 'a rare and mighty man, with head, heart, health, all upon a grand scale . . . an admirable specimen of the *mens sana in corpore sano*'.[23] John Diggle, one of his diocesan clergy, wrote of him: he was a 'thoroughly healthy Bishop, as fresh and straightforward in inward principles as he was strong and erect in outward presence. . . . It was this open-air healthiness of moral sentiment which made Bishop Fraser almost irresistibly charming.'[24] Hughes saw at once a kindred spirit— a man passionately fond of horses, convivial with villagers, utterly without pompousness, stern and tough with moral delinquents.[25] Bryce wrote of him: 'He created not merely a new episcopal type, but (one may almost say) a new ecclesiastical type within the Church of England.'[26] He belonged to none of the categories into which members of the episcopal bench were normally supposed to fall. He was not a strong party man, not an aristocrat with Court connections, not a statesman, not a scholar, not a saintly recluse: in Diggle's words, 'Bishop Fraser was the *Citizen-Bishop*: the lawn-sleeved citizen.'[27]

Fraser was immensely popular. So were the schools which were rapidly adapting their curricula and refashioning their systems to produce more Frasers and Tom Browns. Arnold was still set upon a pedestal by many educational reformers, but the reforms which they initiated were largely distortions of Arnold's original intentions. Greater stress came to be laid on the salutary effects of games-playing—especially of Rugby football and cricket. These became organised and compulsory. Manliness and the respect for duty were well served by introducing more regimentation, in particular by encouraging the establishment of a Rifle Corps in which boys could be taught to drill, to shoot, to go on manœuvres and—ultimately—to command. Public school missions were set up to bring the ideals of courage, decency and manliness into the homes of the unprivileged and depressed. The tone of sermons and addresses became noticeably more patriotic and militant; the virtues of loyalty and pride in one's unit were fostered by rousing school songs, Old Boy Associations and annual dinners concluding with patriotic speeches. The public schools entered their golden age. Poets sang their praises and statesmen brought them fame.

Sometimes the language used was a little extravagant; sometimes the sentiments expressed fell below the nobility and sincerity which were unquestionably sought and became banal, or arrogant, or merely cheap. Whatever one may feel about this, two things are certain: firstly, this development reflected the opinion of the upper-middle classes who were saturated with imperialistic notions and who welcomed the spirit of aggressive patriotism which helped to allay their fears of German militarism and foreign commercial and industrial rivalry. Secondly, to those who cleaved to the older ideals of godliness and good learning and who survived into the 1880's and 1890's, many of the new enthusiasms seemed misdirected and inexplicable. Westcott may have written the lyrics of the Harrow song *Io triumphe*, set to music by John Farmer, but he could never have endorsed the sentiments of Edward Bowen (author of *Willow the King*, written in 1867), namely that 'there lives more soul in honest play, believe me, than in half the hymn books'.[28] The decades which witnessed the births of Henry Newbolt's poems on Clifton, Kipling's masterpiece on the careers of Stalky and Co at Westward Ho!, and H. A. Vachell's *The Hill* seem in some respects to be a century removed from the days when Arnold and Lee—and even Benson—struck their blows on behalf of Truth.

Mr. G. F. H. Berkeley's books on Wellington in the 1880's and 90's catch the mood exactly. He is describing the school as it was only some twenty years after Benson had left. 'Wellington was an uncommonly good place during these years', he writes, '. . . a splendid institution for the Nation and for the Empire'.[29] Its main aim, he says, was 'to turn out a hardy and dashing breed of young officers'.[30] The staff were admirably fitted to achieve this aim, being 'competent and muscular Britons all working to create a stamp of boy such as we wanted in the nation and more especially in the Army'.[31] King Edward's, Birmingham, twenty years after Lee had left, had undergone almost as striking a change. Charles Evans bowed to the popular clamour and began to encourage athletics. Mr. Tom Collins, in his recollections entitled *School and Sport*, recalls his appointment to the staff at King Edward's in 1863: 'Athletics in the school were then at their nadir, and I have always put down my election to the fact that I was a Cricket Blue and that the authorities desired the promotion of athletics in the school.'[32] Thereafter the boys no longer spent their afternoons doing surveys in municipal gardens, collecting botanical specimens and walking to local churches.

The promotion of manliness became steadily more intense in the schools. In the Edwardian age, as the prospects of war became more imminent, the patriotic temper mounted. Lord Rosebery's speech at the Wellington Jubilee Dinner in 1909—an occasion when the cheers of the audience nearly lifted the roof off the new dining hall—shows well what was expected of public-school products:

> The stress that patriotism will have to bear in days not distant, and perhaps imminent, will be greater than has yet been known in the history of this country (*hear, hear*). There never was a time when men were more needed to speak and act up to their faith (*cheers*). I think that men will have to be more universally armed in the future than they are now (*hear, hear*). . . . There are encroaching opinions which threaten patriotism, menace our love of country, and imply the relaxation, if not the destruction, of all the bonds which hold our Empire together (*hear, hear*). I would urge that as far as possible the study of patriotism should be promoted (*cheers*). If this is done daily and sedulously in this College it will live up to the conditions of its foundation and the illustrious auspices under which it has hitherto done its work (*cheers*).[33]

This change in the nature of Victorian educational ideals, important and sweeping enough to warrant the description of a revolution, was both noted and deplored at the time. As early as November 1864, Fitzjames Stephen commented in the *National Review*:

> Tom Brown and his imitators, and those from whom Tom Brown drew his inspiration, had so glorified football and cricket, and had mixed up Mr. Kingsley's theories and Dr. Arnold's practice into a composition so attractive to a considerable part of the public, that the public schools had come to be invested in the eyes of the world at large with even more than usual of that halo which individuals are prone to throw over places in which they have passed a pleasant and important part of their lives.[34]

Mark Pattison, in his *Suggestions on Academical Organisation* (1868), had already observed the impact of muscular Christianity on Oxford:

> the mastery which the athletic furor has established over all minds in this place. They have ceased to be amusements; they are

organised into a system of serious occupation. What we call in-capacity in a young man is often no more than an incapacity of attention to learning, because the mind is preoccupied with a more urgent and all-absorbing call upon its energies. As soon as the summer weather sets in, the colleges are disorganised; study, even the pretence of it, is at an end. Play is thenceforward the only thought.[35]

Maitland has shown that the same phenomenon was frowned upon at Cambridge in the 1860's, when Joseph Mayor of St. John's commented on the insidious influence on Greek learning of 'pestilent muscular Christianity', making the butt of his attack Leslie Stephen, whose suggested reforms for a special Tripos course for the 'poll man' were regarded as pandering to the new cult so popular among the undergraduates.[36]

Clearly forces at work in the 1850's and 60's determined the trend of the new ideals and decided the fate of the old. Equally clearly, muscular Christianity was not a sudden phenomenon, a new philosophy of life conditioned by any single set of circum-stances or inspired by the writings and actions of any one man. There had been muscular Christians before Victoria came to the throne, just as there are muscular Christians to-day. Many of the features of school and university life which one associates with muscular Christianity were in existence before the pursuit of manliness became a popular rage.

Games-playing was already a common feature of public-school life. Dr. Nicholas Hans has shown that many of the private academies of the eighteenth century encouraged physical train-ing, notably fencing, gymnastics, riding and team games.[37] In fact some of them—Soho Academy for instance, which Hans describes as a multilateral school—developed Old Boy Associations, a sense of *esprit de corps*, a wide curriculum with opportunities for organised recreation long before these things can be observed in the public schools.[38]

Even if *Tom Brown's Schooldays* conveys a false impression of Arnold's work and ideals, one cannot doubt that Rugby football played an important part in the life of the school. To Tom Hughes it was everything: 'This is worth living for; the whole sum of schoolboy existence gathered up into one straining; struggling half-hour, a half-hour worth a year of common life.'[39] Among the older public schools, Harrow—in particular—was pre-eminent in the early nineteenth century for the encouragement given to games, both football and cricket. Charles Wordsworth, Bishop of St. Andrew's, in his *Annals of my Early Life*, gives abundant evidence of this. 'My pursuit of athletic exercises . . . was rather excessive even for a more vigorous youth', he wrote. To the boys, games were far more important than work. 'Masters and tutors, though they did not slight, but rather encouraged, had not begun to place them on a par with, or even above, intellectual achievements.'[40] The Eton and Harrow cricket match, begun as an annual fixture in 1821, was the first great sporting occasion to attract public attention in schoolboy games. It led to the engagement (at Harrow) of a professional coach. Soon 'other public schools were anxious to enter into the lists'.[41]

Charles Wordsworth has indeed some claims to be considered the first of the really influential muscular Christians in the nineteenth century. We should expect that generations brought up on the classics would learn to sing the praises of *l'uomo universale*—the 'whole man'. Tuckwell's description of Charles Wordsworth in his *Reminiscences of Oxford* portrays him as exactly that. He was not only a brilliant scholar—he took a First in Greats in 1830, having won the university Latin Verse and Latin Essay Prizes—but he was a member of the Oxford Cricket XI in the first cricket match between the two universities (1827) and a member of the Oxford boat in the first inter-university Boat Race (1829). Tuckwell wrote:

> First among the Oxford comrades of that time . . . ranked Charles Wordsworth; . . . the best scholar, cricketer, oar, skater, racquet-player, dancer, pugilist of his day. His proficiency in this last branch of antique athletics was attested by a fight at Harrow between himself and Trench, which sent the future Archbishop to a London dentist in order to have his teeth set to rights. 'That man', whispered Lord Malmesbury to Lord Derby, when Wordsworth had shaken hands with the Chancellor on receiving his honorary degree, 'that man might have been anything he pleased.' His attainments and capacities were set off by an unusually tall and handsome figure.[42]

Charles and his brother Christopher changed schools when they left the university. Christopher became headmaster of Harrow,

Charles was appointed second master at Winchester in 1835. At once Winchester rose to prominence as a great cricketing school.

No finer athlete ever entered a school [wrote Frederick Gale in 1890, looking back to his Winchester days under Wordsworth]. And no master ever did more to promote all that was noble and manly amongst boys. . . . He . . . took an immense interest in cricket and all manly sports, and played a great deal both in practice and in matches, and brought elevens against us.[43]

The prominence which was given to sport at Rugby, Harrow and Winchester in the 1830's and 40's was by no means universal: and Wordsworth's active participation in the games was very unusual. At Shrewsbury cricket was grudgingly permitted by Samuel Butler, but rowing and football were forbidden as being too dangerous or too undignified.[44] Team games had nowhere become the exclusive activities of boys in their leisure hours, and —as has been discussed earlier—the alternatives chosen by boys were often what the late Victorian age would have considered to be unmanly in both senses of the word—childish and effeminate.

Despite the remarks of Pattison and Mayor on the disturbing athleticism of the 1860's at Oxford and Cambridge, it would be entirely wrong to suppose that the average undergraduate of the earlier decades of the nineteenth century conducted his life on the pattern of those—always a minority—who were working for the highest honours. The greatest divergence in way of life was between the gentlemen commoners and the scholars. The gentlemen commoners went their own way—hunting, driving tandem, gambling, playing at billiards and whist, amassing creditors and mistresses, sometimes both. For those who could not stand the pace of the 'fast' set, the sporting clubs provided an outlet for their energies. Hughes's account of Oriel in the 1840's certainly exaggerates the degree of athleticism at that time. Three-quarters of the undergraduates gave over their time entirely to athletics, he tells us.

Above all, the college was the accepted home of the noble science of self-defence in the University, . . . and the other branches of a polite education [were] looked upon as subordinate and inferior.[45]

Tom Collins, writing of Cambridge in the next decade, suggested that the college sports were pretty much the same as now [1905], except that football in those days was almost ignored . . . Cricket and rowing were the great sports, and happy was the man, in the eyes of his fellows, who attained the honour of taking part in either against the sister university.[46]

Both these writers were 'Blues', inclined perhaps to justify the dissipation of their energies and to over-emphasise the importance of the way of life which they themselves had chosen. It is significant that Tuckwell described Oxford in the same period as 'unathletic Oxford', pointing out that the most 'potent factor in University change' was the subsequent development of athleticism.

At that time there was no football and no 'sports'; only one cricket field, the 'Magdalen ground', at the Oxford end of Cowley marsh. Comparatively few men boated. . . . The great mass of men, whose incomes yielded no margin for equestrianism, took their exercise in daily *walks*. . . . At two o'clock, in pairs or threes, the whole University poured forth for an eight or ten miles' toe and heel on the Iffley, Headington, Abingdon, Woodstock roads, returning to five o'clock dinner. The restriction told undoubtedly in favour of intellectual life. The thought devoted now to matches and events and high jumps and bikes moved then on loftier planes; in our walks, no less than in our rooms, then, not as now,

> 'We glanced from theme to theme,
> Discussed the books to love or hate,
> Or touched the changes of the State,
> Or threaded some Socratic dream.
>
> Where once we held debate, a band
> Of youthful friends, on mind, and art,
> And labour, and the changing mart,
> And all the framework of the land.'

Only I fear in unathletic days was possible the affluent talk of a Tennyson and Hallam on the Cam, on the Isis of a Whately and a Copleston, a Newman and a Froude, a Congreve and Mark Pattison, Stanley and Jowett, Clough and Matthew Arnold—brain as against muscle, spirit as against flesh, the man as against the animal, the higher as against the lower life.[47]

When and why did the pursuit of manliness become a cult? Before this could happen, the theory of what men like Charles Wordsworth and Thomas Hughes practised had to be presented to the world in a popular and palatable form. It is true that Arnold occasionally revealed in his writings a lurking sympathy for the tenets of the muscular Christian school. He attached a great deal of importance to the 'liveliness' of boys,[1] and expressed his belief that discipline was excellent for them in developing 'quickness, handiness, thoughtfulness and punctuality. . . . Many a man who went from Winchester to serve in the Peninsula in the course of the last war must have found his school experience and habits no bad preparation for the activity and hardships of a campaign.'[2] He was an ardent patriot and had something of Kingsley's chauvinism: 'no missionising is half so beneficial, as to try to pour sound and healthy blood into a young civilised society: to make one colony . . . a living sucker from the mother country', he once wrote, when he had thoughts of emigrating to Australia;[3] and he had no love for Jews. 'England is the land of Englishmen, not of Jews.'[4] But these are *obiter dicta* rather than part of a carefully-formulated doctrine; and much of what Kingsley and Hughes were to advance in their writings would have offended him greatly.

Charles Kingsley, undoubtedly, was the man who first united godliness and manliness and popularised his philosophy of religion and life in a series of forceful and didactic writings. To him, manliness was an antidote to the poison of effeminacy—the most insidious weapon of the Tractarians—which was sapping the vitality of the Anglican Church. Young men came to the church for spiritual nourishment: they went away perverted. Their enthusiasm was diverted into unnatural, un-English pursuits. They were encouraged to think of themselves as beings set apart from other men, their minds bent on other-worldliness, the beauty of holiness and the satisfaction of self-denial. Scorning all earthly loves, they released their frustrated emotions upon saints long dead and upon the Holy Mother of God ; renouncing the love of women, they clung to each other, casting aside all manly reticence by confessing to each other their secret temptations, and seeking solace in their own passionate attachments which seemed to a normal healthy male (such as Kingsley liked to think himself) undesirably high-pitched.[5]

Kingsley was perhaps unique in the vigour with which he attacked Tractarianism on the score of its unmanliness. In the 1850's, however, the trend that Tractarianism took after the secession of Newman provoked a sufficiently popular opposition to ensure that Kingsley's attacks and imputations would receive a favourable hearing. It is this second stage of Tractarianism— when the Oxford movement went out of Oxford, when 'Puseyite' became the label of its adherents, when ritualism and the adornment of churches became the chief forms in which its impact was felt by the country at large—that provided the greatest stimulus to the doctrine which represented its complete antithesis—that of muscular Christianity.

Professor Chadwick, in his study of the early history of Cuddesdon, has commented on the bitter troubles which beset the college during the 1850's. 'In the diocese it was rumoured that Cuddesdon curates were "unmanly", that their training bred effeminacy.'[6] He quotes a letter written in 1858 by Bishop Wilberforce, the founder of the college, to a friend:

Our men are too *peculiar*—some, at least, of our best men. I shall never consider that we have succeeded until a Cuddesdon man can be known from a non-Cuddesdon man only by his loving more, working more, and praying more. I consider it a heavy affliction that they should wear neckcloths of peculiar construction, coats of peculiar cut, whiskers of peculiar dimensions—that they should walk with a peculiar step, carry their heads at a peculiar angle to the body, and read in a peculiar tone. I consider all this as a heavy affliction. First because it implies to me a want of vigour, virility and self-expressing vitality of the religious life in the young men. . . . Secondly, because it greatly limits their usefulness and ours by the natural prejudice which it excites.

Then there are things in the actual life I wish changed. The tendency to crowd the walls with pictures of the Mater Dolorosa, etc., their chimney-pieces with crosses, their studies with saints, all offend me and all do incalculable injury to the College in the eye of chance visitors. The habit of some of our men of kneeling in a sort of rapt prayer on the steps of the communion-table, when they cannot be *alone* there; when visitors are coming in and going out

208

and talking around them: such prayers should be 'in the closet' with the 'door shut'—and setting apart their grave dangers, as I apprehend them to be to the young men, they really force on visitors the feeling of the strict resemblance to what they see in Belgium, etc., and never in Church of England churches.[7]

These, indeed, were the features of 'seminary life' which men of Kingsley's stamp so deeply abhorred. Pusey and Liddon were regarded by them as dangerous teachers. The best protection against them was to teach young men to resist their advances by bringing them up on a code likely to breed heartiness and virility. Many of their suspicions were in fact unfounded: they judged too swiftly and too superficially. As Professor Chadwick has written: 'there was manliness and manliness—and Christian manliness was consistent with the virtue of meekness, a grace which some might mistake for effeminacy'.[8] In such a way was Edward King, later Bishop of Lincoln, misunderstood. Even Archbishop Tait, who was by no means a disciple of Kingsley, could write to Gladstone in 1873 on King's appointment to the chair of pastoral theology in Oxford, 'What I fear is a way of dealing with doubts which does not settle them but silence them by authority. . . . I fear the Ultra High Church Party foster a womanly defence instead of a manly faith.'[9]

Kingsley, then, regarded manliness as using to the full all those attributes with which God had endowed the masculine character. To all mankind God had given eyes to see with, a mouth to speak with, a brain to think with: wilful blindness, fear of plain-speaking, and mental laziness were all weaknesses to be cured. But especially to man had God given physical strength— to fight in His service, to protect the weak, to conquer nature; and, no less important to Kingsley, as Mr. R. B. Martin has shown in his recent study,[10] it was man's duty to fulfil his sexual function by the procreation of children in that bliss which is the marital state. Celibacy was a crime against nature, a sin against God. As Martin has written, to Kingsley 'Roman Catholicism was really satisfactory for no one except a sex-starved woman'. He once wrote to a clergyman who was on the point of joining the Roman Church:

If by holiness you mean 'saintliness', I quite agree that Rome is the place to get *that*—and a poor pitiful thing it is when it is got—not

God's ideal of a man, but an effeminate shaveling's ideal—Look at St. Francis de Sale's [sic] or St. Vincent Paul's face—and then say, does not your English spirit loathe to be such a prayer-mongering eunuch as *that*? God made man in His image, not in an imaginary Virgin Mary's image.[11]

Kingsley was highly delighted by *Tom Brown's Schooldays* and he wrote to Hughes in 1857: 'I have puffed it everywhere I went, but I soon found how true the adage is that good wine needs no bush, for everyone had read it already. . . . I have had but one word, and that is that it is the jolliest book they ever read.' He went on to say that since effeminacy was the cause of sensuality, conversely 'pietists of all ages . . . never made a greater mistake . . . than in fancying that by keeping down manly θυμός, which Plato saith is the root of all virtue, they could keep down sensuality. They were dear good old fools.'[12]

Kingsley himself found the expression 'muscular Christianity' painful; and, in 1865, he preached a series of sermons in Cambridge on the subject of David, in the course of which he attempted to define this 'clever expression, spoken in jest'. He took the phrase to mean 'a healthful and manful Christianity; one which does not exalt the feminine virtues to the exclusion of the masculine', and proceeded to denounce the effeminate nature of early medieval (and much of modern Roman Catholic) religion with its preoccupation with saint-worship, mariolatry and the monastic life, in which monks unsexed themselves and assumed too often the worst features of the feminine character, and to compare this with late medieval chivalry which, with its consecration of 'the whole manhood . . . thus contained the first gem of that Protestantism which conquered at the Reformation'.[13]

This was the Kingsley who crossed swords with Newman: the other Kingsley was the man who came to Wellington College on the day of its opening and, seeing a group of dispirited boys with nothing in particular to do, threw off his coat and began playing leap-frog with Frederick Temple in the front quad.[14] In both these respects—the exaltation of manly high spirits and the preaching of a sort of religious chauvinism—Kingsley was the prophet of this revolution in educational ideals. One may even lay at his door the advocacy of the Spartan habit of taking cold baths first thing in the morning. In *Great Cities* he wrote:

> that morning cold bath, which foreigners consider as young England's strangest superstition, has done as much to abolish drunkenness, as any other cause whatever. With a clean skin in healthy action, and nerves and muscles braced by a sudden shock, men do not crave for artificial stimulants.[15]

At the same time, Kingsley belonged temperamentally to a world that was passing. Although he once attacked the effeminacy of the middle class by declaring that its education had been lacking in that experience of pain and endurance necessary to bring out the masculine qualities,[16] he was neither an advocate of the 'stiff-upper-lip' nor a believer in organised games. Kingsley was the very quintessence of Victorian emotionalism, shaking with sobs over other people's sorrows, leaping over the churchyard palings in surplice and hood in his exuberance to fight a heath fire which had broken out during morning service.[17] He loved to see boys physically active and alert—but not in playing cricket or football. Kingsley's real joy was nature—the lash of the rain on your cheek as you strode through the storm, the dust of the prairies swirling about you as you galloped under the sun, the raging seas off Hartland Cliffs, the thick wet mud of the flats round Finchampstead. If Kingsley had been a headmaster, he would have taught his boys to jump five-barred gates, to climb trees, to run like hares over difficult country; and there would have been nature rambles, a school museum stocked with specimens collected by the boys, science lessons and occasional lectures on hygiene and drains. Kingsley, living so near Wellington College to which he sent his son Maurice to escape the evils and absurdities of other public schools,[18] was sometimes a little of an embarrassment to Edward White Benson.

That this philosophy of life has affinities with the movement known as Christian Socialism is plain. Kingsley hated dirt and waste and tyranny and injustice quite as much as he loathed Roman Catholics and Tractarians. The beloved disciple of Maurice, he was soon drawn into the philanthropic and educational schemes which his 'Master', with J. M. Ludlow and Charles Mansfield, was devising to improve the lot of the London poor.

Among those who joined them was Thomas Hughes, then a young barrister, who had been deeply moved by Maurice's sermons as chaplain of Lincoln's Inn. Hughes and Kingsley had much in common. Both were liable to be swept off their feet in admiration for strong and sympathetic personalities and both tended to see in others more of themselves than was there. Both presented to their generation in their writings an idealised picture of clean, healthy manliness, displayed in Kingsley's muscular 'sea-dogs' or Hughes's biographical portraits of Alfred the Great, James Fraser, Daniel Macmillan, George Hughes, David Livingstone and—above all—the semi-autobiographical portrait drawn in *Tom Brown*.[19] Hughes's concept of manliness differs somewhat from Kingsley's. Hughes was a full-blooded patriot. He loved England, her lusty rural life, her ancient traditions and her toughness in adversity. He personified—much more than Kingsley did—the type he admired. For Hughes was a wholly lovable man; good-natured, transparently honest; ready to fight for what he believed to be right. And he always fought cleanly. His pugnacity never stooped to meanness, pettiness and coarse prejudice, all of which tarnish many of Kingsley's polemical writings. And Hughes's attitude to religion, best expressed in his moving *Religio Laici*—a simple exposition of the power of unquestioning hope and faith—was of a straightforward, manly, untheological cast, likely to appeal to the working men and women among whom so much of his life was spent—simple people who had neither time nor intellect for subtleties and theological disputes.

Hughes passionately believed in the moral and physical value of games-playing. As a boy he had grown up in an atmosphere of horseflesh, village cricket and fisticuffs; he had been educated, before going to Rugby, at a private school at Twyford which encouraged athletic prowess among the boys. At Rugby he had been captain of Bigside and head of the XI; and at Oxford he had played cricket against Cambridge and stroked the Oxford crew to victory in 1843. Games brought out the manly qualities, developed a spirit of companionship and taught one to control one's temper. And the finest of all sports was the ancient and noble science of self-defence. At the conclusion of his description of the famous combat between Tom Brown and

Charles Kingsley and Dandy

Thomas Hughes

'John Bull guards his pudding' from *Punch*,
31 December 1859

Slogger Williams, Hughes admitted that he had introduced this scene

> because I wanted to give you a true picture of what every-day school life was in my time, and not a kid-glove and go-to-meeting-coat picture; and partly because of the cant and twaddle that's talked of boxing and fighting with fists nowadays. . . . Fighting with fists is the natural and English way for English boys to settle their quarrels. . . . Learn to box, then, as you learn to play cricket and football. Not one of you will be the worse, but very much the better for learning to box well. Should you never have to use it in earnest, there's no exercise in the world so good for the temper, and for the muscles of the back and legs.
>
> As to fighting, keep out of it all you can, by all means . . . But don't say 'No' because you fear a licking, and say or think it's because you fear God, for that's neither Christian nor honest. And if you do fight, fight it out; and don't give in while you can stand and see.[20]

Hughes's code of living was this: Live dangerously—'English boys love danger'[21]; remember that the best work is done by people who get 'hard knocks and hard work in plenty, . . . and little praise or pudding, which indeed they, and most of us, are better without'.[22] England's ancient glory may be preserved as long as there are plenty of 'strapping healthy young men and women' to do her work and fight her battles.[23] By all means encourage animal spirits in the young. He recalled the old yeoman's advice to his mother: 'Bring 'em up sarcy, Marm. I like to see bwoys brought up sarcy.'[24] When Hughes lent his support to the venture of the Working Men's College in London, he became Major Commandant of their Volunteer Corps, leader of their games (it is interesting to note that he, too, had a taste for leap-frog)[25] * and the successful organiser of boxing classes, founded on the grounds that 'round shoulders, narrow chests, stiff limbs were . . . as bad as defective grammar and arithmetic, quite as easily cured and as much our business if we are to educate the whole man'.[26]

In common with other novelists of the period, Hughes liked to break his narrative from time to time by inserting short uplifting

---

* Hughes led a game of leap-frog on the lawn at Ludlow's and his house at Wimbledon when some of the members of the college were being entertained there.

sermons to point the moral of his story. A typical example of this occurs in *Tom Brown at Oxford* (1861), where the reader is treated to a discourse on muscular Christianity while Tom and his friends make their way to the suburbs of Oxford to visit Wombwell's travelling menagerie and to encounter their first great contest between 'town and gown'.

> Our hero [Hughes writes], . . was enrolled for better or worse in the brotherhood of muscular Christians, who at that time were beginning to be recognised as an actual and lusty portion of general British life. . . . I cannot see where he could in these times have fallen upon a nobler brotherhood. I am speaking of course under correction, and with only a slight acquaintance with the faith of muscular Christianity, gathered almost entirely from the witty expositions and comments of persons of a somewhat dyspeptic habit, who are not amongst the faithful themselves. . . . Nevertheless, had (our hero) been suddenly caught at the gate of St. Ambrose's College, by one of the gentlemen who do the classifying for the British public, and accosted with 'Sir, you belong to a body whose creed is to fear God, and walk 1000 miles in 1000 hours;' I believe he would have replied, 'Do I, sir? I'm very glad to hear it. They must be a very good set of fellows. How many weeks' training, do they allow?'

Tom, however, Hughes assures us, was no mere 'muscleman' —the type who 'seems to have no belief whatever as to the purposes for which his body has been given him, except some hazy idea that it is to go up and down the world with him, belabouring men and captivating women for his benefit or pleasure . . . .' The true muscular Christian

> has hold of the old chivalrous and Christian belief, that a man's body is given him to be trained and brought into subjection, and then used for the protection of the weak, the advancement of all righteous causes, and the subduing of the earth which God has given to the children of men.[27]

Hughes would have laughed if anyone had called him a 'seminal mind'. He was, however, very distressed to see in his late middle-age how sadly misdirected the glorification of sport had become. Professional sport—the child of the railways, free Saturday afternoons and the popular press—was anathema to him. And the keen competitive spirit which inter-school and inter-house matches had bred was something very much lower than the ideal of self-reliance which Hughes had sought to encourage. Thus in 1878 he planned his little colony in Tennessee where the Tom Browns without vocation should go to learn the lessons of co-operation in an atmosphere of pioneering endeavour, free from the degrading demands of modern competition.

In the 1850's and 60's, the works of Kingsley and Hughes were enjoying a wide vogue, arousing quite as much disapproval and savage criticism as they won acclaim. At the same time, in Cambridge, the Rev. Leslie Stephen, then a young Fellow of Trinity Hall, was creating a new type of university don. Stephen, unlike Hughes, was not one of nature's John Bulls. He had been a delicate boy at Eton under Dr. Hawtrey. Like Charles Mansfield, whose childhood days had been dogged by ill health and who celebrated his recovery by strenuously attempting 'to make up for the lost years by continuous activity',[28] Stephen became at Cambridge an enthusiastic rowing man, a cross-country runner and a walker of phenomenal powers. Perhaps because he was passed over by the Apostles' Club (the small, mildly esoteric club of the intellectual *élite* in Cambridge), more probably because he found himself a lonely young radical amidst a group of elderly and unsympathetic dons,* Stephen made a fetish of his athleticism. He went out of his way to invite the rowing men to his rooms, to show that he preferred to talk 'rowing' rather than to take part in academic discussion. He became famous in the university as a rowing coach: a sight worth seeing on the river in his old flannel shirt and patched trousers, with a vocabulary (when he was vexed) which was distinctly undonnish and unclerical. There was a touch of Thomas Hughes about him. Hughes wrote to his wife shortly after his best-seller had been published: 'I met Stephen on my way up, . . . he is almost the most enthusiastic party about Tom Brown whom I have met—It is certainly very odd how it suits so many different folk.'[29] And Stephen's vigorous patronage of the Volunteer movement in 1859 clearly shows the kinship. Maitland has recounted an episode when a party of undergraduates collected in Stephen's rooms to do rifle drill. The crash following the command 'Order

* Henry Latham was, of course, an exception. But he was eleven years Stephen's senior in age.

Arms!', more than once given by their zealous instructor, caused the undergraduate with rooms below Stephen's—a man not famed for intellectual diligence—to ask his gyp to complain of the noise. He did not get satisfaction.[30]

In fact, with Stephen and his friends, manliness rapidly became a cult. There was a moral value in hard walking. It prevented undergraduates from becoming effeminate or childishly mischievous. Spartan habits were encouraged—such as sleeping under an open window with snow drifting upon the bed.[31] Stephen, in time, outgrew his Christianity. The muscularity lasted longer. He became an Alpine mountaineer, and founder of the Sunday Tramps. But in the days when he was the centre of a group of amused, but admiring, undergraduates—those who were best in Stephen's world, the 'manly, affectionate young fellows'—his philosophy of life may be best expressed in Maitland's happy phrase: 'the Lord delighteth in a pair of sturdy legs'.[32]

These three men—Kingsley, Hughes and Leslie Stephen—were none of them schoolmasters. Yet if we put together the various ideals which they upheld in their writings or encouraged by their example, the result is this: the duty of patriotism; the moral and physical beauty of athleticism; the salutary effects of Spartan habits and discipline; the cultivation of all that is masculine and the expulsion of all that is effeminate, un-English and excessively intellectual. Thirty or forty years later, the same ideals or something very like them might be taken to be the creed of the typical housemaster of the typical public school.

3

To examine in detail how this came about would require a separate study of every public school—and many grammar schools—in England over the period from 1850 to 1890; for, clearly, what happened in one school is not evidence of what happened in other schools, and even a cursory study of the evidence suggests that the introduction of particular features of the cult of manliness took place in different schools at different times. Fortunately, however, Mr. Edward C. Mack in his work *Public Schools and British Opinion since 1860* has made a detailed study of most of the leading schools during this period and has in addition worked through the mass of literature—articles in educational journals, works of fiction, memoirs and biographies— to which this revolutionary change in educational ideals gave rise. On the whole—as one might expect—the innovations that took place in the major public schools were soon imitated in the lesser known schools, largely it would seem in response to popular demand. Local grammar schools and small day schools, likewise, began to adopt the dress, manners, terminology and institutions of the public schools.[1] The effect of the vast increase in schoolboy literature and of the wide circulation of the *Boys' Own Paper*—all so many variations on an original theme, using a common setting and speaking a common slang—is something difficult to measure but easy to speculate upon.

The work of G. G. Bradley at Marlborough between 1858 and 1870 is significant. A former Rugbeian of Arnold's time and a Rugby master who had been a colleague of Benson, he succeeded George Cotton who was called away from Marlborough to become Bishop of Calcutta. Cotton had already succeeded in saving Marlborough from collapse. He had fought the spirit of lawless independence by encouraging games and had lent his support to assistant masters who were prepared to join the boys in their games. Neither Cotton nor Bradley were muscular Christians. Bradley, indeed, was typical of his age—a fine scholar, a tough and determined autocrat, yet capable of extreme tenderness and kindness when the occasion demanded them. But for moral and disciplinary reasons, both men sought athletes as well as scholars in forming their staff, to carry out—as the historians of Marlborough have written—'their leading endeavour to make the playing fields the chief centre of outdoor attraction for the School'.[2] Bradley, for the same reason, 'took the keenest interest' in the school games, watching all their matches, once exhorting the Marlborough football captain who had left the field to consult his headmaster about stopping a match in which bad feeling had grown out of hand—"Go back; lick 'em first and talk afterwards; they'll say you funked 'em—funked 'em!"[3]

Frederick Temple's career as headmaster of Rugby (1857–69) was—after Arnold's—the most epoch-making in the history of the school; and he more than any other contemporary headmaster bore distinct traces of a kinship with Kingsley and Hughes. Like Kingsley, he was of West Country stock and proud of it. He had to make his own way in the world, being taught by his mother until the age of twelve in the intervals when he was not working as a labourer on his father's farm. He spent five years at Blundell's, winning one of the close scholarships to Balliol, where he amazed his contemporaries by his ability to live without complaining in conditions of extreme poverty and at the same time to win for himself the reputation of one of the finest scholars in the university. Temple, had he remained at Oxford, could have been a mathematician of the highest distinction. After six years as Principal of the experimental Training College at Kneller Hall and a short period in the Education Office, he succeeded to Arnold's place which had been occupied with more dignity than effectiveness by Dr. E. M. Goulburn. There followed twelve golden years. It is difficult to say exactly where the peculiar richness lay. There was a spate of new building; important advances were made in curricular reform, including the introduction of science teaching and the encouragement of music; a number of long-standing traditions which served no useful purpose and aggravated disciplinary problems were quietly abolished. What really made the period memorable was Temple himself. The famous description of his personality— 'granite on fire'—best expresses the extraordinary power which he wielded and the phenomenal devotion which he commanded from both masters and boys. He was rugged, brisk and forthright; utterly without cant or pose.

Although Matthew Arnold wrote in his testimonial on Temple's behalf that 'Mr. Temple, more than any other man whom I have ever known, resembles, to the best of my observation and judgment, my late father',[4] actually the differences between the two régimes were considerable. Dr. Percival, Bishop of Hereford, pointed out that whereas Rugby under Arnold had been—in Carlyle's phrase—'a temple of industrious peace', under Frederick Temple it became 'a nursery of the strenuous life'. 'It was a fine, strong, healthy, rough and vigorous, self-centred, and supremely self-confident society. We felt that we were breathing the strong and wholesome air which makes strong, brave and efficient Englishmen.'[5]

This was largely the effect of Temple's personality. Like Hughes and Kingsley, he had little sympathy for softness and delighted in animal spirits and lusty play. In his first term at Rugby he himself climbed all the elms in the Close to test whether they were safe for boys to do likewise.[6] On a visit to Wellington, when Benson pointed out to him a particularly fine beech tree, Temple surveyed it critically and then cried out

"I can't resist the temptation—look out!" and before Benson could turn round, Temple had made a rush and a leap, and was scrambling up the bole of the tree. In a few seconds Temple had succeeded in reaching the first stage whence the magnificent limbs diverge in all directions, and was grinning with delight at his success.[7]

At Rugby he would scoff at boys who opened gates on their walks and would give a personal demonstration of the art of hurdling; during football matches he would patrol the touch line roaring 'Take your drop! Take your drop!'[8]

Nevertheless, with Temple manliness never became a fetish. He was typically mid-Victorian in giving free vent to his emotions. He was often seen in tears. When cheerful—his usual demeanour—he beamed his pleasure on all around him. "A true Christian should be a happy man," he once said in a sermon, "and he should show his happiness in his face." [9] And if he encouraged games-playing, he always kept athletics firmly in their proper place. To him, as Mr. Kitchener has written, games

were part of the training of character; and the slackness that led a boy to drop a catch at a critical point of a match, or to shirk the game on the last day of a big football match, was as much to be expelled as that which led to false concords or incorrect reasoning . . . but no one ever doubted which the Headmaster put first.[10]

Athletes who neglected their work were obliged to sit in his study working while the important match for which they had been training was being played within earshot; the 'bloods' were never permitted to encroach upon the authority vested in the Sixth.

Percival thought that Rugby under Temple was 'perfect'. He may well have been right. The excesses of the era of 'godliness and good learning' and of the Spartan régime of the late Victorian public school were both avoided. It was an interesting transitional stage. Temple was sufficiently far-sighted, and powerful enough, to preserve the balance. Under successors who lacked his strength and his shrewdness the balance was soon tilted.

The headmaster who most determined the shape of things to come was Edward Thring. The rise of Uppingham to prominence during his headmastership of thirty-four years (1853–87) is an extraordinary story, the details of which may be found in the two major studies of his life and work by G. W. Parkin and J. H. Skrine. Thring himself had a wretched upbringing, enduring at first the excessive discipline of a harsh, unsympathetic father and a miserable private school at Ilminster, penal both in aspect and character; then he was let loose into the unlicensed debauchery of Long Chamber in the days of Dr. Keate. It is not surprising that Thring made it his life's ambition to prove to the world that boys brought up in decent surroundings under a sympathetic régime which offered outlets for their energy and talents derived more from their education and turned out to be better citizens than the products of the old system of public-school education. Thring was clearly of the muscular school. His nickname at Eton had been 'Little Die First', earned by his refusal to give way to a senior boy while playing fives between the buttresses of Eton chapel.[11] He excelled at football and cricket, remained an expert fives-player until late in life, and played all these games with the boys while he was headmaster of Uppingham.[12] * Although, like Hughes, he had a proper contempt for the excessive competitive spirit, he laid great stress on games at Uppingham, insisting that the school should be provided with first-rate playing fields and with a gymnasium, which, when it was opened in 1859, was the first to be possessed by any public school in England.[13]

Thring's special genius lay in his realisation that a school exists to educate *all* its pupils. Arnold's principle that 'the first, second and third duty of a schoolmaster was to get rid of unpromising subjects' was to Thring an entire misconception of a

* Diary entry 14 February 1862: 'I could not help thinking with some pride what headmaster of a great school had ever played a match at football before. Would either dignity or shin suffer for it? I think not.'

schoolmaster's function. To gear the system in favour of the bright intellects within the school was unfair to the average boy whose mental ability could never rise to the attaining of a university award and whose parents had a right to demand from the school an education adapted to his needs. More than that: it was blind. For every boy, however unpromising he might appear, had some latent talent. Every boy could do *something* well. It was the duty of the school to discover what this 'something' was and to develop the boy's ability so that he could offer his talent to the service of the community. Thus there should be a wide curriculum, opportunities for cultural pursuits, workshops for those whose ability lay in working with their hands. 'Accept the stupid and the fools to mercy'—until the schoolmaster took this petition of Jeremy Taylor to heart, his labours might produce a crop of fine scholars, but the system would still be a travesty of the ideal in which a place would be found for every boy, with work for him to do that he was capable of doing.

The wisdom of this may seem obvious to us: in the 1850's there was nothing commonplace about it at all. It was easy, too, for critics to see the dangers. For once a schoolmaster accepts the stupid and the fools to mercy, he may well feel it his duty to be kind to athletes, who prefer winning glory by brawn and physical skill to gaining the minimum of academic distinctions of which they might be capable. There may be no harm in that. The danger arises from the fact that boys naturally glorify athletic distinction and it is but a step from accepting the stupid and the fools to mercy to putting the physically gifted dullard on to a pedestal. Thring wrote in 1858: 'Many a boy whom we must put at a low level in school redeems his self-respect by the praise bestowed on him as a games-player, and the balance of manliness and intellect is more impartially kept.'[14] Even Skrine, a most devoted disciple, felt that Thring was playing with fire when he chose to preach to the boys on the dangers of over-intellectualism. Boys, indeed, are 'rarely tempted to sins of intellectuality'.[15]

Thring's influence was very powerful after the decade or so in which he had to battle with his Trustees to gain support for his reforms. After the successful experiment of the evacuation of Uppingham to Borth, he was listened to with respect by every headmaster in the country. From 1869, when his efforts to form a regular conference-system among headmasters of public schools first bore fruit, he became one of the leading spokesmen on the aims and methods of the public schools. And if one would seek for a brief exposition of what Thring believed the role of the public school in English society to be, the clearest definition comes in a letter which he wrote to Mr. G. W. Parkin, quoted by the recipient in his two-volume biography of his former headmaster:

> There is no point on which my convictions are stronger than on the power of boarding schools in forming national character. . . . There is a very strong feeling growing up among the merchant class in England in favour of the public schools; and hundreds go to schools now who thirty years ago would not have thought of doing so. The learning to be responsible, and independent, to bear pain, to play games, to drop rank, and wealth, and home luxury, is a priceless boon. I think myself that it is this which has made the English such an adventurous race; and that with all their faults . . . the public schools are the cause of this 'manliness'.[16]

Between 1860 and 1880, games became compulsory, organised and eulogised at all the leading public schools. It is interesting to observe that six of the most prominent headmasters of this period had all been boys together at Edward Wickham's private school at Hammersmith—Eagle House. They were George Ridding (Winchester), Montagu Butler (Harrow), A. G. Butler (Haileybury), G. J. Blore (King's School, Canterbury), E. C. Wickham (Wellington) and Edmond Warre (Eton). Of these, Ridding had something of Charles Wordsworth's enthusiasm for athletics, being a keen player of cricket and fives and setting a great value upon games 'as a means of instilling *esprit de corps* and discipline, and as a training of character'.[17] A. G. Butler of Haileybury worshipped Temple, under whom he had served for a few years, and clearly used Temple's Rugby as a model in his work. Montagu Butler, probably the greatest of the six, had been Charles Vaughan's favourite pupil and succeeded his master at the age of twenty-six. He was far too faithful to the tradition in which he had been reared and far too refined a scholar to over-value games, although he himself had been a cricketer of some distinction and shared to the full the spirit of rousing patriotism which was the most characteristic tone of the public schools in the late Victorian period. Harrow was already set in athletic ways before Butler became headmaster. In 1868 Butler stated to his colleagues that he discerned a great moral improvement amongst the boys, in particular stressing that there had been 'far fewer instances of . . . contempt for all that is not physical'.[18] In *The Hill* of H. A. Vachell, written nearly forty years later, such contempt pours forth from almost every page. (We may recall, for instance, the fate of 'Dirty Dick' Rutford, the unpopular housemaster of the 'Manor', who doesn't wash and isn't a gentleman, and eventually falls low enough to leave the 'Manor' to become 'Professor of Greek at a Scotch University'.)[19] The man most responsible for this was undoubtedly Edward Bowen, the Head of the Modern Side at Harrow and the most influential of Butler's housemasters. Bryce's portrait of Bowen in *Studies in Contemporary Biography* shows him to be a fine scholar and a great advocate of science teaching, but also a man whose admiration for Spartan qualities and pluck in games was so intense that his whole sense of values became distorted.[20]

Again, the influence of the staff rather than the headmaster was the factor which accounted for similar changes at Wellington under E. C. Wickham. Wickham was a pure classical scholar, by temperament a don not a schoolmaster, mildly interested in cricket but completely ignorant of any other game. He nevertheless thought it desirable to bring Wellington into line with the changes at work at other schools. The College fellows disappeared from the staff. In their place came a formidable body of 'Blues', soon capable of producing a Common Room XI or XV that could defeat any team of boys. Wickham allowed his subordinates a free hand. After twenty years (1873–93), little of Benson's Wellington remained. The various features which mark the advent of public-school muscular Christianity had all appeared— abundant playing-fields, 'cock' house matches, the establishment of a Rifle Corps, a *Carmen Heroidum*, a school mission, a flourishing Old Boys' Association.[21]

The most interesting example of all, however, is provided by the transformation of Eton under J. J. Hornby and Edmond Warre. Both Hornby and Warre had been fine athletes in their youth, Warre, indeed, exhibiting the tenets of the muscular Christian school in their purest form. He had been an undergraduate at Balliol from 1855 to 1859, securing a First in Mods

and Greats and becoming President of the University Boat Club.
His enthusiasm for rowing was quite as intense as Leslie
Stephen's. It was he, his biographer tells us, who 'convinced
Jowett of the social, and even moral, as well as physical, value of
rowing as part of College life'.[22] He was an ardent patriot and
vigorously seized upon the war-scare of 1859 (Hughes and
Stephen did likewise) as an excuse to foster military interests at
Oxford. He wrote to *The Times* in April 1859:

> I suppose that when next term begins there will be some thousands
> of us strapping young fellows up here, whose average height, weight,
> and activity might, I have no doubt, equal, if not excel, that of any
> regiment in H.M.'s service. In three years they will be scattered
> all over the Empire. What useful results might not ensue from
> their being instructed as well in the *ars militaris* as in the *ars
> logica*. And, as they stand, they would be a corps behind none in
> pluck and vigour to tackle invaders, be they from Europe, Asia,
> Africa, or America. Why should not the Royal Oxford University
> Volunteers be embodied and drilled in Port Meadow? . . . Two
> hours' drill two or three times a week would set us up bravely,
> and a blue flannel tunic and white trowsers would ruin nobody.[23]

Soon he had drill squads operating in the gardens of St. John's
before breakfast each morning, with musketry practice in the
afternoons. And in December 1859 there was a parade of 340
Oxford Volunteers in the quadrangle of All Souls, inspected by
the Prince of Wales, whose horse was as disquieted by the volleys
that greeted him as must have been the more elderly and sedate
occupants of the buildings around.

In 1860 Warre returned to Eton to take charge of a boarding
house in which would live the pupils of Dr. Balston, lately
appointed Fellow of Eton. He had to wait twenty-four years for
the headmastership; but during Hornby's time (1868–84) the
relations between the two men were so close and their ideals so
akin that Warre—who possessed all the vigour that Hornby
lacked—was soon recognised to be the power behind the throne.

In the 1850's Eton showed few signs of what was to come.
Games had little organisation and the staff stood aloof from what
little there was. There was no Rifle Corps, no house matches; a
little rowing and less cricket. Within a decade the whole spirit
changed. There was a flourishing Rifle Corps (founded in 1860,

Warre becoming Commandant in 1873), house cricket trophies, and activities on the river were 'revolutionised'.[24] The Eton Boating Song was written in 1863. At the same time, the eight sons of Lord Lyttelton were winning their athletic triumphs and earning the adulation of their fellows.

It was not all Warre's doing. The cricket triumphs were rendered more permanent when former prominent boy athletes —R. A. H. Mitchell and later Edward Lyttelton—were appointed to the staff. Doubtless many of the staff applauded the innovations if only to vex Oscar Browning who was vehemently outspoken in his detestation of athleticism. In William Cory, Warre found perhaps an unexpected ally. Cory, whom we met earlier as an incomparable teacher of the classics and as the poet who glorified the Platonic relationship between master and pupil in the verses of *Ionica*,[25] was in this respect true to his Plato. He delighted in manly θυμός; loved to see an inquiring, teachable mind combined with physical grace and muscular strength. Therefore he adored athletes with the same emotional abandon that he bestowed on his pupils: perhaps the love was more intense just because Cory was physically incapable of emulating their prowess:

> I cheer the games I cannot play;
> As stands a crippled squire
> To watch his master through the fray,
> Uplifted by desire.[26]

There were, of course, reservations. Cory could never love the athlete who had no brains. On the other hand, one of the most interesting features of Cory's writing and teaching was the combination of this love of physical activity with the expression of sentiments unashamedly jingoistic. Early in his life Cory had been influenced by the Christian Socialists, notably Thomas Hughes. In his diary for 1852, he described a tea-party for silk-weavers at Bethnal Green:

I made acquaintance with Hughes, the new Editor of our Journal, a tall, high-spirited, hearty, plain-spoken man who wears a wide-awake, and smokes a cigar. . . . This is the man I like best, as writer and talker, of our leaders—though he is less philosophical and refined than Ludlow.[27]

He was thrilled by the sight of soldiers marching, and would, when hearing a detachment of Guards passing his pupil-room on the way to Windsor Castle,

> throw down his pen and go down the little staircase, the boys crowding round him. 'Brats, the British Army!' he would say; and stand, looking and listening, his eyes filled with gathering tears, and his heart full of proud memories, while the rhythmical beat of the footsteps went briskly echoing by.[28]

In *Academus*, there is the verse:

> The wonder flushing in the cheek,
> The question many a score,
> When I grow eloquent and speak
> Of England and of war.

Cory wrote the verses of the Eton Boating Song; presented a House cricket cup in 1860. Edmond Warre, however, in his Spartan ways and a certain philistinism which he found difficult to conceal, represented the type of housemaster which was to become common in the schools in the following decades. He was suspicious of boys 'walking and talking'; distrusted the exceptionally brilliant; disliked 'strange' boys who showed no enthusiasm for games; advocated tough exercise as the panacea for all moral delinquencies.[29]

Both Warre and Cory later somewhat regretted the excesses of their youth. When Warre became headmaster there were predictions that Eton would 'lapse into inevitable decay'.[30] In fact, Warre concealed his athletic enthusiasm and took immediate steps to bolster up academic standards. Arthur Benson has observed that in his later years he seldom watched a school match and that most of the boys never knew that he had once been a great athlete.[31] Cory, in his diary, noted in 1875 that undergraduate life at Cambridge had sadly declined in its standards: 'In my day we were not in Cambridge great *boys*, as they have been since athletics prevailed over everything.'[32]

The changes were not always the result of deliberate policy. It is a truism that a school is as good as its staff; and the disappearance of the College fellows from the schools, following the abolition in 1877 of the obligation of resident fellows to remain celibate, was bound to have far-reaching effects. The men who wanted to become schoolmasters were often those who wanted to

226

continue playing the games which they had learnt at school to enjoy. There was a two-way traffic of athletes coming in and going out of the schools. Both school and undergradute life changed accordingly. 'Aren't they big babies?' was Pattison's comment on the behaviour of Boat Club enthusiasts in 1881,[33] and just as Mayor at Cambridge had fastened the blame on to Leslie Stephen, so Pattison found a victim in Jowett. He it was— in Pattison's opinion—who had diverted the attention of university reform away from the ideal of a 'home of higher research and advanced learning', preferring to see Oxford as a sort of 'super public school, with all its more unpleasing characteristics, its juvenilia, its newly-established-old traditions, its competitive games and competitive examinations, its lack of any real culture, its masculine Christianity'.[34]

Others thought that the new phenomenon was caused by boys staying too long at school, the result of the College reforms (at Cambridge) of 1856 which threw open entrance scholarships to non-residents. George Trevelyan, in a speech in the House of Commons in 1877, complained that this longer spell at school served only to teach boys how to waste time in idle pursuits:

> What else can be expected [he asked], when a young man at an age when his grandfather was fighting in the Peninsula or preparing to stand for a borough, is still hanging on at school, with his mind half taken up with Latin verses, and the other half divided between his score in the cricket field and his score at the pastry-cook's?[35]

It was inevitable that things should swiftly grow out of hand. Once the enthusiasm was fostered, who could hold it in check? As Percy Lubbock shrewdly observed, the common temptation of the schoolmaster is to pander to the popular demand and to attempt to create out of it noble lessons worth the teaching. 'He isn't the first ruler who has been helped in his governance by the use of a popular cult, by the discipline of a crowd-compelling faith.'[36]

4

If the schools were changing, so was England. Pattison may have deplored what he saw happening in Oxford, but when he wrote in his *Memoirs* of 'a deliverance from the nightmare which had oppressed Oxford for fifteen years',[1] the recovery of the university from the desolation caused by the *Tracts for the Times*, he was perceiving but one aspect of the decline of the religious influence and the advent of the new forces of secularism. The alliance of godliness and good learning was wholly natural at a time when the religious spirit dominated national life. The dissolution was inevitable when new enthusiasms arose to capture the imagination of the public and when the attention of scholars became increasingly preoccupied with studies which were not only non-religious but also menacing to the time-honoured teaching of the Christian church. In the 1860's godliness was veering towards manliness; at the same time, good learning was passing into the hands of the agnostics.

What were the young men thinking? The youthful aspirations of those who studied at the Oxford of Arnold, Keble and J. T. Coleridge or at the Cambridge of Westcott, Lightfoot, Benson and Hort were as intense and as varied as it is hoped youthful aspirations always will be. But the common assumption was that whatever the mission, it should be conducted within the Church and—almost equally certain—by an ordained member of the Church. The scholars took orders; eventually many of them received preferment. In the 1850's this was not so certain. At Oxford, Newman and Ward had given way to Jowett and Swinburne: in the next decade, the young men were reading J. S. Mill, listening to T. H. Green, emulating the ways of Walter Pater. Balliol was fast becoming the 'famous nursery of public men'. At Cambridge, the Apostles in the 1850's counted among their number Henry Sidgwick, Vernon Lushington, Howard Elphinstone, Vaughan Hawkins, G. V. Youl and Oscar Browning. By 1870 the brilliant young men, the Senior Classics and the Chancellor's Medallists, members of the Apostles and the Chit-Chat Club were wholly different from their predecessors of thirty years before. They read Swinburne in preference to Wordsworth;[2] * they shared the old enthusiasm for long walks, but preferred the more muscular demands of Alpine climbing or

* Certainly the favourite poet of Sidgwick and Gurney. See Walter Leaf's description of a séance at Newcastle when Sidgwick gave a recital of Swinburne's poems to relieve the tedium of listening to Moody and Sankey hymns.

MUSCULAR EDUCATION—THE PRIVATE TUTOR

Domestic. "PROFESSOR MAULEY, MA'AM!"

from *Punch, 26 May 1860*

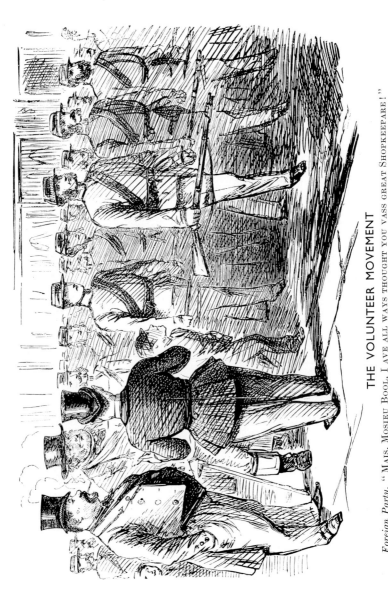

THE VOLUNTEER MOVEMENT

Foreign Party. "MAIS, MOSIEU BOOL, I AVE ALL WAYS THOUGHT YOU VASS GREAT SHOPKEEPARE!"
Mr. Bool. "SO I AM, MOOSSOO—AND THESE ARE SOME OF THE BOYS WHO MIND THE SHOP!—COMPRENNY?"

From Punch, 21 July, 1860

long-distance running. Their gods were Henry Sidgwick and Henry Jackson. Led by Sidgwick and Frederick Myers, almost all of them became keen inquirers in the field of psychical research. Such were the enthusiasms of that brilliant and influential circle that centred on Trinity—the Balfours, Walter Leaf, Edmund Gurney, Arthur Verrall, F. W. Maitland, Henry Butcher and George Prothero.

What had turned their gaze away from the Church? A number of factors has to be taken into account: the impact of the researches of Darwin on the process of natural selection, the coincidence of this revelation with the controversies that raged over Biblical criticism, associated with the names of Strauss, Colenso and *Essays and Reviews*. The effects of new scientific discoveries and of a new approach to the technique of rational inquiry have recently been analysed by Mr. Noel Annan and Professor Basil Willey in their contributions to the symposium *1859: Entering an Age of Crisis*. One had to be bold enough to push out of one's mind a whole host of inherited notions, to transcend the unedifying squabbles to which the onslaught on unquestioning faith and sacerdotalism had given rise, and to re-think the whole meaning and purpose of life. There was in existence a system whose weapons might be turned to fight the new battle— positivism. Darwin's book itself, maintains Mr. Annan, 'was simply another stage in the development of the positivist tradition. . . . There was . . . a disposition of mind towards interpreting all natural and human phenomena in positivist terms: and it was continually gaining strength.'[3] To the philosophers of their generation, the young men turned for help: to Mill, Spencer, Comte, Green and Sidgwick. Everything was worth dispassionate inquiry—the unknown regions of the spirit world, the mystery of the workings of the mind, the science of law and of human behaviour; and—as their enthusiasm waxed and the century grew older—the phenomenon of the group-mind, the telepathic powers of a Mrs. Piper or the Theosophy of Madame Blavatsky.

Walter Leaf has described his abandonment of the evangelical principles which he learnt at home:

> I had no sort of struggle, no remorse. I simply recognised that what I had been taught to say that I believed had no meaning whatever

for me. This did not mean that I became irreligious. No sort of materialism ever made any appeal to me: I was at best a theoretical Agnostic, but with a strong natural bent to Theism of a rather intimate sort. We at Cambridge were still under the dominant influence of Mill . . .[4]

Henry Sidgwick, initially disgusted by the 'virulency of un-reasoning orthodoxy', passed through a stage of admiring J. S. Mill and 'soaking' himself in Comte until his mind was made up not to 'barter my intellectual birthright for a mess of mystical pottage'.[5]

Leslie Stephen went through a similar experience. Writing of his Cambridge contemporaries in the late 50's and early 60's, he observed:

> Some of them shared my scepticism, but continued to be clergymen. . . . The average Cambridge don of my day was (as I thought and think) a sensible and honest man who wished to be both rational and Christian. He was rational enough to see that the old orthodox position was untenable. He did not believe in 'Hell' or in 'verbal inspiration' or the 'real presence'. He thought that the contro-versies upon such matters were silly and antiquated, and spoke of them with indifference, if not with contempt. But he also thought that religious belief of some kind was necessary or valuable, and considered himself to be a genuine believer.[6]

This passage reflects the dilemma of the scholars—they must have been many—who could neither renounce the faith of their fathers nor accept the prospect of ministering in a divided Church whose attitude to rational inquiry was often blind and reaction-ary. After all, the number of convinced agnostics was relatively small. Men like Huxley, W. K. Clifford, Leslie Stephen and John Morley cannot be taken as representative of the intellectual class of England in the 1860's and 70's. Seeley's *Ecce Homo*—a book which Huxley described as feeble and which Shaftesbury con-demned as 'the most pestilential book ever vomited from the jaws of Hell'—was the work which appealed most strongly to the waverers who rejected the proselytism of both churchmen and free-thinkers. To Richard Jebb, for instance, Christianity was acceptable; the Church—as it then stood—was not. He wrote in 1871 to his future wife

I hold my Christianity very much as you hold your belief in God. That is, the Christian morality and the Christian hope appear to me to be divinely adapted to the human heart; I accept them therefore as a divine revelation, on the same ground that supports your faith in a surrounding, protecting, disposing Power. But though I have this definite and constantly evident reason for my belief, I do not pretend or attempt to analyse those details of Christianity which the theological subtlety of centuries has formulated into dogmas of which the very language is unintelligible, without research, to minds of the present day. It is clear to me that the original, the authentic Christianity—the Christianity of the Apostles—was something a great deal simpler and plainer than the Christianity of any modern Church.[7]

Men who would naturally have taken orders ten or twenty years before, therefore, found that doubts and squabbles held them back. This was certainly so, for instance, with R. L. Nettleship, who wrote from Oxford in 1868 to his old headmaster Edward Thring:

I could not with a free conscience go into the Church as I am now or as I am likely to be for some time to come. To do such work requires a foundation of absolute certainty, and that I do not feel that I have. . . . I believe in nothing more strongly than in the necessity at a certain point of belief without proof. But I cannot crush reason and remain a man. I see quite enough at Oxford of doubting for doubting's sake to make me abhor such a thing myself; but the abuse of some must not be allowed to stigmatise all. I cannot help believing myself that there is far more in common between men of different theological opinions than they themselves will allow; that the truth is far wider than any one man or school can comprehend. But until this is more recognised and the Church is some way or other made really Catholic, there must be many who long to go in but are obliged to stay out.[8]

Here the ideal of godliness and good learning killed itself by its excesses. No doubt, too, the bringing up of children in households where the ideal was so firmly accepted that it was assumed to be as compelling to the children as it had been to the parents, planted the seeds of later revolt. Edward Lyttelton certainly believed this to be the cause of Arthur Benson's mild agnosticism. Arthur, as were all the Benson children, was introduced to the intellectual problems of the Christian faith before he had felt the need of a faith to sustain him in his life. 'The tendency was for the children, still in their teens, to discuss fundamental principles as if they were open questions. That is of course the surest way to deprive them of all interest and vitality.' [9] On some temperaments this might not have been damaging; on Arthur Benson's, Lyttelton maintained, the results were wholly unfortunate.

We should be careful not to exaggerate. Good learning never became universally agnostic; churchmen did not as a body abandon good learning. None the less, the new requirements for the study of Biblical criticism put theological researches beyond the reach of the average well-educated clergyman, and scholars—in their turn—saw the necessity of studying problems without reference to fundamental Christian beliefs.

Whereas Adam Sedgwick in 1837 had regarded his geological researches as an elucidation of scriptural truths and had stated that if he ever found his science 'interfere in any of its tenets with the representations or doctrines of Scripture he would dash it to the ground',[10] the aim of scholarship—in almost every branch of academic study—was now changing. The objective was not to demonstrate the truths of Christianity but to seek out truth, however unpalatable the result might be and however inimical to deeply-cherished beliefs. To Huxley it was 'intellectual degradation' to do otherwise,[11] to Mill, no one could be a great thinker 'who does not recognise that as a thinker it is his first duty to follow his intellect to whatever conclusions it may lead'.[12]

It must be emphasised that the pioneers of free-thought were *honest* doubters. Later—in the 1890's and in the Edwardian era —it became quite fashionable to be agnostic and to flout the moral convictions of mid-Victorian England. To do so was to demonstrate one's emancipation from an age which had set too high a store by respectability and which had over-emphasised the duty of conformity to the ideals of one's family, school or class. Men like Francis Newman and Henry Sidgwick, however, were not reacting against the lives and work of the great Christian moralists and teachers of their respective generations. They were no less eager than Arnold, or Lee, or Westcott, or Hort, in their advocacy of goodness and truth. The main differences between them were the premises on which they based their inquiries. The Christian moralist looked no further than the ethical precepts of his faith. Francis Newman, on the other hand, saw the weakness of this restriction, arriving at the conclusion that not only was much of Christian dogma utterly immoral but also that the divine justice as portrayed by the Scriptures was sometimes flagrantly unjust.[13] Once these Christian premises were discarded, the doors were opened on a vast expanse of unexplored terrain.

It was tempting to study the history and culture of other religions; to investigate the sources and the characteristics of primitive forms of worship; perhaps even to draw comparisons. What came about in the course of time was a revolution in the methods and technique of classical scholarship. Writing of the 1870's, Jane Harrison recalled: 'We Hellenists were in truth at that time a people that sat in darkness but we were soon to see a great light, two great lights: archaeology and anthropology. The classics were turning in their long sleep.' [14]

The study of history, too, was turning in its long sleep. Newman had reluctantly conceded that the greatest ecclesiastical historian to his knowledge was the infidel Gibbon. As Coulton reminded his generation, after Gibbon came Maitland,[15] who openly declared himself to be a 'dissenter from both [the English or the Roman], and from other churches'. Maitland, Sidgwick's most brilliant pupil, who later wrote of his master in terms as moving as any of the panegyrics inspired by Arnold or Prince Lee,[16] left Cambridge to become a lawyer and returned as an historian of law. In his *Roman Canon Law in the Church of England*, he refuted the comforting conclusions of the Anglican historians who had drawn up the Report of the Ecclesiastical Courts' Commission of 1883, and demonstrated to historians the truth of Bossuet's great maxim that 'the greatest intellectual failing is that of believing in things because we should like them to be, and not because we have seen that they are in fact'.[17]

These are old battles. If the issues are still real, at least the dust has now settled and the acrimony has everywhere subsided. In the late Victorian age, the way of reconciliation was not plain. Extremism bred extremism. Caught between two fires, the broad churchman might well have wondered to himself—how broad could the church become and still remain a church?

Indeed, the position of the Anglican church was especially vulnerable during these years. Haunted by the fear of disestablishment, its leaders were committed to an official policy of caution—a standpoint increasingly difficult to maintain in view of the presence of extremists both within and outside their body. Within the body, the excesses of sacerdotalists and bibliolaters antagonised the moderates and helped to spread indifference among the laity. Outside, ultramontanism, personified in the Cardinal Archbishop of Westminster who was bold enough to assert that 'dogma must overcome history', offered a secure refuge for those who fled in horror from the profane conclusions of modern scholars. At the opposite extreme, Secularism—the militant atheism of Holyoake and Bradlaugh—even if it affected the intellectual class in England only very remotely—provided for churchmen a terrible example of what materialist philosophy might ultimately lead to if allowed to proceed unchecked.

In the 1880's, while bitterness was passing, indifference was growing. F. J. A. Hort, in a letter written to Benson in December 1882, on the occasion of Benson's acceptance of the primacy, felt obliged to 'croak evil omens'.

> The convulsions of our English church itself [he wrote], grievous as they are, seem to be as nothing beside the danger of its calm and unobtrusive alienation in thought and spirit from the great silent multitude of Englishmen, and again of alienation from fact and love of fact: mutual alienations both.[18]

* * * * *

In time the Church opened her doors to her assailants. Neither Westcott nor Hort had been unduly alarmed by Darwin's *Origin of Species*;[19] Charles Gore, Henry Scott Holland and the other contributors to *Lux Mundi*, by their teaching on the Incarnation, attempted to reconcile revelation and evolution. Both the Cambridge theologians and the Oxford companions of Gore bravely tackled the problem of absorbing within the teaching of the church the new political doctrines of democracy and socialism, Westcott accepting the Presidency of the newly-founded Christian Social Union in 1889, and Gore and Scott Holland becoming Vice-Presidents of the central branch of the Union in the same year. New scientific discoveries, a new political philosophy, even new popular enthusiasms, received the blessing of the Church which now followed the lead given by Westcott in the series of sermons preached in Westminster Abbey, subsequently published under the title *Christus Consummator*.

'The consecration of the entire life of man'[20] is the phrase in which Archbishop Ramsey has recently summed up the doctrine of the Incarnation as it appears in Westcott's *Christus Consummator*. The 'deep sense of the sacredness of all the ordinary relations and the common duties of life' was the description applied in 1858 to the 'muscular Christian' element in Charles Kingsley's writings.[21] Might there not have been some connection between the two ideas? Could it not be said that 'muscular Christianity' itself—as preached and practised by so many clergymen and teachers in the last decades of the nineteenth century—was a manifestation of the Church's coming-to-terms with changing ideals and ideas, in this instance with the popular rage for manliness, athletics and belligerent imperialism?

Those who were charged with the duty of religious teaching in the public schools and whose ministry took them into the newly-founded Boys' Clubs in the East End of London were not likely to underrate the virtuous aspects of manliness, patriotism and sportsmanship. To have done so would have been to separate the pastor from his flock. And here perhaps is the chief explanation of Kingsley's intensity as a muscular Christian. He believed it to be his duty to attack the Tractarians by emphasising the greatest danger of their teaching—their belief in the priesthood as a separate, privileged order, empowered sacramentally to instruct the laity who were dependent upon their ministrations for their very salvation. To argue thus was to set up a priestly caste and to demonstrate this exclusiveness by adopting other-worldly ideals and unnatural habits of life. Both Coleridge and Arnold would have agreed with Kingsley here. But whereas Arnold, who was by nature a passionately intense moralist, strove to lift all men up to the highest standard of moral conduct, Kingsley preferred to keep his ideals more 'down-to-earth' and to deprecate any course of action which might threaten to separate clergy and laity. The ideal of a clergyman was to live within his flock as a member of that flock. He must be a man amongst men; he must be a model for his parishioners, setting the standard of paternal care, domestic piety, manly vigour and unselfish loyalty which he expected his neighbours to emulate.

By the end of the century, the social teaching of Kingsley, Maurice and Hughes had become respectable in the eyes of the Church. Gore and his followers, while admiring Pusey, Liddon and R. W. Church, spoke often in the language of the Christian Socialists. It was the Church's duty to establish missions, to found clubs and to sponsor co-operative enterprises to elevate and to educate the working classes. Cuddesdon, which Kingsley had thought to be the nursery of effeminate seminary priests, was now breeding eager, back-slapping curates who were to begin their ministry by working amongst the urban poor in the diocese of Southwark or in large parishes like Portsea and Leeds. Mission churches, whose ritual provoked the Kensitites * to passionate denunciation, sprang up alongside mission centres, equipped with footballs, boxing-gloves and a pair of parallel bars. Neither Kingsley nor Newman would have felt quite at home in this environment. But the larger part of the generation that succeeded these two great rivals would have cheerfully added both their names to the calendar of saints. Those who became leaders of the Church in the twentieth century could look back together at common youthful enthusiasms. William Temple might have recalled his admiration for Gore and his lifelong friendship with Albert Mansbridge; Cosmo Gordon Lang, a convinced High Churchman, wrote in later life that the book which had first inspired him to take Holy Orders was Mrs. Kingsley's biography of her husband.[22] C. F. Garbett, again a High Churchman, who had shrunk with distaste from the exaggerated heartiness of his Cuddesdon colleagues, 'always regarded Eversley, rather than Hursley, as his spiritual home'.[23]

The Church did not fully appreciate the Christian Socialists until after their deaths. On the other hand, the widespread popularity which the writings of Kingsley and Hughes immediately enjoyed suggests that they were the spokesmen of that large section of their countrymen who, in the middle years of the century, were beginning to feel that England's glory lay in

* The followers of John Kensit, the Protestant agitator, who as secretary of the Protestant Truth Society organised resistance to the growth of ritualistic practices, especially in the diocese of London.

her potentiality to develop under-developed countries and to civilise less civilised peoples, and who were quick to grasp that successful Empire builders needed a touch of Spartan discipline and Spartan qualities to equip them for their task. The belligerence and the militant patriotism which the Crimean War had called forth were indications of what was to come. The incident which best reveals these sentiments, however, was the war-scare of 1859.

The popular bogy was Napoleon III, and the event which convinced Lord Derby's government, and many of the whig opposition, that Napoleon was an unscrupulous conspirator was the Franco-Austrian war waged as a result of Napoleon's compact with Cavour at Plombières in July 1858. Towards the end of that year, there had been rumours of the danger of imminent invasion from France; on the outbreak of the war in Italy, anti-French sentiment reached its peak. Dr. Beales, in a recent examination of the diplomatic manœuvres of these years, observes that the Volunteer Rifle Club movement had by February 1860 enrolled 60,000 men.

> Form! Form! Riflemen form!
> Ready, be ready to meet the storm!
> Riflemen, riflemen, riflemen form!

Thus wrote Tennyson in a poem, published in *The Times* in May 1859. Despite the aggressive language used, the general popular sentiment was in favour of neutrality.[24] But the enthusiasm which the Volunteer movement evoked, seen already in the hearty manner in which it was embraced by Thomas Hughes, Leslie Stephen and Edmond Warre, suggests that sabre-rattling had its attractions in the middle years of the century. One of the most noticeable features of this time was a *malaise*, becoming gradually more widespread among the middle classes, indicating increasing dissatisfaction with conventional morality and the accepted canons of taste and conduct: a craving for revolt, a little blood-letting, a new cause to be passionately embraced; almost as if the middle classes were growing weary of the very security which they had striven for and of the comforts they had saved up to enjoy. There was something elevating in living a little dangerously.

A change in the hopes and ideals of the middle classes meant a corresponding change in the schools to which their sons were sent. It had been so in the 1820's when the period of Arnoldian reform set in. And when the majority of the patrons of the schools ceased to pin their hopes on godliness and good learning and came to agree with Squire Brown that what really mattered was that their sons should turn out to be 'brave, helpful, truth-telling' Englishmen, it was so again.

* * * * *

Both ideals were grand conceptions. We delude only ourselves if we laugh them to scorn. Both enunciated a code of living which was unselfish, active, honourable, useful and good. Both suffered in application from ruthlessness, arrogance, lack of sympathy and perhaps an undue emphasis on the virtues of success. The worst educational feature of the earlier ideal was the tendency to make boys into men too soon; the worst feature of the other, paradoxically, was that in its efforts to achieve manliness by stressing the cardinal importance of playing games, it fell into the opposite error of failing to make boys into men at all. Indeed, one might go further: its code of living became so robust and patriotic in its demands that it could be represented as reaching its perfection in a code of dying. We may recall the closing pages of *The Hill*, when Henry Desmond's death in fighting for his country is made the subject of a moving sermon.

> To die young, clean, ardent; to die swiftly, in perfect health; to die saving others from death, or worse—disgrace—to die scaling heights; to die and to carry with you into the fuller ampler life beyond, untainted hopes and aspirations, unembittered memories, all the freshness and gladness of May—is not that cause for joy rather than sorrow?[25]

This was, indeed, the ultimate of the ideal. The time at which the sentiment was expressed—1905—does not surprise us. If, however, we set beside this an equivalent passage to demonstrate the perfect expression of the earlier ideal, we may find what we seek in eight lines written nearly two centuries before the period in which we have confined our study. These lines—from Milton's *Paradise Regained*—graced the walls of F. W. Farrar's dressing-

room beneath a portrait of the poet.[26] To the author of *Eric; or
Little by Little* they were a constant source of inspiration.

> When I was yet a child no childish play
> To me was pleasing, all my mind was set
> Serious to learn and know, and thence to do
> What might be public good; myself I thought
> Born to that end, born to promote all truth,
> All righteous things; therefore, above my years,
> The law of God I read, and found it sweet,
> Made it my whole delight.

Abbreviations

used in the notes

Bodleian	*Bodleian Library, Oxford. Department of Western MSS. Dep. Benson.*
Chetham's	*Chetham's Library, Manchester.*
Diary	*Trinity College Library, Cambridge. Benson MSS. Box III, no. 1.*
John Rylands	*John Rylands Library, Manchester.*
K.E.S. MSS.	*King Edward's School, Birmingham.*
M.C.L.	*Manchester Central Library.*
T.C.C.	*Trinity College Library, Cambridge.*
W.C. MSS.	*Wellington College Archives.*

The place of publication of books referred to in the notes is London, unless otherwise stated.

Notes

Introduction

1. J. H. Overton and E. Wordsworth, *Christopher Wordsworth, Bishop of Lincoln* (1890), 217.
2. T. Arnold, *Introductory Lectures on Modern History* (1874), 16–17.
3. *Ibid.*, 38.
4. *Ibid.*, 39.
5. R. T. Davidson and W. Benham, *The Life of A. C. Tait* (1891), I.121.
6. J. H. Overton and E. Wordsworth, *op. cit.*, 364.
7. A. Westcott, *Life and Letters of B. F. Westcott* (1903), I.50.
8. E. C. Mack, *Public Schools and British Opinion 1780–1860* (1938), 143–69.
9. R. L. Archer, *Secondary Education in the Nineteenth Century* (1921), 5.
10. N. Hans, *New Trends in Education in the Eighteenth Century* (1951), 13.
11. *Ibid.*, 14.
12. A. P. Stanley, *The Life and Correspondence of Thomas Arnold* (1858 edn.), I.152–4.
13. N. G. Annan, 'The Intellectual Aristocracy', in *Studies in Social History. A Tribute to G. M. Trevelyan*, edited by J. H. Plumb (1955), 247.
14. N. G. Annan, *Leslie Stephen, His Thought and Character in Relation to his Time* (1951), 1.
15. *Ibid.*, 110.
16. R. W. Church, *The Oxford Movement, 1833–1845* (1891), 13.
17. Stanley, *op. cit.*, I.4.
18. Reginald Farrar, *Life of F. W. Farrar* (1904), 4.
19. (Mrs. Kingsley), *Charles Kingsley. His Letters and Memoirs* (1877), I.8.
20. R. E. Prothero, *Life and Letters of Dean Stanley* (1894), I.89.
21. Katharine Lake (editor), *Memorials of William Charles Lake, 1819–1894* (1901), 158.
22. Stanley, *op. cit.*, I.8–9; J. T. Coleridge, *A Memoir of the Rev. John Keble* (1869), I.10–12.
23. W. Tuckwell, *Pre-Tractarian Oxford* (1909), 19.
24. E. S. Purcell, *The Life of Cardinal Manning* (1896), I.39–40.
25. W. C. MSS. C. W. Penny, 'Rough Memoranda about Abp. Benson', 50. He comments: 'I think that Hort's Life shows that

241

the whole atmosphere of Trin. Coll. Camb. in Benson's undergraduate and early fellowship days was imbued with Maurice's
views of theology.'

26. Mark Pattison, *Memoirs* (1885), 236–7.
27. C. R. Sandars, *Coleridge and the Broad Church Movement* (1942), 14.
28. J. H. Newman, *Apologia pro vita sua*, Pt. III, c. 1. In Wilfrid Ward's edition (1913), 113.
29. *Apologia*, 173. See also Owen Chadwick, *From Bossuet to Newman. The Idea of Doctrinal Development* (Cambridge 1957), 83–95.
30. E. S. Purcell, *op. cit.*, II.250. Compare John Morley, *Life of W. E. Gladstone* (1903), I.207.n. For Arnold's high opinion of Butler, see Stanley, *op. cit.*, II.56.n.
31. Morley, *op. cit.*, III.464.
32. T. Mozley, *Reminiscences chiefly of Oriel College and the Oxford Movement* (1882), I.210.
33. R. W. Church, *The Oxford Movement*, 22. Church is describing the influence of Wordsworth on John Keble.
34. Stanley, *op. cit.*, I.13.
35. F. J. Woodward, *The Doctor's Disciples* (1954), 84.
36. L. Elliott-Binns, *Religion in the Victorian Era* (1936), 104.
37. A. Westcott, *Life of Westcott*, I.115.
38. A. F. Hort, *Life and Letters of F. J. A. Hort* (1896), I.7.
39. R. Farrar, *op. cit.*, 4.
40. Basil Willey, *Nineteenth Century Studies* (1949), 1. See the references to J. S. Mill's *Dissertations and Discussions* (1867), I.330, 394, 403.
41. E. G. Sandford (editor), *Memoir of Archbishop Temple* (1906), II.424. See also 472, 656, 670.
42. J. H. Newman, *Apologia*, 195.
43. Coleridge, *Aids to Reflection* (Bohn's edition, 1884), 66. Compare Arnold in the Appendix to his Inaugural Lecture (*Introductory Lectures*, 39) where he writes that the end of societies 'should be good rather than truth'. The whole question of the relative positions of goodness and truth in Arnold's thought is discussed by F. J. Woodward in *The Doctor's Disciples*, chapter one.
44. *Aids to Reflection*, 115.
45. *Ibid.*, 124.
46. Sandars, *op. cit.*, 133. Compare also H. P. Liddon, *The Life of E. B. Pusey* (1894–8), I.44. Liddon writes of 'the moral lassitude of Byron'.
47. J. H. Newman, *Apologia*, 120.
48. T. Mozley, *Reminiscences of Oriel College and the Oxford Movement*, I.218.
49. W. C. MSS. C. W. Penny's Journal, II.30.
50. V. H. H. Green, *Oxford Common Room. A Study of Lincoln College and Mark Pattison* (1957), 129.

51. G. M. Young, *Life of Arnold. Victorian England. Portrait of an Age* (1949), 8.
52. Stanley, *op. cit.*, I.27.
53. *Ibid.*, I.39.
54. A. R. Ashwell and R. G. Wilberforce, *Life of Samuel Wilberforce* (1880), I.71.
55. A. R. Ashwell, *op. cit.*, I.19.
56. T. Arnold, *Introductory Lectures on Modern History*, 30–1.
57. S. T. Coleridge, *Aids to Reflection*, 193.
58. A. Westcott, *Life of Westcott*, II.328.
59. K. E. S. MSS. Box 4/4, no. 4.
60. N. G. Annan, 'The Intellectual Aristocracy', in *Studies in Social*
61. See Davidson and Benham, *op. cit.*, I.207.
    History, *op. cit.*, 243.
62. For a fuller discussion of this, see my *History of Wellington College 1859–1959* (1959), 91–2.
63. E. W. Watson, *Life of Bishop John Wordsworth* (1915), 33.
64. W. C. MSS. C. W. Penny, 'Rough Memoranda about Abp. Benson', 77–8. See also E. W. Watson, *op. cit.*, 34. He mentions that Benson's appointment of John Wordsworth (later Bishop of Salisbury) to his staff 'was to have important results for both, and for the English church'.
65. *Ibid.*, 8; cf. 80. See also W. C. MSS., Penny's Journal, I.16.
66. Reginald, Viscount Esher, *Ionicus* (1923), 58–9.

Chapter I

SECTION 1

1. N. Wymer, *Dr. Arnold of Rugby* (1953), 114–17.
2. A. P. Stanley, *Life of Arnold* (1858), I.138.
3. T. Hughes, *Tom Brown's Schooldays* (Oxford edn. 1921), 151–2.
4. N. Wymer, *op. cit.*, 113.
5. W.C. MSS. VII.14.
6. R. Farrar, *op. cit.*, 143.
7. See, for instance, G. F. Lamb, *The Happiest Days* (1959), 213–16.
8. T. Balston, *Dr. Balston at Eton* (1952), 51–2.
9. W. R. Fremantle, *Memoir of the Rev. Spencer Thornton* (1850), 11,15.
10. T. Arnold, *Sermons* (1829–45), IV.13.
11. *Ibid.*, II.122.
12. *Ibid.*, V.65–7.
13. T. Arnold, *Miscellaneous Works* (1858), 331.
14. Basil Willey, *Nineteenth Century Studies* (1949), 54.
15. Stanley, *op. cit.*, I.69.
16. *Ibid.*, I.100.
17. *Ibid.*, I.88 (note).

18. A. Whitridge, *Dr. Arnold of Rugby* (1928), 9–12.
19. W. Tuckwell, *Pre-Tractarian Oxford*, 102.
20. R. Farrar, *Life of F. W. Farrar*, 19–20.
21. R. E. Prothero, *Life of Stanley*, I.68.
22. A. Westcott, *Life of Westcott*, I.248.
23. (Mrs. Kingsley), *Charles Kingsley*, II.26–7.

SECTION 2

1. T. W. Bamford, *Thomas Arnold* (1960), 26. Stanley, *op. cit.*, I.202–3.
2. Stanley, *op. cit.*, I.201.
3. Bamford, *op. cit.*, 39.
4. For a discussion of this phenomenon, see E. C. Mack, *Public Schools and British Opinion, 1780–1860*, 78–85.
5. Arnold, *Sermons*, II.124–5.
6. E.g. T. Hughes, *Tom Brown's Schooldays*, 133–4; 175; 177–93; 268–9. E. C. Mack and W. H. G. Armytage, *Thomas Hughes. The Life of the Author of Tom Brown's Schooldays* (1952), 16–18. T. W. Bamford, *op. cit.*, 78, 179. T. Hughes, *Memoir of a Brother* (1873), 21. E. C. Mack, *op. cit.*, 238–9.
7. Stanley, *op. cit.*, I.220.
8. *Ibid.*, I.223.
9. Bamford, *op. cit.*, 108.
10. Stanley, *op. cit.*, I.86.
11. *Ibid.*, I.98.
12. *Ibid.*, I.100.
13. *Ibid.*, I.95.
14. A. G. Bradley, A. C. Champneys, J. W. Baines, *A History of Marlborough College* (1923), 168.
15. H. P. Liddon, *Life of E. B. Pusey* (1894–8), I.15.
16. E. C. Mack, *Public Schools and British Opinion 1780–1860*, 93.n.; 98.
17. T. W. Bamford, *op. cit.*, 155–8.
18. T. Arnold, *Sermons*, V.66.
19. E. C. Mack, *op. cit.*, 217.
20. G. F. Lamb, *The Happiest Days*, 42–3.
21. F. W. Farrar, *Eric; or Little by Little* (1914 edn.), 87–9.
22. *Ibid.*, 94.
23. Stanley, *op. cit.*, I.143.
24. W.C. MSS. VIII, no. 7, p. 4.
25. W.C. MSS. Benson Notebook, 5–7.
26. W.C. MSS. VIII, no. 12, D. Newsome, *A History of Wellington College*, 108–10.
27. W.C. MSS. X, no. 15. D. Newsome, *op. cit.*, 166–70.
28. See D. Newsome, *op. cit.*, 187, 242–3.
29. T. Mozley, *op. cit.*, I.113. See also K. Lake (editor), *Memorials of W. C. Lake*, 7.

30. *Ibid.*, I.113–14.
31. (Mrs. Kingsley), *Charles Kingsley*, II.5. Kingsley shared the horror of falsehood. See *Ibid.*, II.400.
32. Stanley, *op. cit.*, I.94.
33. T. Hughes, *Memoir of a Brother* (1873), 32–3.
34. T. W. Bamford, *op. cit.*, 49–53.
35. See F. J. Woodward, *The Doctor's Disciples*, chapter one, for a discussion of this point, especially the relation of truth to goodness in Arnold's writings.
36. F. W. Farrar, *Eric; or Little by Little*, 132.
37. E. S. Purcell, *Life of Manning*, I.9.
38. T. C. C. Benson, MSS. III, Vol. I.25; A. C. Benson, *Life of E. W. Benson*, I.45.
39. A. C. Benson, *op. cit.*, I.213; D. Newsome, *op. cit.*, 159.
40. *Ibid.*, I.213.

SECTION 3

1. Sir Francis Doyle, *Reminiscences and Opinions* (1886), 48.
2. E. C. Mack, *op. cit.*, 297.
3. Stanley, *op. cit.*, I.29.
4. *Ibid.*, I.78.
5. R. J. Campbell, *Thomas Arnold* (1927), 59.
6. E. C. Mack, *op. cit.*, 255.
7. T. W. Bamford, *op. cit.*, chapter twelve, especially p. 141.
8. T. Arnold, *Sermons*, II.52–3.
9. Stanley, *op. cit.*, I.97.
10. T. Arnold, *Miscellaneous Works* (2nd edn. 1858), 378.
11. Stanley, *op. cit.*, I.71.
12. A. Westcott, *Life of Westcott*, I.224.
13. A. C. Benson, *The Upton Letters* (1906), 8.
14. R. Davidson and W. Benham, *Life of A. C. Tait*, I.113.
15. (Mrs. Clough), *Poems and Prose Remains of Arthur Hugh Clough* (1869), I.56–7; 68.
16. *Ibid.*, 17–18.
17. K. Lake (editor), *Memorials of W. C. Lake*, 155.
18. This is a résumé of two sermons in Arnold's *Sermons*, IV (nos. 2 and 3), 19–30.
19. R. E. Prothero, *Life of Stanley*, I.105.
20. *Rugby School Register*, 1 April 1675–October 1857 (Rugby, 1923), XXI–XXII.
21. *Ibid.* These figures are calculated from the *Admission Register of Rugby School* from the year 1825, for boys who entered the school in that year were taught by Arnold and won their scholarships or entered the university during the years of Arnold's headmastership.
22. F. J. Woodward, *The Doctor's Disciples* (1954).

23. E. C. Mack, *op. cit.*, 323–4.
24. T. Hughes, *Memoir of a Brother*, 40–1.
25. K. Lake (editor), *Memorials of W. C. Lake*, 7–8.
26. *Ibid.*, 12.
27. R. J. Campbell, *Thomas Arnold*, 58; G. F. Bradby, *The Brontes, and other Essays* (1932), 54.
28. E. C. Mack, *op. cit.*, 301.
29. *Ibid.*, 253.
30. Prothero, *op. cit.*, I.69.
31. See Basil Willey, *More Nineteenth Century Studies* (1956), 171–4.
32. J. Fitch, *Thomas and Matthew Arnold and their influence on English Education* (1897), 269–71.
33. F. J. Woodward, *op. cit.*, 232.
34. Stanley, *op. cit.*, I.33.
35. F. J. Woodward, *op. cit.*, 32.
36. (Mrs. Clough), *Poems and Prose Remains of A. H. Clough*, II.170.
37. *Ibid.*, I.10–11.
38. E. G. Sandford (editor), *Memoirs of Archbishop Temple, by seven friends* (1906), I.52, n.2. See also Davidson and Benham, *Life of A. C. Tait*, I.72.
39. *Ibid.*, I.53.

SECTION 4

1. See F. W. Farrar, *Essays on a Liberal Education* (1867).
2. See especially, Brian Simon, *Studies in the History of Education 1780–1870* (1960), chapter two.
3. G. F. Lamb, *op. cit.*, 165.
4. N. Hans, *New Trends in Education in the Eighteenth Century*, 38–41.
5. F. D. How, *Six Great Schoolmasters* (1905), 117.
6. K. Lake, *op. cit.*, 5.
7. T. Arnold, *Miscellaneous Works*, 342–6.
8. *Ibid.*, 350.
9. *Ibid.*, 354–5.
10. Stanley, *op. cit.*, I.216–7.
11. Arnold, *Miscellaneous Works*, 360.
12. T. Balston, *Dr. Balston at Eton*, 47–59.
13. A. C. Benson, *Life of E. W. Benson*, I.214.
14. *Ibid.*, I.215.
15. W.C. MSS. Benson Notebook, 40–1.
16. A. Whitridge, *Dr. Arnold of Rugby* (1928), 114.
17. D. Newsome, *op. cit.*, chapter three.
18. A. Whitridge, *op. cit.*, 119–20.
19. (Mrs. Kingsley), *Charles Kingsley*, II.162–3.
20. J. H. Overton and E. Wordsworth, *op. cit.*, 335–6.
21. A. Westcott, *op. cit.*, I.15–16.

22. (Mrs. Creighton), *Life and Letters of Mandell Creighton* (1905), I.7.
23. T. C. C. Benson, MSS. III, Vol. 1,4.
24. A. Whitridge, *op. cit.*, 90.
25. W.C. MSS. I.38.
26. *Ibid.*, IX.9.
27. E. Graham, *The Harrow Life of Henry Montagu Butler* (1920), 133; Charlotte Leaf, *Walter Leaf* (1932), 48; A. Westcott, *op. cit.*, I.174.
28. A. Westcott, *op. cit.*, I.269.

SECTION 5

1. Stanley, *op. cit.*, I.24.
2. T. Hughes, *Tom Brown's Schooldays*, 241.
3. W. Benham (editor), *Catharine and Craufurd Tait. A Memoir* (1879), 30–1.
4. A. R. Ashwell and R. G. Wilberforce, *Life of Samuel Wilberforce* (1880), I.8–9.
5. *Ibid.*, 13–14.
6. *Ibid.*, 17.
7. N. Annan, *Leslie Stephen*, 13. See also Charles Smyth, 'The Evangelical Discipline', in *Ideas and Beliefs of the Victorians*, edited H. Grisewood (1949), 103.
8. W. Benham (editor), *Catharine and Craufurd Tait*, 252.
9. *Ibid.*, 257–64.
10. T. C. C. Benson MSS. Box 1.
11. A. C. Benson, *Life of E. W. Benson*, I.602.
12. T. Hughes, *Tom Brown's Schooldays*, 133.
13. *Ibid.*, 135.
14. W.C. MSS. III.22,23.
15. A. C. Benson, *op. cit.*, I.307.
16. Hughes, *op. cit.*, 81.
17. A. Whitridge, *op. cit.*, 9.
18. G. F. Lamb, *op. cit.*, 223–4.
19. W.C. MSS. Wickham Records (edited G. F. H. Berkeley), II.20–24.
20. P. Green, *Kenneth Grahame 1859–1932* (1959), 34, 39.
21. Prothero, *op. cit.*, I.57.
22. T. Hughes, *Tom Brown's Schooldays*, 275.
23. T. G. Bonney, *Memories of a Long Life* (privately printed, Cambridge 1921), 12.
24. T. W. Bamford, *op. cit.*, 69.
25. See pp. 116–7.
26. *Apologia pro vita sua*, 135.
27. (Mrs. Kingsley), *Charles Kingsley*, II.267.
28. E.g. W.C. MSS. Penny's Journal, I.34–6.
29. (Mrs. Kingsley), *op. cit.*, I.24.

30. W.C. MSS. Wickham Records (edited G. F. H. Berkeley), II.5.
31. V. H. H. Green, *Oxford Common Room*, 137.
32. *Letters and Journals of William Cory, author of 'Ionica'*, selected and arranged by F. Warre Cornish (Oxford 1897), 15.
33. Reginald, Viscount Esher, *Ionicus*, 16.
34. F. Compton Mackenzie, *William Cory* (1950), 18.
35. *Letters and Journals, op. cit.*, 233.
36. *Ibid.*, 112.
37. P. Lubbock, *Shades of Eton* (1929), 87–8.
38. F. Compton Mackenzie, *op. cit.*, 18.
39. *Ibid.*, 44.
40. *Letters and Journals of William Cory*, 186.
41. A. C. Benson, *The Leaves of the Tree* (1911), 271.
42. Stanley, *op. cit.*, I.19.
43. Horace, *Satires*, I.v.41–4.

SECTION 6

1. A. Westcott, *op. cit.*, I.355.
2. *Ibid.*, II.28.
3. *Ibid.*, II.253.
4. G. Faber, *Jowett. A Portrait with Background* (1957), 359.
5. A. R. Ashwell and R. G. Wilberforce, *op. cit.*, II.197.
6. A. Westcott, *op. cit.*, I.145.

Chapter II

SECTION 1

1. Lytton Strachey, *Eminent Victorians* (1948 edn.), 7.
2. ΣΑΛΠΙΣΕΙ (*Salpisae*), *A Memorial Sermon preached after the death of the Rt. Rev. James Prince Lee . . .*, by E. W. Benson. 2nd edn., edited by J. F. Wickenden (1870).
3. B. F. Westcott, *Teacher and Scholar: A Memory and a Hope* (Birmingham 1893).
4. The original of Sutton's article is in the Manchester Central Library (Local History section), attached to a letter from Mr. T. C. Greenwood to Mr. Sutton, dated 11 August 1891. The original article was somewhat longer than the one actually printed, and the deletions, with Greenwood's comments, are interesting.
5. A. C. Benson, *Life of E. W. Benson*, I.39–40. The same story is told in A. C. Benson's *The Trefoil* (1923), 176–7, where the clergyman is identified as a Mr. Phillpotts, nephew of the Bishop of Exeter.
6. *Notes and Queries*, 4th Series, XII.145.

SECTION 2

1. K.E.S. MSS. Box. 4/4.
2. *Salpisae*, 31.
3. *Ibid.*, 31.
4. K.E.S. MSS. Box 4/4.
5. Stanley, *Life of Arnold*, I.220.
6. *Manchester Guardian*, 27 January 1912. Article by G. W. E. Russell.
7. Affidavit of Mr. Joseph Hodgson (surgeon) in *The Queen* v. *Thomas Gutteridge*. See report in *Aris's Birmingham Gazette*, 29 November 1847.
8. *Salpisae*, 7–8.
9. *Ibid.*, 40–1.
10. *Ibid.*, 35.
11. T. C. C. Benson MSS. III, Vol. I.13.
12. A. Westcott, *Life of Westcott*, I.248–9.
13. E. W. Benson, *Our Archbishop's Counsels* (Speeches to the boys of King Edward's School) (Birmingham 1883), 19.
14. K.E.S. MSS. Box 4/4.
15. K.E.S. MSS. Governors' Order Book, 1832–41, 366. A good deal about Michell's career at Lincoln can be found in V. H. H. Green, *op. cit.*, esp. 153–8.
16. Stanley, *op. cit.*, II.135.
17. Rugby School, Temple Reading Room; printed in part in N. Wymer, *Dr. Arnold of Rugby*, 171.

SECTION 3

1. T. W. Hutton, *King Edward's School, Birmingham* (Oxford 1952), 7.
2. *Ibid.*, 8, n.1.
3. *Ibid.*, 84. The full proposals of Dr. Jeune can be found in Appendix D of Mr. Hutton's book, pp. 223–9.
4. *King Edward the Sixth's Magazine*, No. 1, September 1842, 4.
5. T. W. Hutton, *op. cit.*, 121–2.
6. A. C. Benson, *op. cit.*, I.26.
7. T. C. C. Benson MSS. III, Vol. I.3.
8. K.E.S. MSS. Governors' Order Book, 477–9.
9. K.E.S. MSS. Box 5/14.
10. *Ibid.*

We may gain some picture of the family background of Prince Lee's pupils from a useful statistical chart compiled by Lee's successor —E. H. Giffard—for publication in the *Transactions of the National Association for the Promotion of Social Science* (1857, p. 131). Although these figures relate to 1857, nine years after Lee had left, there is no reason to suppose that the distribution was markedly different during his time. For a total of 459 boys in the Classical and English Schools, the distribution was as follows:

Occupation of Father	Classical School	English School	Total
Naval Officers	2	—	2
Clergymen	20	—	20
Dissenting Ministers	6	—	6
Lawyers	15	—	15
Physicians and Surgeons	21	2	23
Merchants	13	1	14
Manufacturers	34	31	65
Architects, Civil Engineers, Surveyors, Land Agents	9	3	12
Sharebrokers, Accountants	2	—	2
Tradesmen	51	112	163
Clerks and Travellers	31	38	69
Officers of Police and Inland Revenue	3	1	4
Teachers	1	2	3
Actors	—	1	1
Parents not in business	42	18	60
TOTAL	250	209	459

It was calculated that the average stay of boys in the Classical School was rather more than four years; in the English School, the average stay was three years. The earliest age of admission was eight years old. The average leaving age in the Classical School was 15½. The average age of the school was 11½.

11. These details are taken from *King Edward's School, Birmingham: Tercentenary Commemoration 1852. List of Exhibitions and University Honours from A.D. 1801* (1852), 6–7.
12. W. W. Rouse Ball and J. A. Venn (editors), *Admissions to Trinity College, Cambridge* (1911), IV, 1801–50.

SECTION 4

1. A. Westcott, *op. cit.*, I.25–6. See also B. F. Westcott, *Teacher and Scholar*, from which this extract is taken.
2. *Ibid.*, 27.
3. Tischendorf's first edition of the Greek Testament was published in 1841. See *Salpisae*, 26.
4. A. Westcott, *op. cit.*, I.26.
5. A. C. Benson, *op. cit.*, I.37.
6. A. Westcott, *op. cit.*, I.22.
7. A. C. Benson, *op. cit.*, I.38.
8. *Ibid.*, I.225.

9. *Ibid.*, I.38. See also A. C. Benson, *The Leaves of the Tree*, 26–7.
10. *Salpisae*, 39–40.
11. *Ibid.*, 41–3.
12. *Ibid.*, 40–41.
13. *Ibid.*, 47.
14. *Ibid.*, 53.
15. *Ibid.*, 48.
16. *Ibid.*, 14–15.
17. *Ibid.*, 12–14.
18. A. C. Benson, *The Leaves of the Tree*, 27.
19. A. C. Benson, *Life of E. W. Benson*, II.690–1.
20. A. C. Benson, *The Leaves of the Tree*, 27.
21. A. Westcott, *op. cit.*, I.61.
22. *Ibid.*, I.73.
23. *Ibid.*, I.91.
24. A. C. Benson, *op. cit.*, I.16, 23–4; *Salpisae*, 48.
25. *Ibid.*, I.31–2.
26. T. C. C. Benson MSS. III, Vol. 1, 5.
27. *Ibid.*, III, Vol. 1, 6.
28. *Ibid.*, III, Vol. 1, 12.
29. *Ibid.*, III, Vol. 1, 15.
30. A. C. Benson, *op. cit.*, I.47.
31. *Ibid.*, I.48.
32. *Ibid.*, 50–3.
33. *Ibid.*, 55.
34. *Ibid.*, I.62–3.
35. *Salpisae*, 19.
36. *Ibid.*, 25.

SECTION 5

1. T. Gutteridge, *Letter to James Taylor . . . on the corrupt system of election of the Medical Officers . . .*, Birmingham, 1843.
2. *Proceedings of the Annual General Meeting of the Governors and Subscribers of the General Hospital, Birmingham*, 20 September 1844 (Birmingham 1844), 3. 'Mr. Gutteridge desires an opportunity of proving that he is entitled to be considered a surgeon of the hospital, as successor to Mr. Alfred Jukes.'
3. *Ibid.*, 5.
4. *Ibid.*, 28.
5. *Ibid.*, 6–7.
6. T. Gutteridge, *Letter to the Rt. Hon. Lord Calthorpe on the corruptions and abuses of the General Hospital and the Free Grammar School of King Edward VI at Birmingham*, Birmingham, 1845.
7. T. Gutteridge, *Letter to the Rt. Rev. The Lord Bishop of Worcester*, Birmingham, 1846.

8. T. Gutteridge, *Report of the . . . Public Meeting held in the Town Hall, Birmingham, 19 May 1846 . . .*, Birmingham, 1846.

9. T. Gutteridge, *Letter to . . . Lord Calthorpe*, 6–8.

10. *Ibid.*, 6.

11. *Ibid.*, 12. Gutteridge's 'honourable gentleman' was Richard Michell of Lincoln College, Oxford.

12. *Ibid.*, 12–13.

13. *Ibid.*, 14.

14. *Ibid.*, 13.

15. *Ibid.*, 14.

16. *Ibid.*, 13.

17. T. Gutteridge, *Report of the Public Meeting . . . etc.*, 11.

18. T. Gutteridge, *Letter to the . . . Bishop of Worcester*, 22.

19. *Aris's Birmingham Gazette*, 29 Nov. 1847.

20. T. Gutteridge, *Facts and Opinions relating to the Archbishop's Court of Confirmation* (Birmingham 1869), 10.

21. *Aris's Birmingham Gazette*, 8 November 1847.

22. *Ibid.*, 15 November 1847.

23. *Aris's Birmingham Gazette*, 25 November 1847.

24. T. Gutteridge, *Facts and Opinions . . . etc.*, 13–14.

25. *Ibid.*, 10.

26. K.E.S. MSS. Governors' Order Book, 368.

27. K.E.S. MSS. Box 3/30. List of Masters and Salaries.

28. T. Gutteridge, *The General Hospital, Birmingham. The Crisis . . .* Birmingham, 1851.

29. T. Gutteridge, *Mr. Gutteridge's Lithotomy Fund*, Birmingham, 1859.

30. T. Gutteridge. *The alleged 'Nunnery Scandal' at Birmingham. Correspondence relating thereto and complete refutation of the Slander* (Birmingham 1868), 28–9.

31. *Ibid.*, 30.

32. *Review of the Correspondence between The Bishop of Manchester and the Rev. Messrs. Irvine, Alsop and Rodwell. . . . By a Layman* (Oxford 1849), 24–5.

33. A. C. Benson, *Life of E. W. Benson*, II.100–101.

34. M. C. L. F. 920.04273.01. Cuttings relating to J. P. Lee. Obituary in the *Manchester Guardian*.

35. J. W. Diggle, *The Lancashire Life of Bishop Fraser* (1889), 179.

36. W. Pole, *The Life of Sir William Fairburn* (1877), 451.

37. *Salpisae*, 38.

38. *Barrow's Sermons and Fragments*, collected and edited by the Rev. J. P. Lee (1834).

39. See J. H. Overton's article in *D.N.B.* III.304.

40. *Notes and Queries*, 4th Series, XII.198.

41. Chetham's. Crossley MSS. Crompton to Crossley, 8 July, 1870.

42. S. Crompton, *Letter to the Rt. Rev. James Prince Lee on Old Trafford Chapel* (1862), 2–6. See also S. Crompton, *Some Particulars of the Threatened Expulsion from Hearnshaw's Blind Asylum* (1863). Both pamphlets may be found in M.C.L. Historical Tracts, H.898.
43. Chetham's. Raines MSS. Box 2, no. 20.
44. See G. S. R. Kitson Clark in *Studies in Social History (A Tribute to G. M. Trevelyan)*, edited by J. H. Plumb (1955), 219–20; 237, n.6.
45. *Salpisae*, 29.

SECTION 6

1. T. C. C. Benson MSS. III, Vol. 1, 23.
2. *Ibid.*, Vol. 1, 25.
3. *Ibid.*, Vol. 1, 27.
4. *Ibid.*, Vol. 1, 26.
5. *Ibid.*, Vol. 1, 32.

SECTION 7

1. J. Evans, *Lancashire Authors and Orators* (1850), 153.
2. A. R. Ashwell and R. G. Wilberforce, *Life of Samuel Wilberforce*, II.125,128.
3. J. S. Leathbarrow, *Victorian Period Piece* (1954), 122. Liddon, in his *Life of E. B. Pusey*, III.160, suggested that the popularity of Stanley's *Life of Arnold* largely accounted for Lord John Russell's favours to known sympathisers of Arnold, e.g. Prince Lee and Hampden.
4. Spencer Walpole, *The Life of Lord John Russell* (1889), I.476.
5. *The Centenary of the Diocese of Manchester 1847–1947* (1947), 18. See also Le Neve, *Fasti Ecclesiae Anglicanae* (1854), III. 333–4.
6. J. W. Diggle, *The Lancashire Life of Bishop Fraser*, 65.
7. *Centenary of the Diocese*, 18.
8. J. S. Leathbarrow, *op. cit.*, 123.
9. *Manchester Guardian*, December 1869.
10. A. C. Benson, *op. cit.*, I.42.
11. Thos. Turner, *A Letter on the Collegiate Parish Church of Manchester with remarks on the Bill before Parliament, etc.* (1850), 4–5 (John Rylands, R.64265).
12. Chetham's. Mun.E.3.12 (Manchester Church Reform Assoc. Box 1), 9.
13. M.C.L. MS/F.283.4273.M.28, p. 4.
14. J. P. Lee, *A Charge delivered at his Primary Visitation in November 1851 . . . by James Prince Lee, Lord Bishop of Manchester* (1851), 7.

15. *Ibid.*, 13.
16. *Ibid.*, 16–17. Cf. Ashwell and Wilberforce, *Life of Wilberforce*, II, 355, where Lee's views on the Gorham Judgement expressed in Convocation are alluded to.
17. *Ibid.*, 19–20.
18. *Ibid.*, 19–20.
19. *Ibid.*, 33.
20. *Ibid.*, 40–41.
21. Chetham's, Raines MSS. Box 2, no. 9.
22. Compare Davidson and Benham, *Life of A. C. Tait*, I.156, where Lee is described as 'an avowed liberal'.
23. Ashwell and Wilberforce, *op. cit.*, I.459.
24. A. C. Benson, *op. cit.*, I.195; A. Westcott, *op. cit.*, I.212; 279.
25. J. P. Lee, *A Charge delivered at his second Visitation* (1856), 3. See also J. W. Diggle, *op. cit.*, 45.
26. Chetham's, Raines MSS. Box 2, nos. 19, 21, 23, 25.
27. *Ibid.*, no. 52. This refers to the prosecution of the Rev. Robert Liddell, who succeeded the ritualist W. J. E. Bennett as Vicar of St. Paul's Church, Knightsbridge. See the cases of *Liddell* v. *Westerton*, 1857, and *Liddell* v. *Beal*, 1860. Davidson and Benham, *Life of A. C. Tait*, I.215–9.
28. *Correspondence between the Lord Bishop of Manchester, the Rev. J. M. Rodwell, the Rev. James Irvine, and the Rev. J. R. Alsop* . . . (Manchester 1849), 75–7. (John Rylands, R.72614.)
29. *Ibid.*, 80–1.
30. E. Fellows, *Sayings and Doings of the Lord Bishop of Manchester* . . . (1852), 6–7. (M.C.L. Tracts, H898.)
31. *Ibid.*, 9.
32. *Ibid.*, 10. J. S. Leathbarrow, *op. cit.*, 122, 150–1.
33. *Ibid.*, 2.
34. 'D.C.L.', *Letters on Church Matters* (1851), 7. (M.C.L. Tracts, H.898.)
35. *Ibid.*, 22.
36. *Ibid.*, 25–6.
37. *Ibid.*, 26–7. See also the version of the Broughton episode in Leathbarrow, *op. cit.*, 150–1.
38. *Centenary of the Diocese*, 18.
39. *Manchester Guardian*, 27 January 1912.
40. *Ibid.*
41. *Ibid.*, 7 February 1870.
42. M.C.L. Letter of T. C. Greenwood to C. W. Sutton, dated 11 August 1891, attached to MS. of Sutton's *D.N.B.* article.
43. A. Westcott, *op. cit.*, I.116.
44. *Ibid.*, I.279.
45. T. C. C. Benson MSS. III, Vol. 2, letter dated 19 May 1849.
46. A. Westcott, *op. cit.*, I.28,249.
47. J. W. Diggle, *op. cit.*, 66.

48. *Manchester Guardian,* 27 January 1912.
49. E. S. Watson, *Life of Bishop John Wordsworth* (1915), 255–6.
50. A. Westcott, *op. cit.,* II.60.
51. *Ibid.,* II.98.
52. Harold Nicolson in B. Pollock, *A Twentieth-century Bishop* (1947), 7.
53. A. Westcott, *op. cit.,* I.28.
54. A. C. Benson, *op. cit.,* I.324.
55. *Salpisae,* 5.

Chapter III

SECTION 1

1. T. C. C. Benson MSS. II. Diary covering the years 1871–81; entry beginning Sunday, 17 February 1878, p. 1. Subsequent references to this long entry will appear as *Diary,* followed by the page number in the narrative.
2. W. M. Benham (editor), *Catharine and Craufurd Tait,* 252; *supra,* pp. 76–9.
3. Bodleian, Dep. Benson. Boxes deposited by the Rev. K. S. P. McDowall in 1949.
4. These are: A. C. Benson, *The Life of Edward White Benson,* 2 vols. (1899); *The Leaves of the Tree* (1911); *Hugh: Memoir of a Brother* (1915); *The Life and Letters of Maggie Benson* (1917); *The Trefoil* (1923); and *Memories and Friends* (1924). E. F. Benson, *Our Family Affairs* (1920); *Mother* (1925); *As We Were* (1930) and *Final Edition* (1940).

SECTION 2

1. A. C. Benson, *The Trefoil,* 51.
2. Bodleian, 1/71–80.
3. *Ibid.,* 3/6/4.
4. A. C. Benson, *op. cit.,* 13.
5. *Ibid.,* 10.
6. *Ibid.,* 22.
7. *Ibid.,* 15.
8. Bodleian, 1/118.
9. *Ibid.,* 3/44/2.
10. *Ibid.,* 3/44/1.
11. Diary, 6–8.
12. *Ibid.,* 5.
13. A. C. Benson, *Life of E. W. Benson,* I.243.
14. A. C. Benson, *The Trefoil,* 159.
15. *Ibid.,* 45.
16. *Ibid.,* 46–7.

17. *Ibid.*, 46–7.
18. *Ibid.*, 44–5. See also E. F. Benson, *Our Family Affairs*, 101–4, for numerous other examples.
19. A. C. Benson, *Life of E. W. Benson*, I.204.

SECTION 3

1. Bodleian, 3/44/6.
2. Temple Grove Library Register, April 1872 (the property of Mr. A. A. M. Batchelor, formerly Headmaster of Temple Grove). See also M. R. James, *Eton and King's. Recollections, mainly trivial* (1926), 8.
3. A. C. Benson, *Memories and Friends*, 30–1.
4. See for instance A. C. Benson, *Memories and Friends*, 27–53; E. F. Benson, *Our Family Affairs*, 76–89; M. R. James, *Eton and King's*, 5–14; B. de Sales La Terrière, *Days that are Gone* (1924), 22–29; Sir W. Goodenough, *A Rough Record* (1943), 12–15.
5. W. Goodenough, *A Rough Record*, 14.
6. Maj.-General T. T. Patman's 'Reminiscences of Temple Grove' (a typescript account of the school under Waterfield in the possession of Mr. A. A. M. Batchelor), p. 6.
7. E. F. Benson, *op. cit.*, 86.
8. *Ibid.*, 77.
9. Sir Norman Macleod, 'Reminiscences of Temple Grove School' (typescript in the possession of Mr. A. A. M. Batchelor), 3.
10. A. C. Benson, *Memories and Friends*, 33.
11. Bodleian, 3/43/2.
12. *Ibid.*, 3/44/40.
13. *Ibid.*, 3/44/9.
14. *Ibid.*, 3/43/4.
15. *Ibid.*, 3/44/10.
16. *Ibid.*, 3/44/11.
17. *Ibid.*, 3/44/12.
18. *Ibid.*, 3/44/13.
19. *Ibid.*, 3/44/15.
20. *Ibid.*, 3/44/16.
21. *Ibid.*, 3/44/17.
22. *Ibid.*, 3/43/5.
23. *Ibid.*, 3/44/14.
24. *Ibid.*, 3/43/6.
25. A. C. Benson, *Memories and Friends*, 29.
26. W.C. MSS. Penny's Journal, I.40.
27. A. C. Benson, *The Trefoil*, 250–1.
28. Bodleian, 3/44/22.
29. *Ibid.*, 3/44/27.
30. *Ibid.*, 3/44/45.

31. *Ibid.*, 3/44/46.
32. A. C. Benson, *Memories and Friends*, 43.
33. Bodleian, 3/44/55.
34. *Ibid.*, 3/43/12.
35. E. F. Benson in *Our Family Affairs*, 85–9, describes an attempt upon his innocence. Cf. A. C. Benson's remarks in *Memories and Friends*, 35–6.
36. Bodleian, 3–43–8.
37. *Ibid.*, 3/43. 6 May 1874.

SECTION 4

1. Diary, 5.
2. Bodleian, 3/44/31.
3. *Ibid.*, 3/44/33.
4. Diary, 37–9.
5. A. C. Benson, *The Trefoil*, 72.
6. The story is told in *Ibid.*, 74.
7. A. C. Benson, *The Trefoil*, 76.
8. *Ibid.*, 85.
9. Bodleian, 3/43, 8 May 1874.
10. *Ibid.*, 3/43, 12 May 1874.
11. Temple Grove, *Report of Classical Examiner*, 8 July 1874.
12. Bodleian, 3/43, 13 July 1874.
13. *Ibid.*, 3/43, July 1874.
14. *Ibid.*, 3/43, 26 July 1874.

SECTION 5

1. Lady Laura Ridding, *George Ridding. Schoolmaster and Bishop* (1908), 51–88; A. F. Leach, *A History of Winchester College* (1899), chapter twenty-nine.
2. Lady Laura Ridding, *op. cit.*, 51.
3. Bodleian, 3/43, 24 September 1874.
4. *Ibid.*, 3/44/37.
5. *Ibid.*, 3/44/36.
6. *Ibid.*, 3/44/35.
7. *Ibid.*, 3/43, 9 October 1874.
8. *Ibid.*, 3/43, 4 October 1874.
9. *Ibid.*, 3/44/44.
10. *Ibid.*, 3/43, 14 October 1874.
11. *Ibid.*, 3/43, 31 October 1874. Arthur went to Eton at the same time as Martin went to Winchester.
12. *Ibid.*, 3/43, 15 January 1875.
13. *Ibid.*, 3/43, undated.
14. *Ibid.*, 3/43, 13 November 1875.
15. *Ibid.*, 3/43, 25 November 1875.

16. E. G. Sandford (editor), *Memoirs of Archbishop Temple*, I.352.
17. A.S. and E.M.S., *Henry Sidgwick. A Memoir* (1906), 11. Cf. the obituary of Martin in *The Wykehamist*, no. 118, February 1878: 'Owing to his taking small part in School games, he was perhaps but little known to many; but those who knew him will not soon forget the quiet modesty and unassuming gentleness of his disposition.'
18. A.S. and E.M.S., *op. cit.*, 139.
19. A. C. Benson, *The Trefoil*, 246. Arthur Mason, Benson's Canon-Missioner at Truro, was subsequently Master of Pembroke College, Cambridge.
20. Bodleian, 1/62. Bundle labelled 'Martin's things'.
21. C. Oman, *Memories of Victorian Oxford* (1941), 66.
22. E. F. Benson, *Our Family Affairs*, 72. An example of Martin's ridiculous poems may be found in E. H. Ryle (editor), *Arthur Christopher Benson, as seen by some friends* (1925), 4.
23. Bodleian, 3/43, 30 May 1876.
24. *Ibid.*, 3/44/50.
25. Diary, 8–10.
26. *Ibid.*, 2.
27. Bodleian, 3/43, 20 February 1877.
28. *Ibid.*, 3/43, 10 October 1877.
29. *Ibid.*, 3/43, 11 May 1877.
30. *Ibid.*, 3/43, 20 July 1877; see also letter dated 18 September 1877.
31. *Ibid.*, 3/47, 16 September 1877.
32. *Ibid.*, 3/47, 30 September 1877.
33. *Ibid.*, 3/47, undated.
34. Diary, 12.
35. *Ibid.*, 5–6.
36. *Ibid.*, 13.
37. *Ibid.*, 39.
38. *Ibid.*, 6.

SECTION 6

1. Diary, 2,4.
2. *Ibid.*, 2–4.
3. *Ibid.*, 16–30.
4. E. F. Benson, *Our Family Affairs*, 74.
5. Ps. 118, v. 106 (Vulgate).
6. Ps. 21, v. 2 (Vulgate).
7. Ps. 22, v. 6 (Vulgate).
8. Diary, 31–2.
9. A. C. Benson, *The Trefoil*, 249.
10. *Ibid.*, 248; E. F. Benson, *op. cit.*, 75.
11. Diary, 35.

12. A. C. Benson, *The Life and Letters of Maggie Benson*, 40.
13. A. C. Benson, *Hugh, Memoir of a Brother*, 52.
14. A. C. Benson, *The Life and Letters of Maggie Benson*, 117.
15. A. C. Benson, *Hugh*, 174.
16. A. C. Benson, *The Life and Letters of Maggie Benson*, 367.
17. *Ibid.*, 392; See also E. F. Benson, *Mother*, 222–9.
18. E. H. Ryle (editor), *Arthur Christopher Benson*, 102–3; also Percy Lubbock (editor), *The Diary of Arthur C. Benson* (1927), 21; 296–8.
19. T. C. C. Benson, MSS. II, Diary, 1889, 14 July.
20. A. C. Benson, *The Trefoil*, 289.

Chapter IV

SECTION 1

1. F. D. How, *Six Great Schoolmasters* (1905), 189.
2. H. D. Rawnsley, *Edward Thring. Teacher and Poet* (1889), 12.
3. E. Graham, *The Harrow Life of Henry Montagu Butler* (1920), 190.
4. R. T. Davidson and W. Benham, *Life of A. C. Tait*, I.104.
5. R. W. Church, *The Oxford Movement, 1833–1845*, 8.
6. B. A. Smith, *Dean Church. The Anglican Response to Newman* (1958), 19.
7. R. W. Church, *op. cit.*, 74.
8. *Ibid.*, 291.
9. *Ibid.*, 321.
10. S. T. Coleridge, *Aids to Reflection* (Bohn's edn.), xv–xvi.
11. *Ibid.*, xvi.
12. *Ibid.*, 5.
13. *Ibid.*, 6.
14. T. Hughes, *Tom Brown's Schooldays*, 103–4.
15. W.C. MSS. Kingsley Papers, nos. 2, 8.
16. E. W. Benson, *Boy Life. Its Trials, its Strength, its Fulness* (1874), 372.
17. T. Hughes, *The Manliness of Christ* (1879), 27–33.
18. F. W. Maitland, *The Life and Letters of Leslie Stephen* (1906), 137–8.
19. *Edinburgh Review*, Vol. CVII. January 1858, 190.
20. E. C. Mack, *Public Schools and British Opinion, 1780–1860* (1938), 328.
21. E. C. Mack, *Public Schools and British Opinion since 1860* (1941), 148.
22. J. Diggle, *The Lancashire Life of Bishop Fraser* (1889), 9.
23. *Ibid.*, 3.
24. *Ibid.*, 9.

25. T. Hughes, *James Fraser. A Memoir 1818–1885* (1889), esp. 7–9; 29–37; 116–18.
26. J. Bryce, *Studies in Contemporary Biography* (1903), 196.
27. J. W. Diggle, *op. cit.*, 22.
28. J. Bryce, *Studies in Contemporary Biography*, 352.
29. G. F. H. Berkeley, *My Recollections of Wellington College* (Newport, Monmouthshire, 1945), 21–2.
30. *Ibid.*, 23.
31. *Ibid.*, 34.
32. Tom Collins, *School and Sport. Recollections of a Busy Life* (1905), 38–9.
33. *Wellington Year Book*, 1909, 43–4.
34. *National Review*, November 1864, 280, quoted by E. C. Mack, *Public Schools and British Opinion since 1860*, 134.
35. M. Pattison, *Suggestions on Academical Organisation* (1868), 316–17, quoted in V. H. H. Green, *Oxford Common Room*, 245.
36. F. W. Maitland, *Life and Letters of Leslie Stephen*, 77.
37. N. Hans, *New Trends in Education in the Eighteenth Century* (1951), 63–5; 67; 72–3.
38. *Ibid.*, 87–90.
39. T. Hughes, *Tom Brown's Schooldays*, 122; E. C. Mack and W. H. G. Armytage, *Thomas Hughes* (1952), 19.
40. Charles Wordsworth, *Annals of my Early Life 1806–1846* (1891), 9.
41. *Ibid.*, 10.
42. W. Tuckwell, *Reminiscences of Oxford* (1900), 85–6.
43. Charles Wordsworth, *op. cit.*, 235.
44. G. F. Lamb, *The Happiest Days*, 222.
45. T. Hughes, *James Fraser*, 26–7.
46. T. Collins, *School and Sport*, 18–19.
47. W. Tuckwell, *Reminiscences of Oxford*, 124–6.

SECTION 2

1. A. P. Stanley, *Life of Arnold*, II.150–1.
2. T. Arnold, *Miscellaneous Works*, 376.
3. R. J. Campbell, *Thomas Arnold* (1907), 118.
4. *Ibid.*, 133–4.
5. On this feature of the Tractarians, see G. Faber, *Oxford Apostles* (Pelican edn., 1954), chapter six; R. B. Martin, *The Dust of Combat* (1959), 238–9.
6. Owen Chadwick, *The Founding of Cuddesdon* (1954), 92.
7. *Ibid.*, 92–3; A. R. Ashwell and R. G. Wilberforce, *Life of Samuel Wilberforce*, II.367–8.
8. O. Chadwick, *op. cit.*, 93.
9. Letter of A. C. Tait to Gladstone, 22/11/1873. Add. MSS. 44,331. I owe this reference to Mr. Peter Marsh of Emmanuel College,

Cambridge, who discovered this in the course of his work on Archbishop Tait for a Ph.D. thesis.

10. R. B. Martin, *The Dust of Combat*, 70–8; 107; 132–3; 208–9.
11. *Ibid.*, 107.
12. (Mrs. Kingsley), *Charles Kingsley*, II.26–7.
13. *Ibid.*, II.212–3.
14. D. Newsome, *op. cit.*, 101.
15. *Great Cities, Miscellanies*, II.330, quoted in (Mrs. Kingsley), *op. cit.*, II.33n.
16. (Mrs. Kingsley), *op. cit.*, II.275.
17. *Ibid.*, II.316; A. C. Benson, *The Leaves of the Tree*, 249.
18. See the letter in the Royal Archives, Windsor Castle (Well. Coll. Box 2, no. 196) in which Kingsley explained to Gerald Wellesley why he had chosen to send his son Maurice to Wellington. A long passage from this appears in D. Newsome, *op. cit.*, 80–3.
19. On this very marked tendency in Hughes's work as a biographer, see the interesting remarks by E. C. Mack and W. H. G. Armytage, *Thomas Hughes*, 269–70.
20. T. Hughes, *Tom Brown's Schooldays*, 307–8.
21. *Ibid.*, 99.
22. *Ibid.*, 20.
23. *Ibid.*, 45.
24. T. Hughes, *Memoir of a Brother* (1873), 10.
25. J. F. C. Harrison, *A History of the Working Men's College 1854–1954* (1954), 38.
26. *Ibid.*, 64.
27. T. Hughes, *Tom Brown at Oxford*, new edn. 1869, 112–13. See the discussion of the importance of this work among nineteenth-century university novels in M. R. Proctor, *The English University Novel*, Berkeley and Los Angeles 1957, 105–13.
28. R. B. Martin, *op. cit.*, 39.
29. E. C. Mack and W. H. G. Armytage, *op. cit.*, 89.
30. F. W. Maitland, *op. cit.*, 64.
31. *Ibid.*, 67.
32. *Ibid.*, 138.

SECTION 3

1. E. C. Mack, *Public Schools and British Opinion since 1860*, 119–20.
2. A. G. Bradley, A. C. Champneys, J. W. Baines, *A History of Marlborough College* (1923), 177.
3. F. D. How, *op. cit.*, 259–60.
4. E. G. Sandford (editor), *Memoirs of Archbishop Temple*, I.153.
5. *Ibid.*, I.222.
6. *Ibid.*, I.159.
7. W.C. MSS. C. W. Penny, 'Rough Memoranda about Abp. Benson', 81.

8. F. D. How, *op. cit.*, 205.
9. E. G. Sandford, *op. cit.*, I.173.
10. *Ibid.*, I.212.
11. G. W. Parkin, *Edward Thring, Life, Diary and Letters* (1898), I.26–7.
12. *Ibid.*, I.118–19.
13. *Ibid.*, I.76.
14. G. W. Parkin, *op. cit.*, I.91.
15. J. H. Skrine, *A Memory of Edward Thring* (1890), 120.
16. G. W. Parkin, *op. cit.*, II.195–6.
17. Lady Laura Ridding, *George Ridding, Schoolmaster and Bishop*, 87.
18. E. Graham, *op. cit.*, 183.
19. H. A. Vachell, *The Hill* (1937 edn.), 102.
20. J. Bryce, *op. cit.*, esp. 350–3.
21. More details and comments are given in D. Newsome, *op. cit.*, 221–4.
22. C. R. L. Fletcher, *Edmond Warre* (1922), 37.
23. *Ibid.*, 38.
24. F. Compton Mackenzie, *William Cory*, 41.
25. *Supra*, 86–8.
26. *Ionica*, 'Academus'.
27. *Letters and Journals of William Cory* (edited F. Warre Cornish), 57–8. Compare p. 79, where Cory expresses his admiration for Kingsley's writings.
28. P. Cory, 'In search of a Grandfather', in *Blackwood's Magazine*, no. 1572, October 1946, 264. Miss Cory is quoting Arthur Benson in this passage. Compare also *Letters and Journals*, 244, where Cory observes—on watching the Guards' Band at St. James's (August 1868)—"No girl has a steadier 'scarlet fever' than I."
29. C. R. L. Fletcher, *op. cit.*, 51; 64–5.
30. *Ibid.*, 106–7.
31. A. C. Benson, *Memories and Friends*, 121.
32. *Letters and Journals*, 375.
33. V. H. H. Green, *Oxford Common Room*, 285.
34. *Ibid.*, 260.
35. D. A. Winstanley, *Later Victorian Cambridge* (Cambridge 1947), 274.
36. P. Lubbock, *Shades of Eton*, 155.

SECTION 4

1. M. Pattison, *Memoirs* (1885), 236.
2. Charlotte Leaf, *Walter Leaf. A Memoir* (1932), 94–5.
3. N. Annan, 'Science, Religion, and the Critical Mind', in *1859: Entering an Age of Crisis*, edited P. Appleman, W. A. Madden and M. Wolff (Indiana 1959), 32, 34.
4. Charlotte Leaf, *op. cit.*, 106.

5. A.S. and E.M.S., *Henry Sidgwick. A Memoir*, 47, 90.

6. F. W. Maitland, *Life and Letters of Leslie Stephen*, 150–1.

7. Caroline Jebb, *Life and Letters of Sir Richard C. Jebb* (Cambridge 1907), 103–4.

8. G. W. Parkin, *op. cit.*, I.275.

9. E. H. Ryle (editor), *Arthur Christopher Benson, as seen by some friends* (1925), 152.

10. A. W. Benn, *The History of English Rationalism in the Nineteenth Century* (1906), I.372.

11. J. Bronowski, 'Unbelief and Science', in *Ideas and Beliefs of the Victorians*, edited H. Grisewood (1949), 167.

12. N. Annan, 'The Strands of Unbelief', in *ibid.*, 155.

13. Basil Willey, *More Nineteenth-century Studies* (1956), 26; N. Annan, in *Ideas and Beliefs, op. cit.*, 153.

14. J. G. Stewart, *Jane Ellen Harrison* (1959), 2.

15. G. G. Coulton, 'Some Problems in Medieval Historiography', in *Proceedings of the British Academy*, vol. XVIII, Raleigh Lecture on History, 1932, 2.

16. H. A. L. Fisher, *Frederic William Maitland* (Cambridge 1910), 7–9.

17. G. G. Coulton, *op. cit.*, 4.

18. A. C. Benson, *Life of E. W. Benson*, I.560–1; A. W. Benn, *op. cit.*, I.vii.

19. A. F. Hort, *Life and Letters of F. J. A. Hort* (1896), I.414; H. G. Wood, *Belief and Unbelief since 1850* (Cambridge 1955), 50.

20. A. M. Ramsey, *From Gore to Temple. The Development of Anglican Theology between 'Lux Mundi' and the Second World War* (1960), 1.

21. *Supra*, p. 198.

22. J. G. Lockhart, *Cosmo Gordon Lang* (1949), 74.

23. Charles Smythe, *Cyril Forster Garbett* (1959), 29. For Garbett's impressions of Cuddesdon, see *ibid.*, 56–9.

24. Derek Beales, 'An International Crisis: The Italian Question in 1859', in *1859: Entering an Age of Crisis*, 192–3.

25. H. A. Vachell, *The Hill*, 236.

26. R. Farrar, *Life of F. W. Farrar*, 21.

Bibliography

A. MANUSCRIPT SOURCES

1. BODLEIAN LIBRARY, OXFORD, Department of Western MSS.
The Benson family papers, deposited by the Rev. K. S. P. McDowall
(great-nephew of Edward White Benson) in 1949, are housed in 3
boxes, the main items in which are these:

Box 1: 'Martin's Things'—a parcel of personal belongings of
M. W. Benson (1/62).
Mary Benson's diaries from 1859 (1/71–80).
Miscellaneous school exercise books, etc. (1/110–126).

Box 2: Extracts from the diaries of Abp. Benson (made by E. F.
Benson), 2 vols. (2/73–4).
Photographs and engravings (2/80).

Box 3: 65 miscellaneous letters of E. W. Benson (3/6/1–65).
Mary Benson's letters to her children when Martin Benson
died (3/19).
136 letters from E. W. Benson and Mary Benson to Martin
Benson (3/43).
57 letters from Martin Benson to his father and mother
(3/44).
Letters from Mary Sidgwick and other members of the
Sidgwick family to Martin Benson and others (3/45).
Letters written by A. C. Benson, E. F. Benson, R. H.
Benson and Margaret Benson as children (3/46).
42 letters written by Mary Eleanor Benson as a child, 1870–
1878 (3/47).

2. KING EDWARD'S SCHOOL, BIRMINGHAM, Governors' Muniment
Room
The bulk of the school records relating to the period of Prince Lee's
headmastership was destroyed in a fire which broke out shortly after
the school moved from the New Street premises to Edgbaston, when the
school and its records were housed in temporary wooden buildings.
The main items among those which remain are as follows:
Governors' Order Book, 1832–41.
School Committee Minute Book.
Printed list of boys and of honours and awards (2/32 and 2/33).
Correspondence relating to the appointment of J. P. Lee as head-
master (4/4).

Memoranda relating to masters and salaries (3/30).
J. P. Lee's correspondence with G. E. Anson, 1843 (5/14).

3. MANCHESTER CENTRAL LIBRARY, Local History Library

The documents on Bishop Lee are almost all printed pamphlets, listed in the second section of this bibliography. The manuscript material of any interest is confined to the letters that passed between Mr. T. C. Greenwood and Mr. C. W. Sutton, the author of the article on Prince Lee in the *Dictionary of National Biography*. There are also some papers of interest in the bound collection of documents (MS. F.283.4273.M.28) which contain Lee's correspondence with the Secretary of the Cathedral Commission.

4. MANCHESTER. CHETHAM'S LIBRARY

    (a) James Crossley's Correspondence. Very little relating to J. P. Lee is contained in this collection, but the letters that passed between Crossley and Samuel Crompton have some interest.

    (b) Canon F. R. Raines MSS, 2 boxes. Box 2 contains a bundle of 60 letters of Bishop Lee to Canon Raines (1848–68), and a smaller bundle of letters from the Rev. John Booker to Canon Raines.

5. TEMPLE GROVE SCHOOL, UCKFIELD, SUSSEX

Mr. A. A. M. Batchelor, late headmaster of Temple Grove, has a number of interesting documents relating to the school during the period when Martin Benson was a pupil. The manuscript sources which I consulted were:

Temple Grove Library Register, April 1872.
'Reminiscences of Temple Grove' by Maj.-General T. T. Patman.
'Reminiscences of Temple Grove School' by Sir Norman Macleod.
Report of the Classical Examiner, 8 July 1874.

6. TRINITY COLLEGE, CAMBRIDGE

A large collection of the personal and private papers of Edward White Benson were deposited in the Trinity Library by Arthur Benson when Master of Magdalene College, Cambridge. These consist of three chests containing the following material:

    Box 1: Papers and Notebooks. 29 bundles and notebooks, mainly commonplace books, special diaries and personal memoranda.

    Box 2: Archbishop Benson's Diaries, 16 volumes. Volume One relates to the decade 1871–81 and contains the 34-page

account of Martin Benson's life and death, quoted extensively in the third study in this book. The remaining 15
volumes, each covering one year, relate to the period
1882–96.

Box 3: Archbishop Benson's Letters, 11 bound volumes. These
letters were typed from originals by A. C. Benson while
working on the two-volume life of his father. Vols. 1–9
extend over the years 1842 to 1896, being arranged
chronologically. Vols. 10 and 11 consist of various undated
letters. The Benson-Lightfoot correspondence, of which
much use has been made in the second study in this book,
may be found in the first two volumes of this collection.

7. WELLINGTON COLLEGE, CROWTHORNE, BERKS

A full description of the Wellington College Archives, to which a
number of references have been made in this book, can be found on
pages 393–4 of my *History of Wellington College, 1859–1959*,
London, 1959. The sources which I have used on this occasion are:

(*a*) The Benson papers.
    (i) 6 bound volumes of MS letters dating from 1858 to 1873.
    (ii) The Benson Scrapbook.
    (iii) Memoranda and official reports, 2 vols.
(*b*) The Penny Papers.
    (i) The Journal of the Rev. C. W. Penny, entitled 'Benson-
    iana', 3 MS volumes written in 1896.
    (ii) 'Rough Memoranda about Archbishop Benson', one volume
    of cuttings and reminiscences.
(*c*) Wellington Records: Wickham, compiled by G. F. H. Berkeley,
    volume 2, containing the 'Recollections of Mr. Henry Richards'.
(*d*) Miscellaneous Papers (ii). Kingsley MSS. A bundle of letters
    written by Charles Kingsley to E. W. Benson, 1860–72.
(*e*) The Benson Notebook. This item, described above on p. 45,
    could not be found when I was working on the history of
    Wellington, and therefore does not appear in the bibliography.
    It has since come to light and gives a good deal of information
    about Benson's plans during his first years as Master of
    Wellington.

8. MISCELLANEOUS

The MS letter of J. P. Lee to Dr. Arnold, dated 19 June 1838, is in
the Temple Reading Room at Rugby School.

The letter of Charles Kingsley to Gerald Wellesley, Dean of Windsor, dated 29 September 1859, is in the Royal Archives, Windsor Castle (Wellington College Box 2, no. 196).

B. PAMPHLETS AND PRINTED SOURCES

1. BIRMINGHAM REFERENCE LIBRARY

Benson, E. W. *Our Archbishop's Counsels, Speeches to the Boys of King Edward's School, Birmingham*, Birmingham, 1883.

Gutteridge, Thomas. *Letter to James Taylor . . . on the corrupt system of election of the Medical Officers at the General Hospital, Birmingham*, Birmingham, 1843.

—— *Letter to the Earl of Dartmouth on the corrupt system . . . at the General Hospital, Birmingham*, Birmingham, 1844.

—— *Letter to the Rt. Hon. Lord Calthorpe on the corruption and abuses of the General Hospital and the Free Grammar School of King Edward the Sixth at Birmingham*, Birmingham, 1845.

—— *Letter to the Rt. Rev. . . . The Lord Bishop of Worcester . . . on corruption and abuses and Clerical Delinquency*, Birmingham, 1846.

—— *Report of the Proceedings of the Public Meeting held in the Town Hall, Birmingham, 19 May 1846, to take into consideration the Abuses of Public Charities, especially The General Hospital and King Edward's Free Grammar School . . .* , Birmingham, 1846.

—— *Three Pamphlets containing the charges of immorality publicly brought against J. P. Lee . . . etc.*, Birmingham, 1847.

—— *The General Hospital, Birmingham, The Crisis. Another Warning addressed to the Governors*, Birmingham, 1851.

—— *Mr. Gutteridge's Lithotomy Fund. Printed List of Subscribers*, Birmingham, 1859.

—— *The Alleged 'Nunnery Scandal' at Birmingham. Correspondence relating thereto and complete refutation of the Slander*, Birmingham, 1868.

—— *Facts and Opinions relating to the Archbishop's Court of Confirmation, allegations against J. P. Lee . . . etc.*, Birmingham, 1869.

King Edward's School, Birmingham. *Tercentenary Celebrations, 16 April 1852. List of Exhibitions and University Honours from 1801*, Birmingham, 1852.

King Edward's School, Birmingham. *Scheme for Teaching in the Free Grammar School . . . etc.* Birmingham, 1836.

Lee, J. Prince, *Letter to J. S. Pakington, M.P. on the plan of Education regarding Dissenters at King Edward's School*, lithographed 1843.
—— *Report on the Religious Teaching given in King Edward's School, Birmingham*, Birmingham, 1843.
Proceedings of the Annual General Meeting of the Governors and Subscribers of the General Hospital, Birmingham, 20 September 1844, in reference to certain statements published and circulated by Mr. Thomas Gutteridge . . . and Mr. John Joseph Ledsam . . . etc., Birmingham, 1844.

2. LAMBETH PALACE LIBRARY

Lee, J. Prince, *A Charge delivered at his primary visitation in November 1851 to the clergy of the Diocese of Manchester . . . etc.*, London, 1851.
—— *A Charge delivered at his second visitation in December 1855 etc.*, London, 1856.
—— *A Sermon preached in the Parish Church of Manchester . . . 1861, being the day appointed for the funeral of . . . The Prince Consort*, Manchester, 1862.
—— *A Letter to the Rev. A. T. Parker, Incumbent of St. Peter's Burnley*, undated.

3. MANCHESTER CENTRAL LIBRARY, Local History Library

Crompton, Samuel, *Letter to the Rt. Rev. James Prince Lee . . . on Old Trafford Chapel*, Manchester, 1862.
—— *Some particulars of the Threatened Expulsion from Hearnshaw's Blind Asylum*, Manchester, 1863.
'D.C.L.', *Letters on Church Matters*, London, 1851.
Fellows, Edward. *Sayings and Doings of the Lord Bishop of Manchester in the Administration of his Diocese, but more particularly with reference to Ringley Chapel*, 2nd edn., London, 1852.
Irvine, J. *Correspondence between The Lord Bishop of Manchester, the Rev. J. M. Rodwell . . ., the Rev. James Irvine . . . and the Rev. J. R. Alsop . . . etc.*, Manchester, 1849.
—— *A Review of the Correspondence between the Bishop of Manchester and the Rev. Messrs. Irvine, Alsop and Rodwell . . . etc.*, Oxford, 1849.
—— *A Letter to the Lord Bishop of Manchester . . . with an Appendix of letters and documents*, London, 1849.

4. MANCHESTER, CHETHAM'S LIBRARY

Manchester Church Reform Association papers, 2 boxes (Mun.E.3.12 and E.4.1.): a collection of printed papers, circulars, pamphlets and drafts of bills, relating to the provision of churches and revenues for the parish of Manchester.

5. MANCHESTER, JOHN RYLAND'S LIBRARY

Two bound collections of printed pamphlets:
- (a) R.72614. A collection of pamphlets relating to the dispute between the Bishop of Manchester and the Rev. J. Irvine, Vicar of Leigh.
- (b) R.64265. A collection of pamphlets relating to the Manchester Church Question.

C. NEWSPAPERS AND PERIODICALS

1. Folder of cuttings from *The Manchester Guardian* and *The Manchester Examiner and Times*, in the Local History Library of the Manchester Central Library.

2. Folder of cuttings (from various newspapers) entitled 'Manchester Cathedral and Bishops', in Chetham's Library, Manchester.

3. *Aris's Birmingham Gazette*, 8 November 1847; 15 November 1847; 22 November 1847; 29 November 1847. (Copies filed in the Reference Library, Birmingham.)

4. Miscellaneous:

Blackwood's Magazine, no. 1572. October 1946.
King Edward VI's Magazine, no. 1. September 1842.
Notes and Queries, 4th Series. Vol. XII.
Owen's College Magazine, April 1870.
Proceedings of the British Academy, Vol. XVIII, 1932.
Transactions of the National Association for the Promotion of Social Science, 1857.
Wellington Year Book, The, 1909.
Wykehamist, The, February 1878.

D. WORKS OF REFERENCE

Dictionary of National Biography, The.
Gardiner, R. B. (editor), *The Admissions Register of St. Paul's School 1748–1876*, London, 1884.
Historical Register of the University of Oxford 1220–1900, The, Oxford, 1900.

Le Neve, John (and T. Duffus Hardy), *Fasti Ecclesiae Anglicanae*, Vol. iii, Oxford, 1854.

Manchester Diocesan Directory, The, Manchester 1871.

Rouse Ball, W. W. and Venn, J. A. (editors), *Admissions to Trinity College, Cambridge*, Vol. iv. 1801–50, London, 1911.

Rugby School Register, The, Vol. 1. April 1675–October 1857, Rugby, 1933.

Wainewright, J. B. (editor), *Winchester College 1836–1906. A Register*, Winchester, 1907.

Waterfield, H. W. (editor), *The Temple Grove Register 1905*, London, 1905.

E. SECONDARY PRINTED WORKS

This list includes only those books to which references are made in the text or in the footnotes. The name of the publisher is given where permission has been granted to reprint certain extracts.

Annan, N. G. 'The Strands of Unbelief', in *Ideas and Beliefs of the Victorians*, edited H. Grisewood, London, 1949.

—— *Leslie Stephen. His Thought and Character in relation to his Time*, London (MacGibbon and Kee), 1951.

—— 'The Intellectual Aristocracy', in *Studies in Social History. A Tribute to G. M. Trevelyan*, edited J. H. Plumb, London, 1955.

—— 'Science, Religion and the Critical Mind', in *1859: Entering an Age of Crisis*, edited P. Appleman, W. A. Madden and M. Wolff, Indiana, 1959.

Archer, R. J. *Secondary Education in the Nineteenth Century*, Cambridge, 1921.

Arnold, Thomas. *Introductory Lectures on Modern History*, 6th edn., London, 1874.

—— *Sermons*, 6 vols., London, 1829–45.

—— *Miscellaneous Works*, 2nd edn., London, 1858.

Ashwell, A. R. and Wilberforce, R. G. *The Life of Samuel Wilberforce*, 3 vols., London, 1880–82.

Balston, T. *Dr. Balston at Eton*, London, 1952.

Bamford, T. S. *Thomas Arnold*, London, 1960.

Beales, Derek. 'An International Crisis. The Italian Question in 1859', in *1859: Entering an Age of Crisis*, edited Appleman, Madden and Wolff, Indiana, 1959.

Benham, W. (editor), *Catharine and Craufurd Tait . . . A Memoir*, London, 1879.

Benn, A. W. *The History of English Rationalism in the Nineteenth Century*, 2 vols., London, 1906.

Benson, A. C. *The Life of Edward White Benson*, 2 vols., London, 1899–1900.

—— *The Upton Letters*, London, 1906.

—— *The Leaves of the Tree*, London, 1911.

—— *Hugh: Memoir of a Brother*, London, 1915.

—— *The Life and Letters of Maggie Benson*, London, 1917.

—— *The Trefoil*, London (John Murray), 1923.

—— *Memories and Friends*, London (John Murray), 1924.

—— *The Diary of Arthur Christopher Benson*, a selection by Percy Lubbock, London, 1927.

Benson, E. F. *Our Family Affairs*, London (Cassell), 1920.

—— *Mother*, London, 1925.

—— *As We Were. A Victorian Peep-Show*, London, 1930.

—— *Final Edition*, London, 1940.

Benson, E. W. *Boy Life. Its Trials, its Strength, its Fulness. Sundays in Wellington Chapel 1859–1873*, London, 1874.

—— *ΣΑΛΠΙΣΕΙ. A Memorial Sermon preached after the death of the Rt. Rev. James Prince Lee*, 2nd edn., with appendix containing memorial notices edited by J. F. Wickenden, London, 1870.

Berkeley, G. F. H. *My Recollections of Wellington College*, Newport (Mon.), 1945.

Bonney, T. G. *Memories of a Long Life*, privately printed, Cambridge, 1921.

Bradby, G. F. *The Brontes, and other Essays*, London, 1932.

Bradley, A. G., Champneys, A. C. and Baines, J. W. *A History of Marlborough College*, London, 1923.

Bronowski, J. 'Unbelief and Science', in *Ideas and Beliefs of the Victorians*, edited H. Grisewood, London, 1949.

Bryce, James. *Studies in Contemporary Biography*, London, 1903.

Campbell, R. J. *Thomas Arnold*, London, 1927.

Centenary of the Diocese of Manchester, The, 1847–1947, Manchester, 1947.

Chadwick, Owen. *The Founding of Cuddesdon*, Oxford, 1954.

—— *From Bossuet to Newman. The Idea of Doctrinal Development*, Cambridge, 1957.

Church, R. W. *The Oxford Movement. Twelve Years 1833–1845*, London, 1891.

(Clough, Mrs.). *The Poems and Prose Remains of Arthur Hugh Clough*, 2 vols., London, 1869.

Coleridge, J. T. *A Memoir of the Rev. John Keble*, 2nd edn., 2 vols., London and Oxford, 1869.

Coleridge, S. T. *Aids to Reflection*, Bohn's standard edn., London, 1884.

Collins, Tom. *School and Sport. Recollections of a Busy Life*, London, 1905.

Cory, William Johnson, *Ionica*, London, 1891.

———— *Letters and Journals of William Cory, Author of 'Ionica'*, selected and arranged by F. Warre Cornish, Oxford, 1897.

(Creighton, Mrs.). *The Life and Letters of Mandell Creighton*, 2 vols., London, 1905.

Davidson, R. T. and Benham, W. *The Life of Archibald Campbell Tait*, 3rd edn., 2 vols., London, 1891.

Diggle, J. W. *The Lancashire Life of Bishop Fraser*, 3rd edn., London, 1889.

Doyle, Sir Francis. *Reminiscences and Opinions*, London, 1886.

Elliott-Binns, L. *Religion in the Victorian Era*, London, 1936.

Esher, Reginald, Viscount. *Ionicus*, London (John Murray), 1923.

Evans, J. *Lancashire Authors and Orators. A Series of Literary Sketches*, London, 1850.

Faber, Sir Geoffrey. *Oxford Apostles. A Character Study of the Oxford Movement*, Pelican edn., London, 1954.

———— *Jowett. A Portrait with Background*, London, 1957.

Farrar, F. W. *Eric: or Little by Little*, 1914 edn., London, 1914.

———— (editor), *Essays on a Liberal Education*, London, 1867.

Farrar, R. *The Life of Frederic William Farrar*, London (J. Nisbet), 1904.

Findlay, J. J. *Arnold of Rugby*, Cambridge, 1897.

Fisher, H. A. L. *Frederic William Maitland. A Biographical Sketch*, Cambridge, 1910.

Fitch, Sir Joshua. *Thomas and Matthew Arnold and their influence on English Education*, London, 1897.

Fletcher, C. R. L. *Edmond Warre*, London (John Murray), 1922.

Fremantle, W. R. *A Memoir of the Rev. Spencer Thornton*, London, 1850.

Goodenough, Sir William. *A Rough Record*, London, 1943.

Graham, Edward. *The Harrow Life of Henry Montagu Butler*, London, 1920.

Green, Peter. *Kenneth Grahame (1859-1932)*, London, 1959.

Green, V. H. H. *Oxford Common Room. A Study of Lincoln College and Mark Pattison*, London (Arnold), 1957.

Hans, Nicholas. *New Trends in Education in the Eighteenth Century*, London, 1951.

Harrison, J. F. C. *A History of the Working Men's College 1854-1954*, London, 1954.

Hort, A. F. *The Life and Letters of Fenton John Anthony Hort*, 2 vols., London, 1896.

How, F. D. *Six Great Schoolmasters*, London, 1905.

Hughes, Thomas. *Tom Brown's Schooldays*, Oxford edn., 1921.

———— *Tom Brown at Oxford*, New edn., London, 1869.

———— *Memoir of a Brother*, 2nd edn., London, 1873.

———— *The Manliness of Christ*, London, 1879.

———— *James Fraser. A Memoir*, London, 1889.

Hutton, T. W. *King Edward's School, Birmingham 1552–1952*, Oxford, 1952.

James, M. R. *Eton and King's. Recollections, Mostly Trivial, 1875–1925*, London, 1926.

Jebb, Caroline. *The Life and Letters of Sir Richard Claverhouse Jebb*, Cambridge, 1907.

(Kingsley, Mrs.). *Charles Kingsley. His Letters and Memories of his Life*, 3rd edn., 2 vols., London, 1877.

Kitson Clark, G. S. R. 'The Romantic Element 1830–1850', in *Studies in Social History. A Tribute to G. M. Trevelyan*, edited J. H. Plumb, London, 1955.

Lake, Katherine (editor). *Memorials of William Charles Lake 1819–1894*, London, 1901.

Lamb, G. F. *The Happiest Days*, London, 1959.

La Terrière, B. de Sales. *Days that are Gone*, London, 1924.

Leach, A. F. *A History of Winchester College*, London, 1899.

Leaf, Charlotte. *Walter Leaf 1852–1927. Some chapters of Autobiography with a Memoir*, London, 1932.

Leathbarrow, J. S. *Victorian Period Piece*, London, 1954.

Liddon, H. P. *The Life of Edward Bouverie Pusey*, 4 vols., London, 1894–8.

Lockhart, J. G. *Cosmo Gordon Lang*, London, 1949.

Lubbock, Percy. *Shades of Eton*, London (Jonathan Cape), 1929.

Mack, Edward C. *Public Schools and British Opinion 1780–1860*, London (Methuen), 1930.

———— *Public Schools and British Opinion since 1860*, London and New York, 1941.

———— and Armytage, W. H. G. *Thomas Hughes. The Life of the Author of 'Tom Brown's Schooldays'*, London, 1952.

Mackenzie, Faith Compton. *William Cory. A Biography with a Selection of Poems*, London (Constable), 1950.

Maitland, F. W. *Roman Canon Law in the Church of England. Six Essays*, London, 1898.

———— *The Life and Letters of Leslie Stephen*, London, 1906.

Martin, R. B. *The Dust of Combat. A Life of Charles Kingsley*, London, 1959.

Morley, John. *The Life of William Ewart Gladstone*, 3 vols., London, 1903.

Mozley, Thomas. *Reminiscences chiefly of Oriel College and the Oxford Movement*, 2 vols., London, 1882.

Newman, J. H. *Apologia pro Vita sua*, Wilfrid Ward's edn., London, 1913.

Newsome, David. *A History of Wellington College 1859–1959*, London, 1959.

Nicolson, Sir Harold, *Good Behaviour*, London, 1955.

Oman, Sir Charles. *Memories of Victorian Oxford*, London, 1941.

Overton, J. H. and Wordsworth, Elizabeth. *Christopher Wordsworth, Bishop of Lincoln 1807–1885*, New edn., London, 1890.

Parkin, G. W. *Edward Thring. His Life, Diaries and Letters*, 2 vols., London, 1898.

Pattison, Mark. *Memoirs*, London, 1885.

Pole, William. *The Life of Sir William Fairburn*, London, 1877.

Pollock, Bertram. *A Twentieth-Century Bishop*, with a foreword by Sir Harold Nicolson, London, 1947.

Proctor, M. R. *The English University Novel*, Berkeley and Los Angeles, 1957.

Prothero, Rowland E. *The Life and Correspondence of Arthur Penrhyn Stanley*, 2nd edn., 2 vols., London, 1894.

Purcell, E. S. *The Life of Cardinal Manning*, 2 vols., London (Macmillan), 1896.

Ramsey, A. M. *From Gore to Temple. The Development of Anglican Theology between 'Lux Mundi' and the Second World War*, London, 1960.

Rawnsley, H. D. *Edward Thring. Teacher and Poet*, London, 1889.

Ridding, Lady Laura. *George Ridding. Schoolmaster and Bishop*, London, 1908.

Ryle, E. H. (editor). *Arthur Christopher Benson, as seen by some of his friends*, London, 1925.

Sandars, C. R. *Coleridge and the Broad Church Movement*, Durham, N. Carolina, 1942.

Sandford, E. G. (editor). *Memoirs of Archbishop Temple*, 2 vols., London, 1906.

(Sidgwick), 'A. S. and E. M. S.', *Henry Sidgwick. A Memoir*, London, 1906.

Simon, Brian, *Studies in the History of Education 1780–1870*, London, 1960.

Skrine, J. H. *A Memory of Edward Thring*, London, 1890.

Smith, B. A. *Dean Church. The Anglican Response to Newman*, London, 1958.

Smyth, Charles, 'The Evangelical Discipline', in *Ideas and Beliefs of the Victorians*, edited H. Grisewood, London, 1949.

—— *Cyril Forster Garbett*, London, 1959.

Stanley, A. P. *The Life and Correspondence of Thomas Arnold*, 8th edn., 2 vols., London, 1858.

Stewart, J. G. *Jane Ellen Harrison. A Portrait from Letters*, London, 1959.

Strachey, Lytton. *Eminent Victorians*, new edn., London, 1948.

Tuckwell, W. *Reminiscences of Oxford*, London (Cassells), 1900.

—— *Pre-Tractarian Oxford*, London, 1909.

Vachell, H. A. *The Hill*, 1937 edn., London (John Murray), 1937.

Walpole, Spencer. *The Life of Lord John Russell*, 2 vols., London, 1889.

Watson, E. W. *The Life of Bishop John Wordsworth*, London, 1915.

Westcott, Arthur. *The Life and Letters of Brooke Foss Westcott*, 2 vols., London, 1903.

Westcott, B. F. *Teacher and Scholar: A Memory and A Hope. An Address given at the Opening of the Grammar School for Girls, Camp Hill, Birmingham*, Birmingham, 1893.

Whitridge, A. *Dr. Arnold of Rugby*, London, 1928.

Willey, Basil. *Nineteenth Century Studies*, London, 1949.

—— *More Nineteenth Century Studies*, London, 1956.

Winstanley, D. A. *Later Victorian Cambridge*, Cambridge, 1947.

Wood, H. G. *Belief and Unbelief since 1850*, Cambridge, 1955.

Wordsworth, Charles. *Annals of My Early Life 1806–1846*, London, 1891.

Woodward, F. J. *The Doctor's Disciples*, London, 1954.

Wymer, N. *Dr. Arnold of Rugby*, London, 1953.

Young, G. M. *Victorian England: Portrait of an Age*, London, 1949.

Index

Page references in italics indicate the principal reference
to a particular entry. The abbreviation H.M. stands for
Headmaster

276